Negotiating Empire

Negotiating Empire

The Cultural Politics of Schools in Puerto Rico, 1898–1952

SOLSIREE DEL MORAL

THE UNIVERSITY OF WISCONSIN PRESS

Publication of this volume has been made possible, in part, through support from the Anonymous Fund of the College of Letters and Science at the University of Wisconsin–Madison and from the Department of History at the Pennsylvania State University.

The University of Wisconsin Press
1930 Monroe Street, 3rd Floor
Madison, Wisconsin 53711-2059
uwpress.wisc.edu

3 Henrietta Street
London WC2E 8LU, England
eurospanbookstore.com

Library of Congress Cataloging-in-Publication Data
Del Moral, Solsiree.
Negotiating empire : the cultural politics of schools in Puerto Rico, 1898–1952 / Solsiree del Moral.
p. cm.
Includes bibliographical references and index.
ISBN 978-0-299-28934-8 (pbk. : alk. paper) — ISBN 978-0-299-28933-1 (e-book)
1. Puerto Rico—History—1898–1952. 2. Puerto Rico—Colonial influence. 3. Education—Puerto Rico—History. 4. Americanization—History. I. Title.
F1975.M59 2013
972.9505′2—dc23
                                                            2012017511

To the teachers of Puerto Rico, on the Island and in the Diaspora

Contents

Illustrations

Tables

Acknowledgments

When I discuss my research with friends, colleagues, and students, inevitably, at some point in the conversation, I declare unapologetically: "Puerto Rico is the center of the world!" A historian of empire must consider the case of Puerto Rico. "The oldest colony in the world," Puerto Rico has much to offer historical understandings of Spanish colonialism in the Caribbean and the United States as empire since 1898.[1] A historian of nation and nationalism cannot ignore how national identities, national narratives, and cultural nationalism emerged in a modern colony. A historian of diaspora has to make sense of how Puerto Ricans can be considered, simultaneously, "foreign in a domestic sense," US citizens, and immigrants.[2] In so many ways, the history of Puerto Rico and Puerto Ricans challenges the traditional boundaries of historical concepts such as empire, nation, and diaspora.

A historian of Puerto Rico working in the United States, I have learned to take radical positions about Puerto Rico, to demand it be inserted into all conversations in a way that transforms our original arguments. It is a necessary reaction. Contemporary colonialism has real consequences for the discipline of history. Although the literature on US empire has expanded, dominant narratives of US history rarely reflect on Puerto Rico. Many historians do not know that the diaspora is the result of the historical link between Puerto Rico and the United States, or that Puerto Ricans are US citizens, or that the island is not an independent country. Latin American scholars may consider Puerto Rico in conversations about the nineteenth century but routinely exclude it from the boundaries of Latin American historical narratives after 1898. Within this framework, in academic exchanges, I want to suggest ways that scholars of both regions might reconsider how Puerto Rican history contributes to and challenges what we think we know.

In my approach to this book, I have been mindful of centering Puerto Rico in historical narratives of US empire. At the same time, I want to locate teachers, parents, and students at the core of the story. My challenge has been to tell the story without presenting homogenized and polarized characterizations of either local educators or US colonial officials. The hopes and visions of local and imperial actors came together in the classroom. Schools became the institution through which both Puerto Rican teachers and US colonial administrators intended to promote their visions of nation, citizenship, and empire. Those visions were, at times, contradictory, at others, complementary. In the end, original positions were transformed. Parents and students confronted and contributed to the definition of those visions in the classroom. Through the historical cycles of the first half of the twentieth century, the classroom remained the location where they negotiated state goals and individual dreams. I am a student of Puerto Rican history, and my intention is to present a story of schools, teachers, and students in the first half of the twentieth century without losing sight of the power dynamics between island and empire.

This book began as a history dissertation at the University of Wisconsin–Madison, where I had the privilege to work with leading historians of Latin America and the Caribbean Francisco A. Scarano, Florencia Mallon, and Steve Stern. The Graduate School, the History Department, and the Latin American and Caribbean Studies Program supported my research with the Graduate School Domestic Research Travel Grant, the Tinker Travel Research Grant, and the Advanced Opportunity Fellowship. I also thank the University of Wisconsin System Institute on Race and Ethnicity Graduate Scholar-in-Residence Program and Luis Villar, the Latin American bibliographer at Memorial Library. The gift of time spent at the University of Wisconsin was the community of scholars and friends whose academic exchanges helped me better understand Latin American and Caribbean history as well as my contribution to the scholarship. I thank Ileana Rodríguez-Silva, Lillian Guerra, Gabrielle Kuenzli, Gladys McCormick, Jaymie Heilman, Andrés Matías-Ortiz, Marc A. Hertzman, Ana Schaposchnik, Claudio Barrientos, Kathleen Kae, and Tiffany Florvil.

Navigating libraries and archival collections in Puerto Rico requires a community of support. I thank the archivists and staff at the Archivo General de Puerto Rico, the librarians and student staff at the Colección Puertorriqueña at the University of Puerto Rico, and the staff at the Centro de Reproducciones at the Biblioteca Lázaro. At the Asociación de Maestros de Puerto Rico (AMPR), I thank the staff at the Public Relations office in San Juan and Mrs. Nancy Bosch, Mr.

Reyes Rodríguez, and the Secretaria de Actas for granting me access to the minutes of the AMPR. In addition, I thank my personal team of researchers. First, my grandmother, Angela Idalia Sánchez Rivera, connected me to teachers, administrators, libraries, and community members in Arroyo, Patillas, and Guayama, in addition to collecting materials and documents. Second, my aunt, Antonia del Moral Colón, introduced me to educators in San Juan and Río Piedras. Third, my friend, Lesli Ann Vázquez Vargas, helped me secure historical documents without which my research would have been incomplete.

At the Pennsylvania State University, the postdoctoral fellowship at the Africana Research Center provided space, funding, workshops, and colleagues. I thank my fellow postdocs, Shirley Moody-Turner, Carina Ray, and Eden Renee-Pruitt, for many conversations about researching the African Diaspora. In the History Department, Sally A. McMurry and Michael Kulikowski provided leadership as they helped me navigate the process of preparing the book for publication. At different moments, Lori Ginzberg, Mrinalini Sinha, and Nan E. Woodruff have served in the important role of mentor. I also thank Eric Novotny, Humanities Librarian at Penn State, for locating research materials at Penn State and elsewhere. At Penn State, I am lucky to have been part of a community of scholars of race and gender in the African Diaspora. Gabeba Baderoon, Alyssa Garcia, Kathryn T. Gines, and Shirley C. Moody-Turner read multiple drafts of chapters and provided insightful feedback along the way. More significant yet has been their friendship, camaraderie, and wisdom. In addition, I thank Christine Buzinde, Grace Delgado, Kimberly Griffin, Russell Lohse, Leticia Oseguera, Antoinette Pressley-Sanon, Matthew Restall, Cheraine Stanford, and Jeanine Staples. I thank my graduate and undergraduate students. Through the courses I offered on the history of Puerto Rico, the Caribbean, Latin America, the African Diaspora, and US empire, they have forced me to reflect, refine, and shape my arguments and construction of narratives. My work has also been shaped by exchanges with colleagues at various conferences over the years. I thank those who challenged my arguments at the conferences of the American Historical Association, the Latin American Studies Association, and the Association for the Study of the Worldwide African Diaspora but especially the Puerto Rican Studies Association. My work has been transformed through these multiple forms of academic engagement.

I thank Gwen Walker, acquisitions editor at the University of Wisconsin Press, for insightful feedback and direction since the early stages of this project. The final version of the book manuscript is much different from the first version submitted to Gwen, thanks to the careful and insightful comments of the anonymous reviewers. Thank you also to Matthew Cosby, Adam Mehring, Mary M.

Hill, and other staff at the University of Wisconsin Press for their expertise at each stage of the production process.

Finally, I thank my parents, William del Moral Colón and Nayda Alicea Sánchez, and my brothers and sister. Ileana Rodríguez-Silva, a fellow historian of Puerto Rico, is also family. It is to her that I am most indebted intellectually. I thank her for unwavering engagement with the history of race and colonialism in Puerto Rico. Gladys McCormick walked with me at every step of the project. Thank you to my family and friends for years of support and inspiration.

Negotiating Empire

Hacer patria

During the first week of December in 1920, teachers, parents, and students came together to celebrate the progress and promise of schools. Local committees organized conferences, exhibitions, and parades that acknowledged schools as "a great factor in the progressive action of the people of Puerto Rico."[1] In Mayagüez, teachers and staff of the Reform School held a parade and school festival in the town plaza. During the morning of December 6, school students, or, rather, *asilados* (inmates), paraded through city streets carrying banners that read: "Pueblo que no educa a sus hijos, crea su propia desgracia" (A people that does not educate its children creates its own misfortune), "Escuelas significan progreso; Analfabetismo, desgracia" (Schools signify progress; illiteracy, misfortune), "Hombres que vais al poder: ¡Más escuelas! ¡Más escuelas!" (Attention men in power: More schools! More schools!), and "Se necesita el pan de la enseñanza" (Education is our nourishment).[2]

The children's parade, testifying to the value of schools in the community and to student demand for instruction, generated positive reviews. A newspaper article titled "Hacer patria" (To build the nation) celebrated the school activities, for they best typified the practice of creating citizens and building the nation. "The practice of making *patria* is entrusted, in part, to the mentors of our youth. Making *patria*, developing patriots, is the noblest of missions that the guides and shepherds of peoples can have. . . . And you make *patria* by creating a youth that is vigorous, strong, dedicated, enterprising, a lover of progress, reverential of the virtue of citizenship, and defender of its land and its home." The key to forming a modern community of citizens committed to the progress of the nation was education, that is, schools and teachers. Patriots were "created neither in the battlefields nor in the military." Rather, "the patriot and the *patria* were created [*se forman*] in the school." As the Mayagüez Reform School transformed its "juvenile delinquents" into "citizens useful to society," it was practicing the "regeneration of humanity." The article concluded with an enthusiastic call for all to support schools in the nation-building process: "Let us build *patria* through the school. . . . Let us make patriots through instruction."[3]

Other activities, framed within a similar enthusiasm for schools and progress, were organized in communities throughout the island. Teachers in the town of Coamo, for example, distributed flyers announcing the week's local events. Addressed to interested and committed members of the community, the flyer called on "fellow citizens" to attend and "demonstrate their interest (today more than yesterday) in the progress of our School." It introduced the guiding concepts that defined the relationship between schools, teachers, the *patria*, and citizenship. "Distinguished patriots: New times demand new ideas. Institutions are sustained on the spirit of ideas, and they, ideas, eternally evolve as they obey the invariable laws of progress. Today a new era begins, an era of great moral as well as spiritual significance for the progress of our society. Different today from yesterday are time, circumstances, and methods." The post–World War I period was a historical moment guided by new ideas and methods. It promised to be a "modern era," one that demanded sweeping change, transformation, and adjustment. Teachers acknowledged that the people of Puerto Rico had "transcendental problems to resolve such as the social, economic, cultural, political, and so on." And they designated themselves as the dynamic actor of the community who would lead in the evolution and progress of the island and its people. "The teachers of Puerto Rico [*la clase magisterial*], an undeniable *factor* in the progressive evolution of the Puerto Rican people, will never remain indifferent to these problems."[4] Parents, too, were responsible for participating in the changes that defined the era through which they were living. They called on parents to awaken, gain consciousness, and take action.

The activities in Mayagüez and Coamo embodied the framework that shaped the relationship between schools, communities, colonialism, and modernity in early twentieth-century Puerto Rico. Teachers proposed that "progress" and "modernity" were just around the corner for the island and its people. They were within reach of everyone. Schools represented wheels of change and progress. They were the sites through which all positive, modern, and "regenerative" methods were practiced. Modern education, in particular, was the key to transformation. However, it was the teacher who could unlock all these promises for students and their families. The changes teachers and schools promised students were greater than the individual. These changes imagined the transformation of the *patria*. The *patria* must progress and join other modern civilizations. Education, therefore, was a practice in citizenship building. The flyers and announcements called for the formation of citizens and for community participation in nation-building processes while locating teachers and public schools as the actors and institutions that would lead.

Teachers suggested that although the people of Puerto Rico did not yet meet the intellectual, physical, and moral requirements of citizenship, with the help of public instruction they could be transformed into a healthy, moral, and intelligent community of citizens who could together compose the future Puerto Rican nation. Teachers would help their students evolve from colonial subjects into national citizens, from illiterates into intellectuals capable of comprehending and practicing their civic duties. Teachers and educators would reach into the island's most distant, isolated, rural, and traditional communities and incorporate them into a modern, progressive, and democratic nation. Both the Mayagüez newspaper report and Coamo flyer suggested that teachers and educators imagined an alternative nationalist project to the US colonial policy of Americanization. This was one of many examples where local teachers promoted their own political vision for Puerto Rico.

This framework, however, also proposed a series of questions. It required clarification about how teachers defined the relationship between US empire, Puerto Rico as its colonial territory, and citizenship. Teachers called for the formation of citizens and the progress of the *patria*. But how were they conceptualizing the *patria*? They identified Puerto Rico as the *patria*. However, their definition of *patria* did not deny the island's colonial relationship to the United States. In fact, teachers engaged an expansive and dynamic definition of *patria* and "nation" that was deeply informed by the island's late nineteenth-century history with autonomism. They saw no contradiction in the formation of a national identity rooted in a territory that remained "under the protection" of a larger, imperial power. Given this conceptualization of *patria*, what kind of citizens did teachers imagine they would create? Colonial citizens? US citizens? Puerto Rican citizens?

In addition, how did teachers define regeneration, progress, and modernity? Their writings, lectures, and practices suggest that citizenship building required a regeneration of sorts. The concept of regeneration was deeply informed by neo-Lamarckian eugenic language.[5] Teachers made assumptions about who and what was holding back the wheels of progress. It was the people themselves. Both rural peasants (*jíbaros*) and urban workers represented physical manifestations of dysgenic genes and practices. Teachers looked at students in the classroom and identified in their bodies the alleged effects of poverty, tradition, and ignorance. The scientific racial theory of neo-Lamarckian eugenics, as interpreted locally by educators, promised regeneration. Through the sanitation of the home and streets, communities could be cleansed. That implied doing away with "social poisons" like alcoholism, prostitution, gambling, and *concubinaje*. Modern education methods and progressive visions promised to contribute to the sanitation of the community, the home, and the individual. Through the hygienic and scientific instruction of physical education, domestic science, and rural agriculture, teachers could lead the transformation of the students, their communities, and, by extension, the *patria*.

This quest for regeneration, in turn, generated other questions. Who were teachers to allege that students and their families were "degenerate"? How were teachers different from the students they taught every day? Teachers, in fact, held great cultural capital in early twentieth-century Puerto Rico. Unlike the majority of the population, they were literate. They were professionals in charge of local schools. They owned their skill and knowledge. Teachers, however, also generated a paternalistic relationship with students and parents. They were better educated, representing social behaviors of a class different from the majority of their nonelite students. Teachers were not doctors and lawyers; instead, they were poorly paid and badly treated civil servants. They did hold some authority over their students and the respect of the community. Teachers were in an intermediate position: they were required to implement education policies directed at them from above (the Department of Education) while dependent on the reception of those from below (students and parents). Teachers were also modern actors. They located themselves at the center of change in Puerto Rico. If the island was to progress, to modernize, it would be at the hands of teachers. As a professional group, teachers were dynamic and undergoing their own transformation. Throughout the first half of the twentieth century, the profession experienced great changes in its demographics and training. Along the way, teachers reconceptualized their definition of citizenship and their vision for the *patria*.

The Coamo and Mayagüez examples introduce some of this book's guiding concerns. By centering teachers, schools, and education at the heart of the discussion, we can better understand how intermediate actors in colonial Puerto Rico contributed to the dynamic relationship between empire, nation, and citizen while promising to enact regeneration, progress, and modernity.

Puerto Rico as Colony and Nation

In 1898 the United States invaded Puerto Rico during the Cuban Wars of Independence, acquired the island from Spain through the Treaty of Paris, and occupied it through a military government for two years. From 1900 until 1952 Puerto

Rico was defined as an "unincorporated territory" of the United States. There were changes in constitutions, from the Foraker Act to the Jones Act. Puerto Ricans born on the island were granted US citizenship in 1917. Puerto Rico, however, was to remain an unincorporated territory. It was not on the path to independence like Cuba; it would not be incorporated like Hawaii. It would remain a colony. Puerto Rico was valuable to the US empire for multiple reasons: access to the Panama Canal, a site for military bases, a US presence in the Caribbean region. It was important for US capital, businesses, and corporations. Like so many countries of the Caribbean and Central America, Puerto Rico was a location for US capital to invest in export commodities, particularly sugar. For military and economic reasons, it was important to establish a colonial state on the island that remained under the control and authority of the US Congress and served the interests of the US empire.[6]

Education and schools were at the heart of US imperial intentions in Puerto Rico. US imperial actors were invested in generating support for US colonialism on the island. One goal was converting colonial subjects into "tropical Yankees" through the teaching of English and the celebration of US history and patriotism.[7] US educators and administrators aggressively promoted the new colonial state ideology of Americanization. Americanization ideologies could be broad or narrow as well as constructive or destructive. Educators imagined the transformation of colonial subjects into second-class citizens under the assumption that they were not to be fully incorporated into the United States. This perspective informed education projects both in the colonies and on the mainland. Puerto Ricans were one of several new colonial peoples of the US empire. Liberal US policy makers asked themselves: What should be done with the new colonial peoples, that is, Puerto Ricans, Cubans, Filipinos, and Hawaiians? Existing education projects in the United States for nonwhite peoples informed this concern. Therefore, schools and curriculum in Puerto Rico evolved in conversation with the experiences that guided Native American boarding schools and African American industrial training institutes in the United States as much as they reflected the long-standing vision of Americanization and schooling in Hawaii. In Puerto Rico, the goal of the US colonial state was to carry out a school project that intended to uplift the new colonial subjects within the broader framework of white supremacy in the nation and empire. Americanization reflected the racial, ethnic, and cultural hierarchies and practices of early twentieth-century US educators.[8]

More specifically, Aida Negrón de Montilla defined Americanization as the intention to displace a native Puerto Rican culture with an American one or the assimilation of Puerto Rican culture into the dominant US culture. Americanization, as a form of cultural assimilation, was meant to generate support and loyalty

for US colonialism in Puerto Rico. She documented the multiple ways US commissioners of education intended to inculcate students with a love of all things
American through the teaching of US history, the supplanting of Puerto Rican
patriots with American ones, the daily ritual of reciting the pledge of allegiance,
and the celebration of patriotic holidays and parades. The underlying assumption
guiding Americanization policies, according to Negrón de Montilla, was an ideology that maintained the superiority of US cultural values and the inferiority of
Puerto Rican ones. It was the leadership of the Department of Education, particularly the commissioners, who were responsible for implementing these policies.[9]

After 1898, with the founding of a US colonial state on the island, Puerto
Rico's history shared a trajectory with other members of the US empire. This
imperial framework, however, did not erase Puerto Rico's four hundred years
of history in the Caribbean and Latin America. In many ways, Puerto Rico's
early twentieth-century educators shared ideas and practices with others in the
neighboring Caribbean and Latin American countries. In the quest to better
understand state formation and national identities in Latin America, scholars
often reference the centrality of education, public schools, and teachers to those
processes. In Brazil, Mexico, and Argentina, for example, since the late nineteenth century, efforts to consolidate the national territory, popularize a national
historical narrative, and define the uniqueness of national identities required the
cooperation of schools and teachers. Schools and history lessons in particular
were in the service of the nation.[10]

Schools were equally significant in early twentieth-century Puerto Rico, if not
more so. As they had in other Latin American countries, schools, particularly the
expansion of a secular public school system accessible to all, became a priority
of the state in the early twentieth century.[11] In Puerto Rico, however, the new
state was colonial.[12] Under the banner of "benevolent imperialism," the United
States founded new public schools and trained both US and Puerto Rican teachers. The intention was to expand the reach of the government into rural areas,
to manage urban populations, and to consolidate the authority of the central
state. The ideology and curriculum that shaped the early schools—Americanization—intended to generate support for US colonialism. To accomplish this colonial state-building goal, a large number of state agents—public schoolteachers—
were recruited, hired, and trained by the Department of Education in collaboration with the University of Puerto Rico. They were then deployed throughout
the island as leaders of new urban and rural schools.[13] Teachers, however, were
met with suspicion by local leadership. When they arrived in rural communities,
in particular, and demanded that children be removed from working in the fields
and plantations and sent to school, they faced opposition from the landed elite

and some parents. Teachers' intentions, and those of the colonial state, did not always complement the existing role of children and labor in rural communities and urban households.

During the early years, the US government attempted to import as many US teachers as possible to Puerto Rico. However, it could not recruit enough teachers to fill all the vacancies, and new recruits were not always prepared to work in Spanish-speaking rural communities. At the same time, commissioners of education sent as many Puerto Rican teachers to the United States as possible to receive training in US methods, while in the island they employed US teachers as the instructors of Puerto Rican ones. Nevertheless, this was too limited. Eventually, the Department of Education and the University of Puerto Rico recruited "locals," Puerto Rican men and women, into the profession. Many of the new teachers in the early years of the US empire were local teachers who had been decertified with the arrival of US forces in 1898.

By the 1920s, most teachers were young adults from middle-class and intermediate backgrounds.[14] Many came from top schools in urban towns. Although many were bilingual (they had to pass English-language requirements to be certified to teach in local schools), the majority were Spanish speakers. They were trained at the University of Puerto Rico by both Puerto Rican and US educators and instilled with the ideology of Americanization. However, they were not empty vessels, for they came to the profession with the class, gender, and race biases that informed the social hierarchy of turn-of-the-century Puerto Rico. Teachers, therefore, also represented an obstacle for the Americanizing intentions of the US colonial state.

The fact that the majority of teachers were Puerto Rican rather than American, however, does not imply that they were inherently guided by different philosophies and intentions. In fact, Puerto Rican teachers shared many similarities with early US teachers as well as members of the teaching profession in other Latin American countries.[15] Teachers owned important social capital. They were literate, educated, employed by the state, in charge of schools and classrooms, and responsible for educating a new generation of children. They held authority and status outside of the schools as well as members of the professional class in local communities. Puerto Rican teachers, however, were members of a highly patriarchal society that defined the location of its members on a social hierarchy according to a dominant honor code deeply informed by race, class, and gender.[16] The new generation of Puerto Rican teachers negotiated their relationship with both local communities and the centralized colonial state in a way different from that of US teachers. Local teachers, therefore, posed a grave challenge to the state goal of Americanization. They advocated for a citizenship-building project that

would serve emerging national Puerto Rican identities in the early twentieth century. While teachers allowed for a definition of "Puerto Rican identity" that was
associated with the United States, they did not promote the creation of either
"tropical Yankees" or Americans.

The differences between Puerto Rico and other Latin American examples
(a colonial versus a national state, Americanization versus nationalism, foreign
versus "native" teachers), while significant, did not mean that Puerto Rico's experience was unique. There were crucial and significant intentions that drew Puerto
Rico ever more closely to other Latin American cases. For example, local teachers and educators in Puerto Rico stood out as the historical actors that might
challenge the top-down intentions of the US colonial state project. Teachers,
therefore, were not simple transmitters of US colonial policy but, rather, critical
actors who challenged and negotiated Americanization ideologies daily through
the schools. In this way, teachers became emblematic of how local actors daily
negotiated the intentions of the state and contributed to the process of state formation, although specifically the construction of a US colonial state rather than
a nation-state.[17] Equally significant, however, is recognizing how the teaching
community constantly reconstructed itself. Teachers were not simple representatives of the US colonial state, but they were also not a simple undifferentiated
class. Members of the teaching profession represented multiple generation, class,
race, and gender visions. They proposed nuanced projects for the regeneration
of the *raza*, or "national race." These debates and divisions and how they were
negotiated through colonial schools, therefore, were emblematic of the process
of colonial state formation in Puerto Rico.

Fundamentally, this study asks: How can the history of schools and teachers
in Puerto Rico help scholars understand the practices of US empire, the process
of colonial state building, and the construction of national identities in Puerto
Rico, the Caribbean, and the United States more broadly? This is the guiding
question that informs this study of schools, race, nation, and empire.

AMERICANIZATION, US EMPIRE, AND HISTORIOGRAPHY

Since the 1990s, scholars of Puerto Rico have proposed critiques of the history
of US empire in conversation with broader Caribbean and Pacific literature.[18]
US empire has been conceptualized beyond economic, political, and military
"hard" policies and practices. In addition to the histories of political intervention
and occupation of Caribbean island nations, the practice of modern US empire
is equally intrusive and present through the imagined promises of "benevolent"
and cultural imperialism.[19] Scholarship has also identified US empire as one of

multiple competing elite political projects in the region, for it was operating in relation to the already present Spanish, French, and English versions. US imperialism, additionally, engaged in an uncomfortable but complementary relationship with the economic, political, and social interests of the local, elite, liberal class.[20]

More specific to the formation of Puerto Rican identities in the early twentieth century, scholars have proposed that, despite the malleability of US imperial practices, politicians, intellectuals, and professionals in those years began to define the history, heritage, and culture of the island in direct comparison to the United States. This emerging national identity of Puerto Ricanness was strongly debated, contested, and reconstructed.[21] Nevertheless, at its foundation it claimed clear elements of difference from Americans. Puerto Rican "cultural identity," according to scholars, was defined as of Latin/Hispanic heritage, Spanish-speaking, Catholic, and shaped by the *gran familia puertorriqueña*. The *gran familia* was a concept that romanticized the family and labor relationships of the nineteenth century, where the male head of household held authority over his wife and children while addressing the material needs of his indebted laborers on the plantation. This racialized, gendered, and classed image of the unity of Puerto Ricans was constructed as one of many fundamental differences between Puerto Ricans and the United States as the Other.[22] Within this island-based critique of the construction of national identities, scholars have highlighted how nonelite actors, particularly workers and laborers, also deployed the dominant honor code and the concept of the *gran familia* in defense of their own rights before both the Spanish and the US colonial states as well as the local elite.[23]

Scholarship about Puerto Rico has been dynamic and innovative in the forms of critique and reflection it provides for our understanding of the malleability of US imperial practices on the island and, more broadly, in the region throughout the early twentieth century. While acknowledging the political framework that emerged when the United States acquired, occupied, and retained the island as an unincorporated territory, scholars have proposed the multiple ways that local actors engaged with and negotiated the top-down intentions of the new US colonial state. Nevertheless, while authors have reevaluated the negotiated processes of state formation, colonialism, and empire building in Puerto Rico, few have proposed that one of the principal symbols of US empire—education and Americanization—was also negotiated. Scholars have not challenged the dominant interpretation that US colonial school policies, specifically Americanization, were frighteningly oppressive, repressive, top-down, and somehow omnipresent.[24] This interpretation of Americanization—which proposes that it was a self-serving US colonial policy that advocated for the cultural genocide of the Puerto Rican people's culture, heritage, language, and history—generated a complementary narrative. It allowed for the conceptualization of teachers as heroic actors who defended and cultivated emerging Puerto Rican national identities at the risk of professional censure.[25] The trope of Americanization, despite the fact that it falls within the larger conversation of US imperial policies, has survived and reproduced the oppression/resistance dichotomy. Why?

Americanization retains a hegemonic location in early twentieth-century conceptualizations of US empire in Puerto Rico for multiple reasons. Let's identify two. The first speaks to questions of historiography, methods, and sources. The second is informed by the politics of empire and cultural nationalism in contemporary Puerto Rico. Early twentieth-century Puerto Rican history is often approached through the lens of Americanization, not only through the framework of the specific intentions of Americanization through education but, more broadly, the Americanization of the island's economy, politics, and society. At the core of the critiques of the narrative of "benevolent imperialism" on the island, however, is Americanization through schools. And the most significant contribution to this historical conversation has been Aida Negrón de Montilla's *La americanización en Puerto Rico y el sistema de instrucción pública, 1900–1930* (The Americanization of Puerto Rico and the public school system). Negrón de Montilla's study is a history of top-down policies promoted by US commissioners of education. She carefully and painstakingly documented, through a clear and concise narrative, how in the early twentieth century, despite some variations in the visions of individual commissioners, Americanization was the primary political framework that shaped the founding and expansion of public schools. She recognized that there were variations of the definition of Americanization at play within the elite group of US educators. Ultimately, she argued, they were guided by the intention to cultivate a new generation of students who could be pro-American and supportive of US colonialism, what José Manuel Navarro coined "tropical Yankees."[26] This cultivation of pro-American colonial subjects was imagined to come to fruition through tight control over a new curriculum that promoted US patriots and civic history and US definitions of progress, democracy, and modernity. At the core of the curriculum was English as the language of instruction.

It is significant that Negrón de Montilla concluded her study by recognizing the limitations of one of her primary documentary sources, the annual reports of the commissioners of education.[27] The annual reports, specifically, represented the voice of elite US administrators. They recorded a conversation between regional directors on the island, the commissioner, and the US president. The reports, therefore, celebrated the alleged successes of Americanization efforts in Puerto Rico. Negrón de Montilla called on researchers to unearth alternative sources that could attest to the history of resistance to Americanization and to document other perspectives about the history of colonial education in the early twentieth century. Despite her recognition, as a historian, that her source base restricted the framework of her argument, her interpretation of Americanization policies in Puerto Rico remains dominant: the US goal was to Americanize Puerto Ricans; without teacher and student resistance, Americanization would have generated the "social death" of a generation.

Negrón de Montilla's study was significant for how it contributed to a foundational narrative about the evils of US imperialism in Puerto Rico. Her conceptualization about the practices of Americanization highlighted that it required the deprecation of local culture. US educators imagined that there was very little value in Puerto Rican culture that could be reproduced in the schools. Instead, children represented a clean slate, for despite their inferiorities, they could be uplifted and molded into a colonial version of young Americans. Americanization through schools was also informed by the assumption that Puerto Rico would remain a permanent colony of the United States, unlike Cuba and the Philippines. Therefore, Americans assumed the right to redefine the future "personality" of Puerto Ricans, erase past history, celebrate the alleged liberation of the island from Spain, and promote a measured assimilation of the new colonial subjects.

Negrón de Montilla's arguments and narrative remain at the core of the history of education and the history of early twentieth-century Puerto Rico, so much so that scholarship does not stray far from her framework. In addition, research has continued to rely on the same source base—the annual reports of the commissioners of education. The annual reports, in fact, are omnipresent in Puerto Rico's scholarship. They are some of the most researched, cited, and mined sources, and with good reason. They are readily available at most research institutions in hard copies, on microfilms, and through interlibrary loan. In fact, the annual reports are truly an invaluable source for Puerto Rican history, for in addition to serving as brilliant examples of Americanization ideologies, they document the dynamic growth of the school system in those early years. The colonial government founded new schools and trained and hired a new generation of teachers. Hundreds of thousands of children attended school for the first time. The reports also detail changes in policies, reflecting how historical moments shaped curriculum. War-work campaigns took center stage during World War I. Elitist athletics became more inclusive physical education programs after the war. School lunchrooms and cafeterias were founded in ever larger numbers in the 1930s. In so many ways, the annual reports document how Puerto Rican society transformed.

However, there are significant limitations to the source, particularly voice and vision. As mentioned earlier, the reports were written by commissioners of education appointed by the US president. They were crafted for consumption by the US president and other colonial officials. The narrative was intended to confirm the supremacy of US imperial policies on the island, to document the success of assimilation and colonial state building in Puerto Rico as a model for other campaigns in the mainland and colonies. The colonial school project in Puerto Rico, scholars remind us, was practiced in conversation with competing projects in Hawaii, the Philippines, the Pacific Northwest, the Northeast, and the Southwest. The annual reports, therefore, glorified the alleged successes of Americanization campaigns. They were produced through the voice of US imperialists and meant to highlight the "benevolence" of the United States as a "modern" empire. Uncle Sam was paternalistic and dominant without losing compassion for his colonial subjects.[28]

As students of Puerto Rican history and of US imperial history more broadly, we have to be aware of the limits of this historical source. It does not tell the entire story. No matter how carefully we try to employ critical historical methods and read between the lines, we cannot find the varied perspectives of Puerto Rican teachers who had already been practicing when US forces arrived. It homogenizes the important identities and divisions within a new generation of teachers that emerged in the 1920s. It cannot fully represent the demands and expectations of parents and students in the 1940s.

Therefore, the questions for us today—and the call proposed by Negrón de Montilla in the conclusion of her study—are: What have these government-produced sources and top-down conceptualizations of Americanization left out of the story? Whose voices have been excluded, sanitized, and silenced? How have scholars inadvertently reproduced these silences in the analysis of the sources? Can we, as students of history invested in providing a critical and nuanced understanding of both US imperial practices and Puerto Rican society in the early twentieth century, produce a more balanced story? How do we move past the oppression/resistance dichotomy? Did the early twentieth-century history of schools not share the dynamic struggles and challenges that have been proposed for the history of the working class?[29] Were Puerto Rican teachers, parents, and students simple receptors of top-down Americanization policies? Or did they offer their own interpretations and visions along with manipulations of the concept? Why would Americanization through schools be the only location where dynamic hegemonic processes were not in play?[30] Providing a critical history of early twentieth-century Puerto Rico, one that privileges the contributions of nonelite historical actors, requires that we ask broader questions and search for different sources.

Those perspectives, demands, and negotiations, which are at the core of the "cultural politics" of colonial schools in Puerto Rico, have not yet been exposed.[31] I propose a reinterpretation of the history of early colonial schools. In conversation with scholars of the history of education, empire, and the subaltern, I propose to unmask the "hidden history" of Puerto Rico's schools during the first half of the twentieth century, a moment that is most notoriously understood to be symbolic of the ideological violence of Americanization and US colonialism.[32]

CULTURAL POLITICS OF SCHOOLS, CULTURAL NATIONALISM, AND MODERN COLONIALISM

The historiography, therefore, has reproduced theories, methods, and narratives that serve to further consolidate a monolithic interpretation of the centrality of Americanization practices in early twentieth-century Puerto Rico. However, the narrative of Americanization, the dichotomy of oppression and resistance, is also reproduced in the contemporary politics of cultural nationalism in a colonial/postcolonial context. While Puerto Rican cultural-nationalist identities are vibrant and dynamic, they are also fragile. They are constructed, practiced, and reproduced within a modern version of a colonial state, for despite the celebration of cultural nationalism in modern (post-1950s) Puerto Rico, fundamentally, the island lacks political sovereignty over its territory. While it functions as a semi-independent state associated to the United States, it remains a colonial territory. Everyday reminders of US authority and presence on the island—evident in the existence of military bases or through fear of "contamination" in popular culture and language—generate tremendous anxiety and require that cultural nationalists continue to clearly reestablish the boundaries between "Puerto Rican" and "American" ways.[33]

Puerto Rican intellectuals and scholars collaborated with Governor Luis Muñoz Marín and the Partido Popular Democrático (PPD, Popular Democratic Party) in the 1950s to define a new "cultural nationalism." Cultural nationalism became a state-sponsored identity that has served both the colonial government and multiple sectors of society. At the core of the celebration of cultural nationalism is a definition of Puerto Rican "authenticity" that is constructed in direct opposition to that imagined to be "American." Very simply, Puerto Ricans speak Spanish; Americans speak English. Puerto Ricans embody a history of racial harmony; Americans are white supremacists and maintain rigid racial hierarchies. Puerto Rican women flourish within the *gran familia puertorriqueña* and find freedom of expression through "social feminism"; US feminist ideologies fall outside of the national "family." The dichotomy produces unrealistic and uncritical generalizations of both groups. According to the cultural-nationalist narrative, in addition, Puerto Rican cultural identities, best personified through the performance of difference (language, racial harmony, and gender roles), have survived in spite of the virulent and oppressive Americanization campaigns carried out in the early twentieth century. As scholars have proposed, emerging Puerto Rican national identities were constructed in opposition to the Other, the *Americanos*.[34]

Two cultural markers particularly susceptible to contamination within the framework of cultural nationalism are language and history. English-language instruction was a requirement of Americanization policies. Therefore, the imposition of English-language instruction in the early twentieth century was a direct challenge to Puerto Rican culture and identity, for Spanish was the vernacular in homes, government, and business. English-language instruction provoked fears of cultural genocide. The US intention to impose English-language instruction generated resistance from teachers, parents, politicians, intellectuals, and others. The resistance to English was not a myth but a fact. Teachers led the opposition to English-language instruction and suffered the consequences—professional repression, blacklisting, and firings.[35] Spanish-language policies continue to inform contemporary cultural-nationalist debates. In turn, a defiant resistance to English, a glorification of Spanish, and a rejection of "Spanglish" are important national performances. While scholars have proposed the malleability of US imperial policies, few have critiqued the heroic history of teachers' resistance to English. The potential corruption of Spanish language among Puerto Ricans "here and there" (island and mainland) is also a contemporary fear. This fear was at the root of destructive 1970s cultural identity debates and is part of everyday conversations within families who have members living "en la isla y afuera." Language remains at the heart of cultural-nationalist identities.[36]

History, historical narratives, and public school history textbooks are equally contested. Whose history is taught in island schools? In the first half of the twentieth century, history texts written by Puerto Rican scholars that proposed an island-centered interpretation of history were denied distribution in colonial schools. Those textbooks that were approved instead proposed a different interpretation of history and Puerto Rico's location within it. The commissioner of education had the authority to approve "appropriate texts" for colonial public schools. The approved textbook, *Historia de Puerto Rico* (1922), written by commissioner of education Paul G. Miller, proposed a narrative that framed local history as a model study of modern and benevolent US imperial practices.[37] Miller's textbook also dismissed the island's history before the arrival of US forces as insignificant and traditional while it minimized Puerto Rico's particularly Caribbean history. The cultural nationalism of the 1950s, however, revolutionized the history curriculum.[38] Historical narratives and the language of instruction remain two markers of national identity that have had to be defended from US imperial impositions and cultural contamination.

It is at this location in cultural-nationalist narratives that the history of Americanization policies takes a central role. Fundamentally, the early history of Americanization is one of the best examples that represent the dichotomous construction of oppression and resistance, of us versus them, of colonialism versus nationalism. History and language remain deeply connected to contemporary debates about authenticity, identity, and nation. This suggests that a revision of Americanization scholarship might appear—initially and at a superficial level—to undermine the nationalist narrative built on notions of difference and cultural heritage.

Instead, I propose that a critical study of the "cultural politics" of colonial schools in the first half of the twentieth century can help liberate that history from rigid nationalist narrative constructions by allowing for a more well-rounded understanding of how local actors chose to engage with colonial schools and, by extension, the emerging colonial state. While fully aware of the power relations between the colony and the metropole, I nevertheless suggest that teachers and parents engaged colonial schools in a way that condemned racist Americanization policies while contributing to and complementing a broader racial and social uplift project. This collaboration, a negotiated process, reflected how intermediate actors in the colonial hierarchy practiced the Puerto Rican political ideology of autonomism rather than outright revolution or annexation. This daily negotiation of local actors with the colonial state was carried out through local schools. The colonial state project was dependent on the collaboration of teachers and parents. It was not a simple transmission of top-down policies to the middle (teachers) and from the middle to the bottom (parents and students). Instead, the three sectors found ways to negotiate their interests and visions without undermining the authority and framework of the colonial state. It is this process of engagement and negotiation—best exemplified in colonial schools—that led to the founding of a modern and reformed US colonial state in the Caribbean in the 1950s in the form of Puerto Rico's Estado Libre Asociado (ELA, Free Associated State). A revision of the history of Americanization, therefore, can help us understand how intermediate actors contributed to the formation and resilience of the modern colonial state.

A PUERTO RICAN STORY: SOURCES AND ARGUMENTS

What is the story beyond Americanization? That depends on historical sources. Schools were at the heart of early twentieth-century debates about the successes, failures, and intentions of the colonial state. Elites, professionals, teachers, and parents were engaged in an ongoing conversation that evaluated the "progress" of local society through the lens of schools and public instruction. These conversations were recorded in different documentary sources. Not only was the vision of the colonial state recorded in the annual reports, but, more significantly, it became policy. The vision informed the drafting and approval of the new school laws for Puerto Rico. This colonial legislation, discussed in chapter 1, represented conversations held between US colonial educators who traveled and practiced throughout the US empire. School legislation in Puerto Rico was part of a broader vision for the incorporation of colonial peoples inside and outside the borders of the US mainland, including the US South, Hawaii, the Philippines, Native American communities, and the new immigrant communities throughout the mainland.

The perspectives of local teachers, however, were also recorded in multiple venues. As the historical body of scholarship produced by Rubén Maldonado Jiménez best exemplifies, local teachers had shared their opinions, protests, and agendas through the publication of education newspapers since the 1890s.[39] By 1919 teachers published regularly in the newspaper *El Mundo*. In addition, in collaboration with the Department of Education, they published articles and speeches in the education journal *La revista escolar de Puerto Rico/Porto Rico School Review* (*PRSR*). As the visions of the department and teachers began increasingly to move in different directions by the late 1920s and 1930s, sharing this journal became highly contested. In addition, when teachers joined forces in an island-wide labor union in 1911, they began to collect the minutes of their meetings, which are today stored in the private archives of the Asociación de Maestros de Puerto Rico (AMPR, Association of Teachers of Puerto Rico). Finally, teachers from different generations published memoirs that told of their history and practice in schools since the late nineteenth century. These important sources document how generations of teachers held competing visions and perspectives about the value of schools and instruction.

However, I am mindful that these sources provide the perspective of the elite few, the leadership of the *magisterio*. The number of teachers grew from 1,623 in 1910, to 3,220 in 1920, and to 8,881 by 1946.[40] While I try to provide as many competing voices of individual teachers as possible, I recognize that the opinions most often found in primary sources were those of the teaching leadership, which I refer to as "elite teachers" to distinguish them from the rest of the teaching class. These are the sources that inform chapters 2, 3, and 4.

Parents and students were equally demanding of their rights before the colonial state. In the 1940s, in particular, their voices are documented in the archives. They wrote letters to the commissioner of education and to the senator and first elected governor of Puerto Rico, Luis Muñoz Marín. Their letters expressed how they defined the values of school and instruction for themselves, their families, and their communities. Parents and students, additionally, were clear about their expectations that the colonial state make schools accessible to all. They claimed their rights, as members of Puerto Rican society, to public instruction. Chapter 5 highlights their demands and how they contributed to the process of negotiation with what became the new, modern colonial state in Puerto Rico, the Estado Libre Asociado. The story told in chapter 5, therefore, is important to the early history of education and colonialism in Puerto Rico, for student and parent voices boldly emerged and challenged the assumptions held by Puerto Rican educators and US colonial administrators in prior decades. When their voices become accessible in the archives, they proposed a dynamic understanding of the relationship between citizenship, schools, and colonialism.

This combination of sources allows for the construction of multiple interconnected narratives about schools, the colonial state, and teachers in the early twentieth century. I offer three main lines of argument. First, schools were at the heart of the colonial state project. In the first half of the twentieth century, the US colonial state in Puerto Rico evolved through different stages: a military occupation (1898–1900), a colonial civil government (the Foraker Act of 1900, the Jones Act of 1917), and a modern colonial state under Puerto Rican leadership (the ELA, formed in 1952). Each of these versions of the colonial state required the collaboration of teachers through schools, for it was in the classroom that colonial state ideologies were intended to be transmitted to and reproduced by the next generation—children. Throughout the study I emphasize the centrality of schools to the project of building the colonial state.

Second, teachers and educators proposed a citizenship-building project. Social hierarchies that differentiated its members according to race, class, and gender were already present and vibrant in nineteenth-century Puerto Rico. Dominant honor codes, the ideal *gran familia puertorriqueña*, the political vision of creole liberal elites, and the social project of the professional classes shaped turn-of-the-century Puerto Rico. It was teachers, however, who, as intermediate actors, claimed the right and the moral authority to create citizens in the early twentieth century. Elite teachers, in particular, promoted a vision for regeneration, social uplift, and progress that was informed by late nineteenth-century neo-Lamarckian eugenic ideologies. The new schools founded under the US colonial state became the venue through which elite teachers promoted their citizenship-building project. Teachers negotiated the intentions of Americanization in a way that simultaneously allowed for the promotion of their visions through schools.

However, definitions of citizenship were always dynamic. As the role of schools, teaching demographics, and social context changed, so did the definition of citizenship. While citizenship in the late 1910s and 1920s represented a balance between Americanization and regeneration arguments, the framework changed a decade later. Resistance against colonial repression of political ideologies exploded in the 1930s. University students called for a reevaluation of the limits of colonial forms of citizenship. By the 1940s parents and students had highlighted the constructed and reciprocal relationship between colonial state and citizen. Citizenship was a deeply contested concept, and teachers and others redefined its intentions according to changes in colonial society. Throughout the process, however, what does not change is the centrality of schools and public instruction to definitions of citizenship and the colonial state.

Third, with the intention of moving beyond the oppression/resistance dichotomy, I highlight the process of community building within the teaching profession, which required the clear establishment of hierarchies and differences. While the teaching leadership spoke in a united voice when they opposed the policies of the commissioner of education, there were important divisions within the ranks. The definition of progress, modernity, and gender was at the core of the debate. How to train "modern girls"? How to regenerate the *jíbaros*? How to define the limits of modern and progressive gender practices in secular, coeducational, public schools? These questions informed the debates that emerged within the teaching profession and reflected a reaction to the dynamic women's social movement of the 1910s and 1920s. Schools became a location where the gender politics of citizenship-building ideologies could be clearly established.

These three lines of argument come together in the broader process of colonial state formation. The history of schools in the early twentieth century suggests that nonelite actors, like teachers and parents, were equally invested in shaping the policies of colonial schools. They proposed their intentions to contribute to the citizenship-building project. However, as they negotiated curriculum, teaching appointments, funding, and access to schools, teachers and parents were contributing to a negotiated process that led to the reproduction and consolidation of a colonial state. Public schoolteachers were not revolutionaries. In the tradition of middle-ground autonomist ideology, they found ways to work within the boundaries of colonialism. This negotiation, however, was important and contributed to the popular politics that supported and consolidated a Puerto Rican–led colonial state by 1952. The US imperial visions of the early 1900s were never truly foreign. They were malleable, complementary, and in conversation with the legacy of Spanish colonialism, which generated the island's colonial reformist leadership. However, colonial reform was carried out not only by local political leadership. As this story suggests, intermediate actors in the colonial hierarchy—teachers—also shaped the political process.

ORGANIZATION OF THE BOOK

I tell the story of the everyday interactions between teachers, parents, and US colonial officials at the heart of the process of building the colonial state through four historical moments. The first period, the 1890s to 1916, highlights early challenges to the expansion of US empire in Puerto Rico (chapter 1). At the turn of the century, US imperial agents (American teachers and administrators) enthusiastically embarked upon the new "white man's burden" in the Caribbean. They imagined the Caribbean colony to be a tabula rasa, an island of children with no history and little experience with modern education and government. However, they soon realized that the intellectual and political legacy of late nineteenth-century Puerto Rican teachers, educators, and intellectuals denied them the space to unconditionally implement their vision of creating "tropical Yankees" (chapter 2). Teachers and educators composed a small but significant community of local intellectuals. They challenged new US colonial school policies, which intended to disenfranchise them and deny them their traditional patriarchal authority in the training and molding of Puerto Rican children. These two chapters examine how turn-of-the-century US imperial agents and Puerto Rican educators engaged each other's visions of modern education within the emerging US empire. This early negotiation established the parameters that shaped the cultural politics of schools throughout the first half of the century.

In the second period, 1917 to 1930, US imperial agents were driven by a stronger urgency than ever before to promote Americanization. Puerto Ricans were no longer colonial subjects. As the United States prepared to enter World War I, in March 1917 the US Congress granted Puerto Ricans born on the island US citizenship. The war consolidated Puerto Rico's military value to the United States in the Caribbean. However, this Americanization push was challenged by a new generation of Puerto Rican teachers who emerged and united under the newly founded AMPR. This labor union represented Puerto Rican educators' visions for public schools. It was an institution that created the space in which to formulate a citizenship-building project that had little to do with Americanization. At this significant moment in the construction of a US colonial state in Puerto Rico, intermediate actors (teachers) intervened, mitigated the harsh intentions of US colonialism, and promoted a citizenship-building project.

Chapter 3 examines the teachers' citizenship-building project and, particularly, the multiple conflicts and contradictions (generational and gendered) that emerged. Modern education and racial regeneration ideologies came together in discussions over the potential transformative benefits of teaching home economics, modern agriculture, and physical education. Teachers were optimistic that they could "regenerate" and "whiten" the Puerto Rican national body through the teaching of health, hygiene, and sanitation. They could transform the allegedly physically weak and submissive Puerto Rican girls into modern and progressive homemakers by teaching domestic science in schools and bringing that science directly into homes through extension work. They intended to modernize male *jíbaros* into efficient farmers through the teaching of scientific agriculture in rural schools. They could strengthen the weakened national "race" through the teaching of science, health, hygiene, and physical education. Finally, they could teach literacy and civics with the intention of transforming illiterate students into well-rounded citizens in the service of a potential Puerto Rican nation.

Teachers believed that by introducing the modern science that informed these school topics to students and, by extension, their parents, they could directly address the problems of the home, health, and labor and teach families modern strategies for regeneration. It was this goal, the "racial regeneration" of the citizenry, instead of traditional characterizations of Americanization, that Puerto Rican teachers advocated in the late 1910s and 1920s. Nevertheless, the process of defining and consolidating this citizenship-building project struggled to address the newly emerging generational, gender, and class debates within this intermediate sector of the colonial hierarchy.

The third moment was defined by local responses to the 1930s international economic crisis, which brought to light the dire material conditions of the majority of the working class. Collaboration between Puerto Rican colonial reformers, public health professionals, and a new generation of modern educators emerged as public schools became key sites through which communities received support (nutrition), medical services, and job training. Americanization goals lost priority as a new generation of Puerto Rican colonial reformers implemented economic reconstruction policies. In turn, this experience consolidated the patriarchal role of the colonial state through the public schools.

In the early twentieth century, however, the history of Puerto Ricans was not restricted to the geographic boundaries of the island. Workers migrated throughout the US empire in search of employment. The early Puerto Rican diaspora became a lightning rod for debates over citizenship, race, and empire in the US mainland. Chapter 4 follows Puerto Rican workers to the Northeast. Island-based definitions of citizenship, race, and imperialism were always constructed in relationship with debates on the mainland. This chapter examines how a 1935 psychological study of Puerto Rican children in a New York City public school generated grave anxieties for US racial eugenicists and immigration restrictionists as well as for Puerto Rican educators. Students, education, and schools were sites through which many attempted to define citizenship, nation, race, and empire.

During the fourth period, the 1940s through the 1950s, a new generation of Puerto Rican colonial reformers rose to power through the discourse and promises of populism (chapter 5). Luis Muñoz Marín emerged as the charismatic leader of the newly founded PPD. Muñoz Marín and the PPD gained the political support of the working class as they ushered forward a new reformed colonial state— the ELA. What was the relationship between citizen, colonial state, and schools in the 1940s? This chapter highlights personal letters parents and students wrote to Muñoz Marín in the late 1940s and early 1950s in which they appealed for attention to their concerns about teachers and schools. They demonstrate how the new political discourse of citizen and nation promoted by Muñoz Marín empowered Puerto Rican parents and students, who then used those concepts to challenge the limitations of the newly founded colonial state. By the 1950s, when Muñoz Marín's administration brought to fruition the new Puerto Rican colonial state, the ELA represented, I argue, the tradition of generations of teachers and educators who daily negotiated and curbed the intentions of earlier versions of US colonialism. The voices of students and parents in the 1940s highlight the centrality of schools and education to the definition of citizen in the new, reformed, modern colonial state of the 1950s.

The conclusion ties together the book's narrative line—that the consolidation of US colonialism in the Caribbean represents generations of negotiation between intermediate actors and US imperial agents. I also examine how Puerto Rico contributes to and challenges comparative Latin American and Caribbean historical conversations about race, citizenship, and nation building.

chapter 1

The Politics of Empire, Education, and Race

The spectacle of clashing political projects shaped the historical moment that was turn-of-the-century Puerto Rico. Puerto Rican liberals in the late nineteenth century successfully negotiated a reformed colonial relationship with the declining Spanish empire. Spanish imperial authority in the Caribbean was deteriorating as Puerto Rican liberal reformers and Cuban radical revolutionaries struggled against an oppressive Spanish colonialism. Meanwhile, the expansionist United States was emerging as a new imperial power in the Caribbean and the Pacific, challenging the political projects of local elites within the colonies and the broader Spanish imperial intentions in the regions. While Spanish and US imperial actors battled each other for supremacy in the Caribbean, creole liberal reformers and revolutionaries struggled to maintain their authority within each island's political hierarchy.

The 1880s and 1890s were years of intense political activity in Puerto Rico. Liberal reformers, reorganized into the Partido Autonomista Puertorriqueño (Puerto Rican Autonomist Party) in 1887, demanded that the Spanish colonial state redefine the relationship between empire and colony. Guided by the political ideology of autonomism, liberal reformers called for greater local and municipal control over the island's political and economic affairs without fully rejecting Spain's political authority as empire. In response to the political pressure of liberal reformers, the highest representative of Spanish colonial authority on the island, the appointed governor, launched a campaign against the proponents of liberal reform. Through the notorious Guardia Civil (Civil Guard), Governor Romualdo Palacios persecuted those opposed to absolute Spanish authority. Despite the repression, liberal reformers achieved their goals in 1897 when the queen of Spain granted Puerto Rico and Cuba a new constitution, the *Carta Autonómica* (Autonomic Charter). This new constitution altered Spain's relationship to the Caribbean colonies. While Spain maintained sovereignty over both colonies, it granted them the right to establish an insular government with elected representatives. The Autonomic Charter, which was a Spanish reaction to the political pressure of both Puerto Rican liberal reformers and Cuban revolutionaries, fulfilled some basic tenets of autonomist ideology. The year 1898 began with a new promise for autonomism, a political project that different sectors of the creole elite nevertheless contested and redefined.[1]

The liberal reformers' political project, however, was quickly undermined by the expansionist intentions of the United States. Since the 1850s, the political and physical boundaries of the United States had been expanding west, spilling across the Pacific Ocean. Beyond the territory of Hawaii, US imperial aggression reached the Philippines. US imperial actors first challenged the Spanish colonial government, then the Filipino "insurgency," with the intention of acquiring the archipelago. After the success of the US military in Manila, US imperial intentions turned to Cuba. The US intervention in the 1895 Cuban War of Independence became the "Spanish-American" War of 1898. Before negotiating the Treaty of Paris with Spain, the US military invaded its number two target in the Caribbean, Puerto Rico. At the end of the "splendid little war," the United States and Spain signed the Treaty of Paris on December 19, 1898. The treaty called an end to the war between the two empires and ceded Puerto Rico, Cuba, and other Spanish territories in the Caribbean and the Pacific to the United States. The treaty also provided the legal foundation for the new US military occupation of Puerto Rico. For eighteen months the United States maintained a military occupation of the island. On April 12, 1900, the US Congress approved a new civil government for Puerto Rico with the Foraker Act. The founding of the new civil government confirmed what several Puerto Rican liberal reformers feared. Through the act and the judicial clarification of the 1901–4 "Insular Cases," the island was defined as an unincorporated territory of the United States. The Foraker Act consolidated US imperial intentions to retain the island as a "permanent colony."[2]

The United States entertained several objectives for Puerto Rico. For some Americans, the island held the promise of economic profit. They imagined Puerto Rico to be ripe for economic investment and agricultural production, a source of cheap labor, and a ready market for US exports. The political project of US empire in Puerto Rico, however, was not clearly defined. Some in the mainland were opposed to US expansion and acquisition of colonial territories, convinced it went against the basic tenets of a liberal democracy. Others, informed by a strong sense of white supremacy and the Anglo-Saxon right to govern over those defined as "inferior peoples," imagined other opportunities in Puerto Rico. Within this range, Americans disagreed over the political projects to pursue in the new permanent colony. Some had faith that Puerto Ricans (at least the elite) were intelligent and demonstrated a capacity for self-government. Others questioned whether, despite requiring the elite to undergo a period of apprenticeship under the tutelage of US colonial officials, Puerto Ricans were capable of overcoming the intellectual and moral deficiencies assumed to shape non-Anglo-Saxon peoples.[3]

These early questions about how to rule the colonial territories, however, were clarified through US imperial practices in the first decade of the twentieth century. US colonial officials in the Caribbean and the Pacific drew clear distinctions between the new US territories. The ideology of Anglo-Saxon supremacy and the US colonial officials' assessments of the new colonial subjects informed how each territory was imagined to be incorporated into the US empire. Through the constitutional debates over the Insular Cases, the Supreme Court defined the new colonial territories' location. Once Puerto Rico was defined as an unincorporated territory and assumed to maintain a permanent relationship to the US empire, US colonial officials were charged with the responsibility to "Americanize" the island and its people.[4]

Americanization had multiple meanings and intentions. Under the Foraker Act, the island's economy and productive capacity were reorganized in the interests of US corporations. Puerto Rico, along with Cuba and the Dominican Republic, became a prominent site of America's "sugar kingdom."[5] Politically, the new civil government established a framework that located US colonial officials in positions of authority over local political leaders. The intention to Americanize politics meant rearranging the political organization and structure of the island government to more neatly correspond to the centralized authority of the United States, whether the US-appointed governor of Puerto Rico or the US president. Although some liberal reformers were initially hopeful that an association with the United States might lead to the fulfillment of their autonomist political project, many were disillusioned by the Foraker Act and its clear colonial intentions. Nevertheless, in the first decade, Puerto Rican liberal reformers (*Republicanos* and *Federales*) demanded recognition from the US colonial officials as the rightful political representatives of the island and its people.[6]

Under the banner of "benevolent empire," Americanization also suggested investment in the health and social welfare of the working class. US colonial officials collaborated with select Puerto Rican professionals to reorganize civil services such as public health, sanitation, and education.[7] The broad goal of Americanizing colonial subjects through education was a core policy of the self-defined modern, civilizing, and benevolent US empire. Broadly, Americanization through education meant the creation of "tropical Yankees," or the creation of colonial subjects who supported US colonialism on the island.[8] Visions for the Americanization of Puerto Ricans, in particular, were shaped by US colonial officials' understanding of imperial practices and racial ideologies. Americanization was more than replacing Spanish as the language of instruction with English. It suggested the uplift and transformation of a Spanish colonial people into members of the modern US empire. Historical actors demonstrate, nevertheless, that in this early historical period (1898–1917), the relationship between Americanization and education was in flux. The multiple actors (Puerto Rican and American) invested in the success of public schools challenged, redefined, and contested the definition of Americanization. Colonial schools became an important and highly contested site for Americanization in Puerto Rico, where competing agendas and political projects were carried out.

Expanding the existing public school system was an overwhelming challenge for the young US colonial government. Many Americans have been celebrated for their contribution to the early colonial school project. However, while elite colonial officials (such as Brig. Gen. Guy V. Henry, Gen. John Eaton, and Head of the Bureau of Education Victor S. Clark) played influential roles, they were guided, informed, and assisted by a core of elite Puerto Rican professionals and educators. For example, some of the first supervisors of the six newly established school districts in 1900 included local intellectuals, educators, and politicians such as José A. Saldaña, Robert H. Todd, Jorge Bird Arias, Enrique Huyke, and Rosendo Matienzo Cintrón.[9] In addition, many "intermediate" historical actors contributed equally to the founding and expansion of the colonial school system, including thousands of Puerto Rican schoolteachers as well as active parents and students. Together these historical actors informed the debates that guided the formation of new schools. Each contributed to the process of defining the goals of Americanization and education. Despite US colonial intentions, Americanization through schools was never defined and imposed from the top down. Instead, it was negotiated by intermediate groups and the working class. The story of how local actors shaped the founding and direction of the colonial school project begins in chapter 2.

Our first step in the analysis of the negotiation of colonial state building through local school projects is an introduction to the turn-of-the-century moment. This chapter presents a brief history of Spanish colonialism and education in nineteenth-century Puerto Rico. Local elites were aware of the Spanish colonial state's negligence toward universal education. The state of schools and education, however, became one of multiple arguments US colonial officials used to justify their intervention and occupation. US colonial officials celebrated their version of tutelary colonialism as modern and progressive and, therefore, deeply distinct from the practices of the Spanish empire. US visions for colonial education, at the same time, were deeply informed by racial ideologies and hierarchies.

This chapter examines the ways US historical actors imagined the new relationship between education and empire in the early years of encounter. The 1898 war, the expansion of the US empire into the Caribbean and the Pacific, and the newly defined "permanent" relationship between Puerto Rico and the United States forced insular and imperial political projects into conversation. In this early moment of encounter, US colonial officials established their authority over colonial schools. Americans launched themselves as the new imperial authority, centered public instruction at the heart of the emerging imperial venture, and highlighted the permanency of Puerto Rico as a colony of the United States. Education was at the heart of an imperial project informed by US racial ideologies.

Colonialism and Education in Nineteenth-Century Puerto Rico

The actions of slaves and African-descended peoples in the French Caribbean in the late eighteenth century deeply transformed the direction of Caribbean and Atlantic history. In addition to the North Atlantic revolutions in the United States and France, freed and enslaved Guadeloupian and Saint Dominguean practices in the 1790s radicalized the liberal ideologies of the Age of Revolution.[10] By the 1820s, driven by economic and political motivations, most Spanish colonies in the Américas had broken away from the Spanish empire. Elite creoles and subaltern groups wrought fragile and tense, yet effective, alliances. Together they fought for national independence.[11]

The liberal ideologies and practices traveling throughout the Caribbean in the early nineteenth century, however, did not lead to revolution in Puerto Rico or Cuba. Instead, these islands became the two remaining colonies, and royalist strongholds, of the Spanish empire in the Caribbean. At the same time, the wounded and declining Spanish empire clung to Puerto Rico and Cuba. Both island colonies became a relative asylum for the remaining conservative royalists in the region. Supporters of Spanish colonialism, in the face of widespread revolutionary forces in Latin America, took refuge on the islands.

In the early nineteenth century, in response to Latin American revolutionary movements and the pressure of Puerto Rican and Cuban creole leadership, the Spanish crown, with the intention to retain the two colonies, provided reformed colonial legislation. Reformist liberal economic policies, like the 1815 Cédula de

Gracias (Decree of pardon), generated economic incentives (land, tax, and trade), facilitated the importation of African slaves into the colonies, and helped create the environment required to revolutionize export-commodity production. In the first half of the nineteenth century, Cuba and Puerto Rico, along with Brazil, became leading sugar exporters, promptly replacing Saint Domingue's sugar supply to the Atlantic markets.[12]

In addition, the island of Puerto Rico witnessed a dramatic demographic change in the first half of the nineteenth century. The Cédula and the economic opportunities it generated attracted a variety of immigrants into the small island. Wealthy immigrants from Europe, the neighboring Caribbean islands, and the United States brought their capital, slaves, and knowledge about the production of sugar and coffee. Significantly, Caribbean laborers also came in large numbers. Workers came alone and with their families, providing the highly valued skilled trades required in the developing economy.[13] In 1802 the island's population was a mere 160,892, the majority of whom were African-descended peoples. Out of these residents, 15.3 percent were enumerated as slaves, 40 percent as free colored, and 44.6 percent as white. A generation later, the population had doubled. By 1830, out of 324,838 residents, 10.6 percent were enumerated as slaves, 39.3 percent as free colored, and 50.1 percent as white.[14]

By midcentury, Puerto Rico's economy had undergone important transitions. The abolition of the slave trade, competition with beet sugar producers, and the gradual emancipation of slaves by 1873 undermined the profitability of sugar production and export. As sugar declined, the coffee highlands became the center of economic and demographic growth. Coffee production in the central and western mountains transformed communities. Free laborers, escaping labor conditions on sugar plantations or seeking employment on coffee farms, moved into the region. However, the experience for coffee workers and small landowners in the late nineteenth century was hardly bountiful. The working conditions, diseases, and loss of land led to the steady impoverishment of coffee labor throughout the late nineteenth century.[15]

Meanwhile, Spanish immigrants, recruited by extended family members, came to the highlands, generated wealth as merchants and large landowners, and returned with their profits to their country of origin. These were years when creole Puerto Rican identities were emerging and local elites began asserting their rights against the privileged *peninsulares*. Creoles defined and advocated for the political ideologies of separatism or colonial reform. Wealthier Spanish immigrants faced great resentment on behalf of separatist creole elites. In addition, the increasingly indebted creole coffee farmers wanted change in the economic structure, which favored Spanish immigrants. Together, these economic conditions, along with the revolutionary ideology of separatists like Ramón Emeterio Betances, led to the 1868 Grito de Lares (Cry of Lares), an important anti-colonial revolutionary movement.[16]

The Spanish colonial government, however, intolerant of anticolonial activity, put down the rebellion. After the revolution, due to repression, persecution, and exile of political separatists, colonial reform (autonomism) became the dominant political ideology of the late nineteenth century. Autonomism, however, represented a range of platforms and intentions (radical autonomism versus assimilation). It was not a homogeneous political ideology, and liberal autonomists like Román Baldorioty de Castro and José Julián Acosta, in their intention to generate a new colonial relationship with the Spanish empire, faced intense repression by the Spanish colonial government on the island.[17]

Historians of nineteenth-century Puerto Rico have carefully delineated the ways colonial liberal society was organized through hierarchies of race, class, and gender.[18] One organizing concept in particular, the *gran familia puertorriqueña* (the great Puerto Rican family), was emblematic of the hierarchies. Similar to Sandra Lauderdale Graham's conceptualization of the household and the "house and street" in colonial Brazil, the image of the *gran familia* extended the familial organizational structure to the rest of society.[19] The *gran familia* organized colonial society under patriarchal authority. The male head of household held the authority over his subalterns, including his wife, children, and employed or enslaved laborers. Local, regional, islandwide, and imperial politics were intended to be carried out between elite male heads of households. Nevertheless, nonelite white males and nonwhite males also jockeyed for voice and influence. And, although the organizational structure required the subordination of women in public and private spaces, women of all classes asserted their views and ideologies. Bourgeois women asserted authority over plebeian women. Meanwhile, plebeian women fought for their honor and demanded that their partners fulfill their duties to wife and children, as court records attest. Although the development of race, class, and gender ideologies was specific to regions and labor relations, white creole male privilege was reproduced through the organizing principle of the *gran familia*.[20]

Although patriarchy was one organizing framework of the late nineteenth century, subaltern men and women challenged its authority. Liberal society in the nineteenth century, the heads of the *gran familia* in particular, was concerned with the great "social question" of labor. Puerto Rico was an exporter of agricultural commodities dependent on the labor of slaves and the peasantry. Planters struggled to control the labor of the free and independent peasantry through vagrancy laws, such as the Reglamento de Jornaleros of 1849. Meanwhile, the control and wealth of elite Puerto Ricans were undermined with the emancipation of slavery in 1873. In the late nineteenth century, the peasantry challenged the restrictive regulations of the Reglamento, while the recently emancipated intensely negotiated their labor contracts, their right to work, their mobility, and the terms of their wages.[21]

Although the elite represented a small but powerful minority on the island, the majority of residents, in fact, were workers—men and women who contributed their labor to the production of agricultural commodities and all their complementary demands. There were important divisions within the working group between skilled artisans, semiskilled laborers, and unskilled workers. Standards of living also varied between urban and rural workers. Some rural workers owned small plots of land or worked and resided on a small plot of their boss's land in exchange for labor and crops. This majority nonelite population was also of diverse racial heritage. Many had early origins on the island. They were descendants of African slaves, European masters and workers, and other Caribbean peoples who had settled on the island over the centuries. The nineteenth-century population, however, grew rapidly. By the end of the century, many were descendants of recent nineteenth-century Caribbean immigrants, also of African heritage, who made the island their home.[22]

However, creole intellectuals—who were articulating emerging Puerto Rican identities, celebrating coffee creole culture, and writing essays and pamphlets describing the conditions of the working class in the late nineteenth century—found little promise for progress when they looked at the majority nonelite population. Intellectuals like Manuel Alonso, author of El gíbaro (The peasant) (1849), did not celebrate the assertiveness of recently freed laborers who established the terms of their labor contracts by defending their mobility, or the stubbornly independent peasants who refused to be tied down to another's land, or the domestic servants who brought their own children into the kitchens and homes of the patrones.[23] Instead, intellectuals penned their concerns about how to build a modern and progressive community of citizens (or, rather, potentially equal subjects as a province in the reformed Spanish empire) out of this working class. When elites turned their attention to the people, they saw obstacles to progress.

One of the leading pseudoscientific racial ideologies in Latin America and the Caribbean provided an explanation for the poverty of the nonelite. The logic was neo-Lamarckian eugenics. This desolate and pessimistic interpretation of the limits of the island's majority nonelite population was medicalized in the writings of late nineteenth-century intellectuals like Manuel Zeno Gandía.[24] It was in the medical discussions and debates, in the tradition of Latin American and Caribbean interpretations of eugenics, that intellectuals imagined a positive reformulation.[25] Neo-Lamarckian eugenics allowed for the suggestion that through the sanitation of public spaces and the hygiene of the individual, the working classes could be reformed. Young girls could become healthy, strong, moral homemakers. Boys could grow into masculine, responsible fathers and husbands. This social interpretation of eugenics imagined that society could be improved through reform and education. It was an ideology that allowed liberal reformers to imagine the regeneration of the working class, for improving the health of the "race" could also lead to a more obedient and productive labor force. This social vision for the regeneration of the nonelite, articulated by the elite in the late nineteenth century, would inform and be appropriated by intermediate actors in the colonial society of the early twentieth century, particularly educators.

This progressive vision for improved sanitation and hygiene of the working class via education, however, also reflected the very real negligence toward public education on the island. Providing colonial peoples access to public education was not a priority of the Spanish colonial state in the nineteenth century. In fact, universal public education was not something the Spanish state provided in the metropole. Instead, through legislative projects such as the Decreto Orgánico of 1865, the Spanish colonial state allowed for the founding of a small number of schools organized around a Catholic education. The schools intended to address the elementary training of male children of elite families in urban centers, although a smaller number of young girls also acquired an education. In 1898 there were 501 elementary schools and 26 secondary institutions. Of these, 384 were schools for boys and 117 for girls.[26] Out of a population of 953,243, only 47,861 children attended school.[27] The colonial central government, the Diputación Provincial, approved teacher licenses. Municipalities, meanwhile, paid teacher salaries and rented rooms or buildings for classroom use. The two main private universities were the Seminario Conciliar (Seminary) (a Jesuit school) and the Instituto Civil de Segunda Enseñanza (Civil Institute of Secondary Education). A leading advocate for university training, especially in the sciences, was Rufo Manuel Fernández, known as Padre Rufo.

Historians of nineteenth-century Puerto Rico, like Cayetano Coll y Toste and Salvador Brau, however, have documented that some of the nonelite gained access to private education.[28] Private individuals, men and women, taught small groups of young children literacy and other subjects in their homes. Private teachers, like Rafael Cordero and his sister Celestina Cordero, founded private schools in homes and workshops in San Juan. These private teachers, most in urban areas, were funded by small donations made by parents of the children they taught in the form of either cash or material goods. And some, like maestro Rafael, supplemented their income as artisans. Significantly, Rafael and Celestina were also of African descent. Brau has documented that while teachers employed by the

Spanish colonial state were often *peninsulares,* independent teachers who taught in private schools were men and women of African descent.[29]

In addition, as historian Fernando Picó argued, while access to schools and education in Puerto Rico was restricted to the elite in the nineteenth century, the working class acquired their education in the fields, factories, and kitchens. Nineteenth-century schools privileged boys and the elite and reproduced clear class and racial differences in Puerto Rican society. Picó concluded:

> The school system, far from guaranteeing equal opportunities to all, erected sharp divisions between those who could gain access to employment in commerce, municipal bureaucracies, printing presses, and more skilled occupations . . . and those who were condemned to swing an ax and a hoe, to bend under the sun of the sugar plantations, or to serve a life sentence in a humid coffee plantation. Two different types of instruction, schooling and the school of life, two cultures, one increasingly refined and European, the other ever more dehumanizing and disenfranchised, two ways of life, two experiences with public health, two types of citizens before an electoral system, the landlord and the landless, those who lived long enough to meet their grandchildren and those who died and left children to be distributed among godparents.[30]

The creole elite's vision for the regeneration of the working class, informed by racist, classist, and gendered hierarchies of late nineteenth-century liberalism, was also a critique of the long-standing neglect for public education that the Spanish colonial administration practiced in Puerto Rico. While the children of the elite were privy to an education, it was less accessible to young girls. Although private instructors tutored small groups of children in their urban homes and workshops, the majority of the working class found itself without those resources. Instead, the children of laborers worked alongside their parents in coffee, tobacco, or sugarcane plantations and workshops or in domestic service in the home. The creole elite's embrace of neo-Lamarckian promises for the regeneration of Puerto Rico's nonelite classes, therefore, reflected the conditions they witnessed in the working class, material conditions that also attested to Spanish colonial policies toward education.

US EMPIRE, EDUCATION, AND RACE

Scholars of US empire have provided narratives of national consolidation and imperial expansion informed by the economics, politics, and racial ideologies of the turn of the century. The United States proudly joined European nations as a

modern empire in 1898. Through a show of US naval power in the Pacific and
the Caribbean, the United States invaded and engaged in war in the Philippines
and abruptly intervened in the Cuban War of Independence. The expansion of
US empire overseas, the violent engagement in war with local peoples and the
declining Spanish empire, and the acquisition of island territories officially designated the United States as a member of the community of modern empires in the
late nineteenth century.[31]

Historians have examined the economic and political reasons the United States
spilled outside of its borders into the Pacific and the Caribbean. At the turn of
the century, the United States was engaged in two different but complementary
processes: national consolidation and empire building. As it acquired territories
west of the Mississippi, the government put them on one of two paths. Some territories were intended to join the United States, or to be "incorporated." Others
were held as "unincorporated" territories, as colonies of the empire. The decision
whether a territory was to be incorporated or not was not dependent on its location. Alaska and Hawaii, separated from the mainland by land and sea, became
states. The decision, rather, was partly informed by how US officials imagined
the cultural differences between the colonies. The racial Others of Puerto Rico,
Cuba, Guam, and the Philippines were never imagined to "fit" into the nation.[32]

Universal education was at the core of both national consolidation and empire
building. Liberal government officials and educators imagined that education
was an important path through which to create "Americans." There were varied
groups/classes that could benefit from education—or instruction in government,
civilization, and industry. At the same time, there were multiple types of school
projects to meet different intentions. There was no universal ideology about public schools that was applied to different classes/groups without distinction. In
fact, the nineteenth-century US common school, imagined to be available for
all students, explicitly denied access to African Americans.[33] Public education
policies reflected the racial, class, and gender hierarchies of US society in the
late nineteenth and early twentieth centuries. In other words, public education
was imagined to be a tool through which to include and exclude groups from the
polity while demarcating everyone's appropriate "place" within that polity. The
new colonial peoples of the "imperial archipelago" joined the broader community of inferiors—women, children, working-class whites, eastern European immigrants, African Americans, Native Americans—who could be trained to fulfill
their class, gender, and racial location within US society.[34]

Why "imagined"? I mean to acknowledge the distinction between educators' intentions from the practice of teachers and the reception of students. The
historiography of Native American education is a case in point. In 1889 US

Commissioner of Indian Affairs Thomas J. Morgan outlined the intentions and objectives of Native American boarding schools in his "Supplemental Report on Indian Education."[35] Some historians, like David Wallace Adams in *Education for Extinction: American Indians and the Boarding School Experience, 1875–1928,* have masterfully examined how the government's intention to assimilate Native Americans required the annihilation of traditional languages, cultures, and values.[36] More recently, some scholars have focused on specific schools, collecting letters and oral testimony of schoolchildren. The new scholarship argues that despite the explicit intentions of cultural genocide, resilient native children were able to resist violent and malicious assimilation practices. As individuals and in groups, they reconstituted community in the hostile environment of boarding schools. Indeed, as adults, some have become leaders in the reconstitution of tribal identities, languages, and practices. K. Tsianina Lomawaima's *They Called It Prairie Light: The Story of Chilocco Indian School* proposes that historical perspective.[37]

Education is at the center of the study of empire in the way that it ties together national and imperial visions. Through no other example is the interconnectedness between nation and empire more evident. The story of Richard Armstrong and Samuel Chapman Armstrong highlights this relationship. While scholars have documented how US goods and values were exported from the mainland to its colonies, the Armstrong family history suggests that national projects were informed by imported colonial examples. In the late nineteenth century, two twin school projects emerged in the United States. One was the founding of African American vocational institutes, for example, the Tuskegee Normal and Industrial Institute in 1881, pioneered by the leading black intellectual Booker T. Washington. The second was the government-sponsored Native American boarding schools founded on Native reservations, with the exception of nonreservation boarding schools, for example, the Carlisle School in Pennsylvania and the Chilocco Indian School in Oklahoma.

A model school for both Tuskegee and Native American boarding schools, however, was the Hampton Normal and Agricultural Institute, founded in 1868. The Hampton School, originally founded with the intention to educate African Americans, eventually also admitted Native American students. The Hampton School provided an industrial education curriculum. Its founder, Samuel Chapman Armstrong, was informed by the vision that African Americans and Native Americans, through rigorous schooling, could shed their "backward" traditions and values and be transformed into second-class citizens, productive and skilled in industry, contributors to the community.

It is significant that Samuel modeled his curriculum and objectives after his parents' example in Hawaii, specifically, after the manual training program at the

Hilo boarding school.[38] Samuel's parents, Richard Armstrong and Clarissa Chapman, were US Baptist missionaries "who spent their lives working and proselytizing among the people of Hawaii." Richard founded "vocational and agricultural education in the island kingdom and played a foundational role in the Americanization of Hawaii."[39] The formation of racialized school projects for nonwhite peoples on the US mainland and in the island colonies, dating to the earlier nineteenth-century example of Hawaii, was interconnected.

While as students of US empire, race, and education we must acknowledge that the twin processes of national consolidation and empire building were interconnected, and while we can identify the individuals, institutions, and policies that wove the school projects together, we must not homogenize them. Lanny Thompson reminds us that while US policy makers were clearly informed by a sense of Anglo-Saxon superiority and felt justified in expansion and occupation at the behest of Manifest Destiny, colonial peoples were not racially homogenized as the singular Other. Rather, US policy makers narrated differences in the racial construction of colonial others in the Caribbean and the Pacific. These different racial constructions, which were deeply classed and gendered, informed individual policy governance for each colony. For example, while the alleged amicable, friendly, and receptive "Porto Ricans" could be governed perpetually as members of an unincorporated colony, the wildly diverse and multiethnic brown and black tribal Filipinos could not.

Along the same lines, I argue that while US school projects across the imperial archipelago and within the US mainland were informed by the racist ideologies of Anglo-Saxon supremacy and Protestant missionary and civilizing visions, they were always specific to both imperial intentions and local conditions. Therefore, the intention to Americanize Puerto Ricans, first into colonial subjects and then into second-class citizens after 1917, was similar to but different from the vocational instruction promoted in the Philippines and in Native American boarding schools. They were all informed by the glorification of Anglo-Saxon white supremacist visions yet were tempered by the demands and conditions of local communities as well as by the larger intention of US policy makers for that colony or people.

The January 25, 1899, issue of *Puck* magazine published a cartoon titled "School Begins." In it, illustrator Louis Dalrymple caricatured the relationship between empire and civilization through the metaphor of education. The classroom was emblematic of both national consolidation and empire building. It was a site through which Uncle Sam could tutor and educate all members of his empire, including colonial and national populations. In the classroom, Uncle

Sam could instruct colonial peoples and US-based nonwhites whose progress demanded lessons in civilization.

Dalrymple's cartoon depicts a classroom where Uncle Sam stands authoritatively at the front of the class. As *the* adult in a room of inferiors, he physically towers over all others, displaying a menacing authority. Uncle Sam stands behind a large desk, which represents power and knowledge. Atop the desk is a book titled *U.S. First Lessons in Self-Government.* Underneath the book is a list of newly acquired territories. A globe of the world, representing the unlimited imperial potential for Uncle Sam, rests next to the desk. Uncle Sam has frightened the students in the front row. They appear to cower and react to his aggressive posturing. In turn, Uncle Sam has advised the students in "his new class in civilization": "Now, children, you've got to learn these lessons whether you want to or not! But just take a look at the class ahead of you, and remember that in a little while, you will be as glad to be here as they are!" The new colonial peoples, he suggests, had no choice about whether or not to join the empire and be ruled by Uncle Sam. His declaration has also erased any history of resistance on behalf of the residents of the incorporated territories.

The spatial organization of the students inside and outside the classroom corresponds to their contemporary location in the nation and empire. The cartoon depicts five groups of students representing an evolutionary cycle of governance:

"School Begins," January 1898.

the states of the Union, territories on the path toward statehood (defined as incorporated in 1901), overseas colonial territories, US-based nonwhite peoples (African Americans and Native Americans), and the excluded category of Chinese Americans. The student representations illustrate how well they had acquired Uncle Sam's lessons in civilization.

Isolated from the main classroom and hidden behind the US flag is an audience of students who represent the contemporary United States. Their features are not distinctive. However, on the wall above them is a reminder of the lesson they have learned about government and consent: "The Confederate States refused their consent to be governed. But the union was preserved without their consent." National consolidation was a priority of the federal government, one that it defended at any cost, including civil war.

Separated from the states and the colonies are the younger states of California and Texas, the territories of Arizona and New Mexico, and the District of Alaska. They are depicted as attentive, self-regulated, disciplined students. Well dressed and groomed young ladies and gentlemen, they independently attend to their lessons. They have already been set on the correct path and appear to require little additional attention or oversight from Uncle Sam. The incorporated territories, in addition to gender differences, also reflect racial distinction. Alaska is represented by a darker-skinned student who is attentive and learning her lessons in the tradition of the other incorporated territories. The students sit in front of the second lesson for the classroom. The chalkboard reads: "The consent of the governed is a good thing in theory, but very rare in fact. England has governed her colonies whether they consented or not. By not waiting for their consent, she has greatly advanced the world's civilization. The U.S. must govern its new territories with or without their consent until they can govern themselves." The modern British method of ruling colonies was the model example for some US policy makers who debated the constitutionality of governing colonies.

The rest of the students, located at the margins of the core of the incorporated, represent greater challenges for Uncle Sam. Centered in the cartoon, the four colonies sit together in the front row of the classroom. Unlike the students representing incorporated territories, who sit in individual desks, the colonies share the same bench. They are all starting their education in civilization from the same location. They seem to be the ones whom Uncle Sam is particularly concerned about. They require the most attention and, according to Uncle Sam's posture, the most discipline. These students represent nonwhite colonial peoples and are drawn with brown and black skin. Unlike the healthy and fit incorporated territories, they are plump and short, and they appear uncomfortable in their clothing and on their school bench. They are not children but rather a Lilliputian version of men. Their facial and body features are not gender neutral, although they are somewhat ambiguous. Yet they contrast sharply with the distinct gender differences depicted in the idealized incorporated territories.

The Philippines are represented by a young man who sports a short black afro and wears a long skirt. He grimaces at the sight of Uncle Sam wielding the teacher's pointer. Hawaii, meanwhile, is represented as a man with straight black hair loosely kept in place by a headband. Hawaii wears a long dress and is barefoot, with gold anklets on both feet. Hawaii is also frightened but, with arms crossed, seems to challenge Uncle Sam. The difference between the representation of Hawaii and the incorporated territories, even the dark-skinned one of Alaska, is great. The illustrator may have questioned Hawaii's future. He does not imply that Hawaii could easily join the students in the back of the classroom. Puerto Rico is represented as a small black man with unruly hair and silver rings in his ears. Although he wears long pants, he is clearly afraid of Uncle Sam. He seems to cower and lean toward Cuba for safety and protection. Cuba is represented as a young black man with curly black hair worn pulled back. Cuba is the most defiant. His expression is not of fear but rather disappointment. He clasps his arms at his waist and seems to observe Uncle Sam with displeasure.

At the margins of the brown and black colonial students and the incorporated territories are other individuals representing African Americans, Native Americans, and Asian Americans. They stand between the states and the territories, signifying how they are outside the imagined core of the US polity. They are also physically segregated from those receiving academic lessons. A young black man, representing African Americans, is not privy to academic instruction. He is physically separated from the other children, working behind Uncle Sam. On a stepladder with a bucket and holding a rag, he cleans the classroom window. As he does so, however, he attentively observes the entire scene, aware of Uncle Sam's threats to the colonies. Maybe a critique of the goals of African American industrial and vocational schools, this student representation suggests that black children were privy to an education that trained them for a subservient occupational position within US society. They represent labor. Located in the left corner of the classroom, outside the interest and attention of Uncle Sam, this student has been left behind. There is no intention to allow him access to the academic and civic lessons that were required for US citizenship. While allowed inside the classroom, he is situated outside the polity.

A Native American student sits alone by the classroom door, far away from the other students. He is wrapped in a blanket, wearing feathers on a headband. He is so unfamiliar with the markers of civilization—literacy and education—that he is unaware that he holds the lesson book upside down. This image represents

the segregation of Native American children into government-sponsored boarding schools. The challenge for educators was the complete transformation of the
Native student. The education of Native Americans was not just about teaching
literacy; instead, it offered lessons in civilization, religion, and loyalty to the United
States. The illustrator implies an ambiguity about the intention of educating Native
children, for the cartoon does not suggest that they will join other students as full
members in the classroom; instead, they remain at the margins.

Completely outside the classroom is a Chinese American student, representing Asian Americans. While the Native American student barely makes it inside
the classroom, the Chinese student is explicitly excluded. He seems to want to
join the others, having brought his own book, and he is looking in through the
doorway. Although he has come prepared to participate in the classroom on civilization, he finds that he has been denied access. The location of the Chinese student represents the Chinese Exclusion Act of 1882, which was extended for ten
years in 1892 as the Geary Act. He is the least likely of all the students to be set
on the path of citizenship and incorporation. Finally, the cartoon is missing one
colonial student—Guam. Imperial legislation records, Lanny Thompson argues,
conceptualized Guam as a military outpost. At most it was a refueling station for
the US Navy on an island inhabited by an allegedly insignificant and unimportant
group of natives.[40] In the cartoon they are erased as consequential students of
US empire.

"School Begins" brings together all of Uncle Sam's students, all members of
the US nation and empire. The states, the incorporated territories, US nonwhites,
the excluded immigrant, the new colonies, and the disappeared are represented
in the classroom. Empire building was modeled after the British and imagined to
require the tutoring of colonial peoples in the values and requirements of US government. Some students required more education than others or different types
of school projects. Nonetheless, they all required, including the states, control by
the central government (Uncle Sam) and continuous education in civilization.
Representations of racial difference and "otherness" suggested the potential for
evolution, assimilation, and the capability of being governed. Empire building was
closely linked to education and schools, for colonial peoples, above all, required
lessons from Uncle Sam in civilization and government.

Unlike "School Begins," a second cartoon, published as the cover of *Harper's
Weekly*, was careful to make distinctions between the colonies, distinctions that
suggested each one's progress toward self-government. "Uncle Sam's New Class
in the Art of Self-Government" was published on August 27, 1898, just six months
after the US Congress declared war against Spain. Six months before the end of
war, the cartoonist was already depicting US assessments of and intentions for

HARPER'S WEEKLY

JOURNAL OF CIVILIZATION

Vol. XLII.—No. 217.

NEW YORK, SATURDAY, AUGUST 27, 1898.

TEN CENTS A COPY.
FOUR DOLLARS A YEAR.

UNCLE SAM'S NEW CLASS IN THE ART OF SELF-GOVERNMENT.

"Uncle Sam's New Class in the Art of Self-Government," August 1898.

the new possessions. Like the first cartoon, "Uncle Sam's New Class" also locates Uncle Sam as the authoritative teacher in the classroom, standing behind the desk, waving his stick. On the back wall of the classroom is a large map of the world. The map of the United States is centered in a way that allows for a full view of its new Atlantic possessions. The Philippines, Hawaii, and Alaska are marked on the map with US flags, as are Cuba and Puerto Rico in the Caribbean.

In the classroom, Emilio Aguinaldo—the anti-Spanish revolutionary leader and president of the Philippines—is depicted as a surly young man, dark-skinned, wearing a dunce cap, made to stand on a stool in the corner. In the front row, the illustrator has depicted two versions of Cubans. One is an older white (Latin) man, likely the famed general of the Cuban War of Independence, Máximo Gómez. He is quietly reading his book, undisturbed and uninterested in the fighting taking place right next to him. For sharing the front bench with Gómez are too additional Cubans—a "guerilla" and an "ex-patriot"—engaged in a fight, fists in the air, books flying. Dark-skinned, barefoot, wearing simple and frayed country clothes, the two seem oblivious to Uncle Sam's stick tapping them on the head. Cuba and the Philippines are juxtaposed to the more docile colonies, Hawaii and Puerto Rico. The islands are represented as two young ladies, beautifully clad in long dresses, crowned in flowers, joyfully reading their lessons. They appear pleasantly engaged in the reading, completely oblivious to the unruly ways of the Cubans and Filipinos. Dark-skinned Hawaii and light-skinned Puerto Rico, therefore, welcome Uncle Sam's instructions in self-government. Gómez (one sector of Cuba) and Puerto Rico are the only students wearing shoes, suggesting they have already acquired lessons in civilization, locating them ahead of the others on the evolutionary scale.[41]

Unlike the first cartoon, this one intends to highlight differences in how the colonies engaged with US intervention, occupation, and authority. Docility and acceptance of the US path to civilization are distinguished by gender. Women, even "darker-skinned beauties" like Hawaii and Puerto Rico, are on the right path. Men, meanwhile, have proved harder for Uncle Sam to dominate. The cartoon acknowledges some differences in the ideologies and practices within Cuba in the presentation of the three different men—white and black, old and young, attentive and disruptive. At the same time, it mocks Aguinaldo's authority over the Philippines, depicting him as a young man unwilling or unable to learn from Uncle Sam.

Racial ideologies and hierarchies informed school projects in the colonies as much as, if differently from, in the mainland. As the second cartoon suggests, US colonial officials characterized colonial peoples in specific ways. These racial characterizations also informed their visions for colonial school projects, visions that became law through the early process of creating new school policies. In the early twentieth century, in addition, racial characterizations of Puerto Ricans varied.

In addition to cartoon representations, Jorge Duany has examined the multiple ways US government officials, scholars, and photographers imagined contemporary Puerto Ricans and their racial heritage. Americans often divided islanders into two groups, the elite and the masses. The elite were linked to a Spanish heritage, while the masses were defined by their racial mixture, sometimes of indigenous descent, maybe of African heritage, but somehow mixed in a way that individual racial heritage was indeterminate. Government displays of Puerto Rico at world's fairs (the 1901 Pan-American Exposition and the 1904 Louisiana Purchase Exposition) in the early twentieth century often reproduced the island elite's narrative of their racial and cultural heritage. Puerto Ricans were represented as whiter and often more civilized than Filipinos, in particular. The island was represented through Spanish architecture, meant to link the island to European and Latin American culture. Anthropologists, meanwhile, produced relatively different depictions. Some described the nonelite as "essentially transplanted Spanish peasants," while others highlighted the racial mixture of the majority of the population. The government and academic representations were, nevertheless, different from the images reproduced in photographs published and collected as part of our "new colonial peoples and possessions." Elites often disappeared from the images, replaced by the dominant characterization of islanders as mulattos and blacks, who, as reflected in their clothing and surroundings, were imagined to be impoverished, uneducated, and backward.[42]

While there was variety in the racial characterizations of Puerto Ricans, the descriptions and images were presented as part of a broader narrative of colonization. The racial characterizations were linked to the assumption that the island was to remain a territory of the United States, that Puerto Ricans needed tutelage, that US colonization was justified, and that while islanders were clearly different from Americans, they were nevertheless pliable colonial subjects. The colonial narrative and imagery were sympathetic and paternalistic. Islanders were depicted as more welcoming, docile, and passive than Filipinos and Cubans, with potential for transformation. Puerto Ricans, the images and descriptions suggested, were practically demanding the intervention of the modernizing United States. It would almost have been irresponsible for Americans not to fulfill the "white man's burden" and govern the colony.[43] US visions, as varied as they were, were also informed by neo-Lamarckian understandings of eugenics, which suggested that nurture and the environment could lead to the limited transformation of the colonial other.[44]

How did the racial characterization of Puerto Ricans inform the construction of the island's school project? Education via colonial schools served a specific goal in Puerto Rico. José Manuel Navarro argues that this goal was the creation of "tropical Yankees," or Caribbean supporters of US colonialism.[45] Although Puerto Ricans were imagined to be racially different from Americans, categorized as colonial others, they could be Americanized. They could be uplifted from their current location as neglected colonial subjects into enlightened tropical Yankees. As such, even though they could not shed their multiracial heritage, they could be somewhat improved, as had other nonwhites in the United States. Americanization, therefore, promised the limited and quantified racial uplift of islanders via education. In this way, the island's new colonial school project, strongly defined by US intentions for Americanization, was informed by US racial characterizations of Puerto Ricans and the US government's political intentions for the long-term relationship with the territory.

Cartoons, photographs, and other discursive representations help us visualize some of the arguments scholars of US empire have proposed, arguments that inform this study. First, nation and empire were interconnected. How distinct was national consolidation from empire building at the turn of the century? They were twin processes. At the turn of the century, the United States had acquired all the territory west of the Mississippi River that was bordered by the Pacific Ocean. When the US Navy extended its authority into the Pacific Ocean and the Caribbean Sea, it did so intentionally and purposefully. There was no confusion or haphazard behavior. In the early twentieth century, through the Supreme Court rulings known as the Insular Cases, the US government carefully legislated the rationale for maintaining incorporated and unincorporated territories. In other words, early twentieth-century legislation allowed representatives of the US government to imagine the nation as an exceptional democracy at the same time that it fashioned colonial legislation and rule. Nation and empire were complementary and interconnected.

Second, education and schooling were part of imperial and national projects. The classroom was not simply a metaphor. US nonwhite peoples allegedly required training and schooling if they were to be converted into contributing members, although not equal members, of US society. Likewise, colonial territories required lessons in self-government. These were lessons to be taught not only to local creole elites and politicians but also to children and teachers. Teachers, as intermediate actors in the colonies, were responsible for inculcating young students in US values, history, and traditions. They, along with other state actors, were held responsible for Americanizing colonial subjects.

Third, the parallel paths of national and imperial projects at the turn of the century suggest that the colonies informed the metropole. As Ann Laura Stoler and Frederick Cooper have long argued, influences and power were not unidirectional from the mainland to the colonies.[46] Lessons learned in earlier colonial territories, like the Hawaii Americanization projects, informed national school projects for African American and Native American communities. They were adjusted for national interests and intentions and then re-exported as school models for the new colonies. School projects, ideologies, and educators traveled throughout the US empire, sharing experiences and learning from each other.

Fourth, while nonwhite US populations and colonial peoples could be carefully located within one common classroom, they occupied different places on a hierarchy. Cultural representations of colonial peoples, in particular, also varied. Hawaii was represented differently from Puerto Rico and the Philippines. Stereotypes of different types of Cubans also emerged. These cultural representations both informed and reflected the particular colonial legislation that would be pursued in individual colonies. While they were all brown and black cartoonish figures, they were different and distinct nonetheless.

Colonial State Building and School Laws

The early bureaucratic process that imagined the founding and governance of the local school project was emblematic of US assertions of superiority in the colonies. Therefore, in the tradition of colonizers justifying their authority over new territories, US officials looked at the material condition of the island's population and explained their intervention by highlighting the need for public instruction. This explanation was informed by the colonial trope of the "empty lands" and of native subjects as "clean slates."[47] In the early twentieth century, US officials in particular were guided by the new sciences of administration and government. Colonial state building was justified on the grounds of racial difference and guided by an ethos of reformism and transformation. Informed by the mainland's progressive reform movement, which envisioned that the efficiencies of the new sciences of government could effect a transformation of individuals and communities, US officials imagined the careful management of a new colonial public school system.[48] Colonial schools served two purposes: as a model for efficient administration and as an engine for the transformation of colonial subjects.

One of the first steps taken by US authorities was to study, assess, and evaluate existing schools and teachers. US occupiers in 1898 found that Puerto Rico had two normal schools in San Juan, one for men, another for women. The main university was the private Jesuit school, El Seminario Conciliar. There was also the secular Instituto Civil de Segunda Enseñanza. In addition to San Juan's industrial school, and as stated earlier, there were 501 schools throughout the island, 384 designated for boys and 117 for girls. The 1899 US review committee, however, reported disappointment with the instruction and methods applied in the Seminario and the Instituto. They were dissatisfied with the "exceedingly elementary character of the instruction" by professors who "rambled from subject to subject, showing no evidence of preparation."[49]

US authorities chose to shut down most existing schools and start fresh: "Before the investigation of the committee, the industrial or trade school was suspended; upon the recommendation of the committee the Institute and the Normal Schools were then suspended in June, 1899, at the close of the academic year."[50] The bachelor degrees granted by the Instituto were annulled and replaced by a certificate provided by the insular board of education listing the coursework a student had completed. Years later, Paul G. Miller, who served as commissioner of education from 1915 to 1921, reproduced the narrative about late nineteenth-century

"America's Greatest Gift to Porto Rico—the Public School, Caguas," ca. 1900.

schools in a key public school text. The history textbook he wrote and assigned, *Historia de Puerto Rico* (1922), explained how at the time of US arrival, the "mediums of instruction were not accessible to the people," "the material conditions of schools were deplorable," and "hardly any of those schools, even those in the capital city, were furnished with supplies and utilities."[51]

The second characteristic typical of colonial governance and bureaucracy was the incorporation of and collaboration by local elites. From the earliest moments, sectors of the local elite were invested in US intervention and made themselves available in the early process of colonization. Historian Gervasio García argues that sectors of the Puerto Rican liberal elite shared a class alliance with US colonizers, whom they believed to be modern and liberal. Both groups, sectors of the Puerto Rican elite and US colonial officials, located themselves at the top of the social hierarchy, often reserving paternalistic and derogatory opinions for the majority of the working class.[52] At the initial moment of evaluation, then, US officials were assisted and directed by leading Puerto Rican educators, politicians, and intellectuals. In that tradition, when US colonial officials began the assessment of existing schools in 1899, they did so through a committee that included two elite Puerto Ricans, Manuel F. Rossy and Francisco del Valle Atiles. Immediately before the US invasion and military occupation, Rossy had been elected the minister of education during the short-lived 1898 autonomous government of Puerto Rico.[53] Rossy had been a leading autonomist, a lawyer, an editor of the newspaper *El País*, and the future cofounder of the annexationist Republican Party. Del Valle Atiles was a eugenicist, an autonomist, and a future mayor of San Juan.

The third aspect of US colonial state building evident in the founding and governance of a colonial school project was the centrality of the framework of paternalism. Mary Renda, through the case study of US occupation in Haiti, argues that paternalism was "a moral and subjective framework for colonial administration" through the metaphor of fatherhood. It was an "assertion of authority, superiority, and control expressed in the metaphor of a father's relationship with his children."[54] At the turn of the century, US interventionist practices in the region were justified through a paternalistic framework that dismissed imperial intentions. US president Woodrow Wilson, in particular, rationalized US "authoritarian action in Latin America and the Caribbean" through a "liberal political philosophy" that was informed by "the unstated, yet, central racialized structures of domination at the heart of liberalism." Renda argues that in the case of Haiti, paternalism was "always embodied in the logic of domination . . . based on the assumptions that Haitians were as of yet in the early stages of their evolutionary development as a people." Colonial tutelage and the "guiding hand" of paternal Uncle Sam would in time result in Haiti coming "into its own as a nation."[55]

Paternalism as justified domination was also at the heart of Puerto Rico's colonial school project. The recently arrived US colonial administrators looked at the legacy of Spanish colonialism in Puerto Rico—a legacy of neglect and poverty for the majority of the population—and through a paternalist lens declared its intention to take on the responsibility of governance (tutelary). Crafting a narrative about the negligence (bad parenting) of the Spanish colonial government, US educators justified what they promised to be a new modernizing, benevolent, and tutelary form of government. Americans (and some elite Puerto Ricans) denied there was any value in the existing schools, complained that local teachers were not qualified to teach, and linked this state of affairs to the practice of Spanish colonialism.

The promises of a US colonial school project for the island, justified and regulated through the discourse of paternalism, became the primary narrative of colonial history textbooks. This was the argument that Miller presented in his history textbook, *Historia de Puerto Rico. Historia* was the first history textbook written by a US colonial official for the island curriculum. However, as the commissioner of education, Miller was a political appointee of the US president and the primary administrator responsible for creating "tropical Yankees" through the colonial school system. Puerto Rican scholars and intellectuals, like Salvador Brau and Cayetano Coll y Toste, had written narrative histories of Puerto Rico years before the publication of *Historia.* However, their versions, informed by late nineteenth-century intellectual conceptions of Puerto Rican history, were not intended to promote the narrative of the benevolent and modernizing US empire. Their versions of Puerto Rican history, therefore, fell outside of the intended historical narrative that shaped the colonial curriculum.

Unlike those of Coll y Toste and Brau, Miller's history textbook presented a carefully crafted narrative of the "benevolent" leadership of US empire in Puerto Rico, juxtaposed against the negligent, apathetic, and abusive policies of Spanish colonial rule. It detailed the alleged progress and modernity Americans brought to the island and its people, separated Puerto Rico from the history of the Caribbean, and located the island's value and worth in its close relationship to the United States. Under Spanish colonial rule, Miller argued, "the progress in instruction in Puerto Rico has been even slower than its economic and political development." This was in comparison to US colonial rule, where "education is a top priority in the insular budget," which attested to the commitment of the United States to liberal and modern public instruction.[56] For Miller, literacy rates confirmed the failure of Spanish colonial education. He decried the 1899 census estimate that 79.6 percent of the population was illiterate. But in particular, in his critique, Miller highlighted how Spanish colonialism privileged the education

of elite male boys to the detriment of women, people of color, and rural populations. In 1860 only 7 percent of women and only 2 percent of "all people of color"
could read. Miller concluded that these numbers "not only denounce a general lack of attention, but also an apathy and neglect, which today is difficult to
comprehend."[57]

In the history textbook Miller wrote and assigned to colonial schools, public
education and literacy rates became emblematic of the stark differences between
the qualities of Spanish versus US colonial rule. While the Spanish legacy was
neglect and apathy, the US promise was modern and progressive in its attention
to equal opportunities for education to all children, including women, people
of color, and rural residents. This guiding liberal philosophy of US educators,
presented through the argument of equality of all Puerto Ricans before the colonial government, however, did not undermine the racial and gender hierarchies
that shaped these opportunities and relationships, for embedded in Miller's philosophy was the racialized, gendered, and classed hierarchies that informed
mainland school project traditions toward nonwhite peoples. Nonetheless, the
paternalist promise that balanced benevolence and domination informed how US
commissioners defined their contribution to the island's colonial school project.

Confident that there was little to no history of public schooling in Puerto
Rico worthy of recognition, US officials embarked on the process of writing new
school laws for the colonial school project they imagined only they could build.
The new legislation, which established the framework that continues to shape
contemporary education in Puerto Rico, codified racialized US imperial visions
and practices. In February 1899, the island's third military governor, Brig. Gen.
Guy V. Henry, created the Bureau of Education within the Department of the
Interior. Months later, Henry approved the Código de Leyes Escolares in May
1899. The 1899 school laws, the first under the US military government, over-
wrote all previous school legislation. Written by Gen. John Eaton and his assistant,
Victor S. Clark, the new school laws created a co-ed, free, graded public school
system. Eaton's school law detailed municipal responsibilities to local schools
and established teaching requirements and salaries. Weeks later, the fourth military governor, Brig. Gen. George W. Davis, initiated the process of consolidating
the school system by creating a *junta de educación* to advise on all matters related
to education on the island. The *junta*, which replaced the initial Bureau of Education, represented the central administration and organization of public instruction. Eventually, the *junta* was composed of nine members, seven of whom were
required to be native-born Puerto Ricans.[58]

The organization and administration of public instruction changed again in
April 1900 with the approval of the Foraker Act. With the Foraker Act, Puerto

Rico transitioned from a military to a civil government. The act, also known as the island's first constitution or first organic act under US empire, was named after its sponsor, Senator Joseph B. Foraker of the state of Ohio. Historian Francisco Scarano argues the Foraker Act is an example of how the racial and cultural perspectives of US superiority became law while confirming the US Congress's willingness to create a colonial government. The Foraker Act defined the political and economic relationship between Puerto Rico and the United States as it organized the island's civil government. It established three government branches: executive, legislative, and judicial. The executive branch was composed of the governor, appointed by the US president and responsible only to him, and the Executive Committee, which also served as the upper house of the legislature. The Executive Committee had eleven members: six Americans and five native-born Puerto Ricans. The legislature was divided into two houses. The upper house was composed of the Executive Committee and the lower house of the elected House of Delegates. The House of Delegates was composed of twenty-four members elected every two years by a majority of the voting population, which was literate males age twenty-one and over. The legislature had the right to create laws for Puerto Rico in all matters that fell outside of federal legislation, but all laws passed by the Puerto Rican legislature had to be approved or could be annulled by the US Congress. The judicial branch was composed of the Supreme Court, which was based in San Juan, five district courts, and local courts.[59]

The Foraker Act created the position of commissioner of education, and the first commissioner further consolidated the authority of that position over the colonial school project. The commissioner of education, appointed by the US president, was a member of the Executive Committee. He was, therefore, in the position to propose and approve legislation as a member of both the legislative and executive branches. The first commissioner under the Foraker Act, Martin G. Brumbaugh, proposed significant revisions to the early 1899 school laws, assuming greater control over teachers, curriculum, organization, and administration at the expense of the authority of municipal school *juntas*. In 1902 the second commissioner of education, Samuel McCune Lindsay, proposed a new school law that meant to consolidate US laws since 1899 and their amendments. The Lindsay law changed the administration of the normal school, later the University of Puerto Rico, and further centralized the authority of the commissioner. The normal school, charged with the training of teachers, would be led by a *junta de síndicos* under the leadership of the commissioner of education. The commissioner would also serve as the chancellor of the university.[60]

Aida Negrón de Montilla argues that these early laws intended to place Puerto Rican children on the path to Americanization. She defined Americanization as the intention to supplant a native Puerto Rican culture with an American one, or the assimilation of Puerto Rican culture into a dominant US culture. Americanization, as a form of cultural assimilation, was meant to generate support and loyalty for US colonialism in Puerto Rico. She documented the multiple ways US commissioners of education intended to inculcate Puerto Rican students with a love of all things American—through the teaching of US history, the supplanting of Puerto Rican patriots with American ones, the daily ritual of singing the US national anthem, and the celebration of US patriotic holidays and parades. The underlying assumption guiding Americanization policies, according to Negrón de Montilla's argument, was an ideology that maintained the superiority of US cultural values and the inferiority of Puerto Rican ones. It was the leadership of the Department of Education, particularly the commissioners, who were responsible for implementing these policies.[61]

From 1898 to 1916 Puerto Rico's schools suffered through changes implemented by six different commissioners of education in addition to the early leadership of Eaton and Clark. Each commissioner contributed to Americanization policies according to his priorities, from the intensity of English-language instruction to the training of local teachers. As José Manuel Navarro argues, "U.S. governmental and educational policy makers who held sway in Puerto Rico from 1898–1908 were not of one opinion regarding the educability, intellectual competence, and moral stature of the colonial wards received from Spain."[62] Each commissioner made his mark and correspondingly was forced to respond to protests and complaints from teachers, parents, and legislators, who often disapproved of the imposition of US imperial visions through school legislation.

The process of consolidating US authority over public schools in Puerto Rico was deeply informed by the way US colonial officials conceptualized the relationship between race and education, both on the mainland and in the colonies, as discussed in the previous section. At the core of this relationship was a definition of US empire-building practices as modern, progressive, and benevolent. In Puerto Rico, in particular, US imperial practices were intended to overcome the legacy of Spanish empire, understood to have had a particularly corrupting and backward effect on the island and its people. In particular, the relationship between US colonial authority, race, education, and empire building was articulated through the process of creating colonial legislation, the writing of school laws. The new school laws US colonial officials wrote and supported intended to consolidate US authority over schools, for the colonial school project was critical to US empire building in the territories. I highlight a few examples from the early history of US educators (Eaton, Brumbaugh, and Lindsay) to further illustrate the centrality of schools to the colonial state building project, the relationship between race and education, and the connection between US national and imperial racial projects.

When during the military occupation Henry created the Bureau of Education within the Department of the Interior and appointed Eaton as its director, he was replicating in Puerto Rico the pattern already pursued in the United States after the Civil War. The US Bureau of Education was a fledgling office in the US Department of the Interior until President Ulysses Grant appointed Eaton to its directorship as the commissioner of education in 1870.[63] Eaton, born in New Jersey and raised in New Hampshire, was a teacher and school principal committed to education and administration. He entered the army as a chaplain and was appointed colonel of the Sixty-Third Colored Infantry regiment. Grant chose Eaton to "run the 'contraband' camps, caring for and organizing the large numbers of African-American men and women who escaped slavery behind Union lines."[64] Eaton became the supervisor and eventually the assistant commissioner of the Freedmen's Bureau. He retired from the military in 1865 and had been elected superintendent of schools in Tennessee when President Grant chose him to oversee the organization and expansion of the US Bureau of Education, which he led for the next sixteen years.

The imperial intention of consolidating authority over the education of nonwhites in the US empire was important enough that, despite Eaton's poor health at the age of seventy, Henry called on Eaton to serve the colonial project in Puerto Rico. On the island, Eaton's responsibilities grew, as "he was known successively as the superintendent of schools, director of public instruction, and chief of the bureau of education."[65] Despite his short tenure in Puerto Rico (January 1899–May 1899), Eaton was extremely influential.[66] He wrote the 1899 school laws, which reorganized the school system and set the standards of evaluation for teachers. His appointment reflected the US federal government's established practices at the end of the twentieth century regarding nonwhite peoples, education, and state building, practices that he exported to and replicated in the colonies.

Let's consider Eaton's particular relationship to those three categories. He rose to national prominence in the United States for his work with black freedmen and freedwomen during the war. His military leadership in the Freedmen's Bureau during the Civil War, his success "managing" newly freed blacks, and his commitment to the role of the US federal government in education won him recognition and appointment as the first US national commissioner of education. In the 1870s, his work was at the heart of the consolidation of a federal school system, which faced opposition from states that struggled against the centralization of schools. Eaton's work and recognition by Grant spoke to the strong relationship between race, education, and nation building during Reconstruction.

Eaton's appointment as the "first American colonial administrator of education in Puerto Rico" intended to reproduce the close relationship between education and state building in the colonies.[67] In particular, the school project in the new colonial territory was informed by US racial practices and ideologies. Therefore, Eaton's successful background "managing" newly liberated blacks in the US South was as important as his administrative skills in education. US colonial officials imagined a strong comparison between the experience of managing freed blacks' path to civilization via education and the potential path Puerto Ricans in the US empire might be allowed to pursue. Puerto Ricans had just been "liberated" from the oppressive and neglectful Spaniards and now, like recently freed blacks in the United States, were in need of the guiding hand of the state. Under the tutelage of US officials, colonial subjects could transition from the innocence and ignorance that characterized the island's uncivilized savagery, imagined to be particularly devastating among the nonelite. Puerto Ricans could gain literacy, English-language skills, and the ability to comprehend their rights and responsibilities to the US empire. The assumption behind Henry's appointment of Eaton was that Puerto Rican colonial subjects, like the liberated blacks in the US South a generation earlier, were uneducated, uncivilized, and incapable of comprehending liberal ideologies and responsibilities without the guiding hand of white US tutors. The US imperial project, in some ways similar to visions for Southern Reconstruction, intended to reproduce specific racial hierarchies within the dominant white supremacist framework.

In addition to Eaton's history, the experiences of the first two commissioners of education, Brumbaugh and Lindsay, further attest to how US colonial officials imagined the broader racial project of US empire at the turn of the century and Puerto Rico's location within it. Puerto Rican colonial school laws were in conversation not only with federal policies for African Americans but also with school policies for Native Americans, Filipinos, and Hawaiians.

Puerto Rico's early commissioners of education were prominent educators from northeastern US universities who, after serving short appointments on the island, went on to pursue powerful careers in academia and politics. Brumbaugh, for example, was a graduate of Harvard University, earned a PhD from the University of Pennsylvania, and was the president of Juniata College when President William McKinley appointed him as the first commissioner of education in Puerto Rico (1900–1901). His fourteen months on the island provided him with experiences in policies that he, in turn, imported to the mainland. In 1902 he returned to the University of Pennsylvania, where "he earned a national reputation as an expert on how to teach American children patriotism along with reading, writing and arithmetic."[68] In 1906 Brumbaugh became the superintendent of the Philadelphia public school system and from 1914 to 1919 served as the Republican governor of Pennsylvania.

President Theodore Roosevelt appointed Samuel McCune Lindsay, professor of sociology at the University of Pennsylvania, the island's second commissioner (1902–4). In those two years, Commissioner Lindsay served concurrently as the president and chancellor of the University of Puerto Rico in addition to his appointment to the Executive Committee of the legislative and executive branches. After his tenure on the island, he returned to the faculty at Penn and then went on to serve from 1907 to 1939 as professor of social legislation at Columbia University, where he was committed to child labor reform.[69]

Brumbaugh is remembered in the history of colonial education in Puerto Rico for addressing two main challenges: the early efforts to rapidly expand elementary schools and the corresponding challenge of hiring enough teachers to attend to the new classrooms. To address the latter challenge, Brumbaugh pushed through the Puerto Rican legislature new policies that provided funding to send Puerto Rican students to pursue secondary education in the United States. He also invited leading US educators to travel with him throughout the island, sponsoring teacher training seminars in order to quickly provide training to the newly hired but feared to be underprepared Puerto Rican teachers. Finally, Brumbaugh advocated for the exchange of teachers between the United States and Puerto Rico. Americans were recruited to come to the island to serve as English-language teachers and to model contemporary US pedagogic methods for local teachers. The second commissioner, Lindsay, carried on Brumbaugh's teacher-exchange initiatives, sending hundreds of Puerto Rican teachers to Cornell and Harvard for summer teaching institutes.[70]

The policies and initiatives carried out by Brumbaugh and Lindsay in Puerto Rico were formulated within the broader turn-of-the-century framework that shaped the relationship between race, education, and empire among US educators, liberals, and progressives who identified themselves as "friends of dependent peoples." Brumbaugh, Lindsay, and the third commissioner, Roland P. Falkner, were each invited to report on the progress of US colonial schools at the annual Lake Mohonk Conference of Friends of the Indian and Other Dependent Peoples. It was at this conference that Brumbaugh proudly reported the success of his policies, which allowed Puerto Rican students to study in the United States while the island received model US teachers. Lindsay shared with the Lake Mohonk conference audience the success of the summer institutes held at Cornell and Harvard, and Falkner testified to "the desire of our people that the [Puerto Rican] schools should represent the full American system of public schools."[71] The commissioners made their presentations about Puerto Rican colonial schools before an audience committed to acknowledging "a sense of the worth of other races than our own, and with a conviction that all those who would be of real service to the people of different races and religions with whom the events of the last decade have brought us into close political relations should study sympathetically the national life, the history, the ideals, and the racial characteristics of those whom they would help."[72] The Lake Mohonk conference created a venue for US colonial representatives to come together and reflect on potential "solutions" to "the Indian Problem," "the Philippine Problem," "Hawaii To-Day," and "Porto Rican Policy."[73]

The close relationship between race and education in "the dependencies" and "Indian Territory" that members of the Lake Mohonk conference represented was also reflected in colonial school legislation. It was under Brumbaugh's leadership that the Puerto Rican legislature approved two laws (H.B. 35 and S.B. 12) that annually allocated fellowships to provide for twenty-five Puerto Rican students to attend schools in the United States.[74] When in 1903 Lindsay revised all school laws and amendments issued since 1899, his legislation specified that Puerto Rican students would be designated to attend the premier model African American industrial and agricultural training and normal schools in the United States. Section 73 of the 1903 school law specified that "the colleges and institutions designated for these students to carry out their studies, shall be the Hampton Institute, Virginia, and the Tuskegee Institute, in Tuskegee, Alabama; as well as other similar educational institutions."[75] One of the additional schools selected for Puerto Rican children to attend was the Carlisle Indian Industrial School in Pennsylvania, "the first Indian school to be founded by the federal government off a reservation." One of the foremost early twentieth-century Puerto Rican educators, Juan José Osuna, attended the school, along with sixty other Puerto Rican students, before it closed in 1918.[76] The formation of racialized school projects for nonwhite peoples on the US mainland and island colonies, dating to the nineteenth-century example of Hawaii, was interconnected. Puerto Rico's foundational school laws were shaped by US colonial officials' racialized imperial vision for nonwhite peoples in combination with the particular challenges that local actors and conditions posed.

In conclusion, the examples of Eaton, Brumbaugh, and Lindsay suggest that, in the early years of US colonial rule, US officials intended to establish their authority through the creation of a public school system. Creating new colonial schools first required delegitimizing the existing schools and disenfranchising local teachers. As US colonial educators created new laws and policies that centralized the colonial school project, they not only consolidated US authority over the new schools but also legislated US racialized ideologies and practices.

Disenfranchising the existing Spanish colonial schools and requiring a generation of teachers who had spent a lifetime practicing in local schools prove they had the skills and competence to work for the new, allegedly modern, and progressive US colonial schools were the US empire's first steps in consolidating their authority over local matters. This process intended to erase the island's history before US arrival, characterizing the island as a relic and abandoned backwater of a declining and degenerate Latin empire. This characterization of pre-US Puerto Rican history would continue to emerge as a contentious interpretation in education debates through the first half of the twentieth century.

US colonial officials abolished the schools they found upon arrival because they imagined a superior model. The US model of colonial schools, critiqued for its narrow Americanization goals, was also an extension of the history of school policies for nonwhite peoples in the broader US empire. Americanization did not simply mean Puerto Ricans would be assimilated into US culture. It was more specific than that. Puerto Ricans were set on the path to reconstruction through education, a path already forged by African Americans, Native Americans, and Hawaiians, and a path meant to locate nonwhite peoples in a particular location in the racial hierarchy. The process of deliberately consolidating US authority over colonial schools was part of the broader US racial project at the turn of the century.

The new school laws written for Puerto Rico replicated Eaton's intentions as the first US commissioner of education on the mainland, laws that reflected his experience legislating policies for the reconstruction of freed blacks through education in the United States. Brumbaugh and Lindsay celebrated the importation of US teachers who could serve as model educators as they spread the English language at the same time that they exported Puerto Rican students into African American industrial schools and Native American boarding schools. The early commissioners shared ideologies, practices, and experiences with a broader community of like-minded progressive whites at the Lake Mohonk conferences. The conferences allowed the commissioners to converse with others who were also working with colonial subjects in the US empire—specifically, Native Americans, Hawaiians, and Filipinos—and who were also creating policy. When Puerto Rican colonial subjects traveled from the island territory to the mainland, they were categorized according to phenotype and parsed out into already existing segregated schools in the United States—Tuskegee, Hampton, and Carlisle.

In these early laws, US colonial officials' intentions to consolidate their authority over local schools were deeply informed by how they imagined the relationship between race and education both on the mainland and in the colonies. Americanization of nonwhite peoples in this early period was very specific. It was more than the general intention found in the scholarship: to erase Puerto Rican history and identities in order to replace them with American ones, however those might be defined. For early US colonial officials, Americanization meant finding particular ways to put colonial peoples on the path to racial reconstruction within the broader US imperial project, a project framed by the ideology of white supremacy.

chapter 2

El magisterio (the Teachers)

A Counterpoint: The *maestro sufrido*

US officials, informed by racial ideologies about nonwhite peoples in the mainland and territories, intended to consolidate and centralize the colonial school project. However, local teachers, educators, politicians, and intellectuals forced US officials to negotiate those intentions. Documenting literacy through census statistics, keeping track of the number of new classrooms founded, and importing US teachers were markers for how US officials interpreted and evaluated their contribution to colonial society. These were symbols of alleged US imperial benevolence and modernity. Puerto Rican teachers and educators, from different urban centers and defined by multiple political inclinations, had their own intentions for colonial schools. Their visions, nevertheless, were also informed by local constructions of race, class, and gender.

Puerto Rican teachers who practiced under the Spanish colonial government in the late nineteenth century were disenfranchised with the arrival of Americans. New school laws required them to pass US-based examinations in order to qualify to teach in the newly established colonial schools. Many were recertified and returned to their profession. It was these very teachers who proposed direct challenges to US officials' visions for colonial schools. Local teachers did not transition into the US colonial schools without critique. While they may have shared some assumptions and characterizations about nonelite Puerto Ricans with US officials (see chapter 3), they nevertheless allocated themselves (local experts) and Americans (foreigners) different locations and responsibilities within the school project. For example, teachers were particularly anxious about illiteracy rates in the student body, as were Americans. That mutual concern, however, did not mean local teachers shared the same vision for colonial schools or that they were willing to hand over authority to US colonial officials.

One way local teachers and educators challenged US assumptions of authority was by establishing their independence from the Spanish colonial government. They did not deny that Spanish colonial officials neglected the founding of a universal school system. However, they proposed an alternative narrative of the history of education on the island and their role within it. Teachers developed a narrative around the heroic and romanticized representations of the teacher as martyr. This image demanded recognition of the history of nineteenth-century teachers, particularly the initiatives and selfless practice of those who labored *in spite of* the neglect and lack of interest of the Spanish colonial state. When they narrated a separation of their history from that of the Spanish colonial state, they were also asserting their independence from the visions and practices of US empire. Teachers understood that US colonial officials crafted an image of themselves as liberators and modernizers. They also recognized that US imperial visions were informed by white supremacist racial ideologies. Puerto Rican teachers were not willing to grant US officials complete authority over definitions of modernity, nor were they willing to accept US racial ideologies that contradicted local narratives of racial harmony.

The myth of racial harmony was an evolving narrative in the late nineteenth century. It was an emerging ideology that popularized the argument that the island, unlike the neighboring Caribbean islands and the United States, had maintained "social" peace and positive relationships among the classes. This peace and harmony was built on a narrative about the benevolence of Puerto Rican liberals, like Segundo Ruiz Belvis, José Julián Acosta, and Francisco Mariano Quiñones, who in 1866 called for the abolition of slavery. The myth of racial harmony in the late nineteenth century, however, was also deeply regulated by a "conspiracy of silence" over racial conflicts.[1] Elites and the leadership of the working class collaborated to manage racial conflict and facilitate political and economic alliances. Intellectuals and politicians embraced the myth of racial harmony as a strategy with which to challenge US colonial officials' assumptions about authority over the colonial school project. Early twentieth-century educators, like Juan José Osuna and Gerardo Sellés Solá, however, also deployed this strategy. As they proposed an alternative narrative of the history of education in nineteenth-century Puerto Rico, teachers further contributed to the construction of the foundational myth of racial harmony.

In particular, teachers and educators promoted the emblematic image of the *maestro sufrido*, the "martyred teacher." This was the teacher who, despite the lack of resources provided by the Spanish colonial government, had dedicated his life to the moral and patriotic labor of bringing literacy and rudimentary elementary instruction to the children of Puerto Rico. The image of the *maestro sufrido* acknowledged that nineteenth-century Puerto Rico suffered from an inadequate school infrastructure. However, the responsibility for these conditions lay in the policies of the negligent Spanish colonial state, not the practice of local educators who struggled to teach despite material limitations and, sometimes, political persecution. The struggle and commitment of the *maestro sufrido* was best captured and promoted through the memory of maestro Rafael, who was a private teacher and a tobacco worker by trade. A free black in the slave society of colonial urban San Juan, he provided instruction to young boys in his home, which was also a tobacco workshop.

The history we know today about maestro Rafael was produced by his former students, who after his death in 1868 eulogized and documented his life in their writings. Narratives about maestro Rafael's life, whether written in the late nineteenth century, reproduced in the first half of the twentieth century, or commemorated in the 1990s, follow a specific trajectory: Rafael Cordero Molina was born in San Juan on October 24, 1790, to freed black parents—Lucas Cordero, a master artisan, and Rita Molina, a seamstress. Slavery was not abolished in Puerto Rico until 1873. As a free black man in early nineteenth-century Puerto Rico, maestro Rafael's education and occupation opportunities were restricted by colonial laws that regulated the rights of freedmen. As a child, he was particularly interested in reading and writing but was not allowed to attend the one school for boys in San Juan, which restricted attendance to children of white families. In response to this institutionalized racial discrimination, his parents created a private school for children of color in their home. Due to his parents' diligence and attention to education, maestro Rafael, his sister, Celestina, and other free black children in San Juan attended the private Cordero school.

As an adult, Rafael became an artisan, a *tabaquero* and shoemaker. In 1810 he opened a school for poor children in his tobacco workshop on Luna Street in San Juan. He is remembered for not discriminating between the poor and rich or the black and white. Turn-of-the-century intellectual Salvador Brau wrote that maestro Rafael "gathered around his tobacco worktable the children of presumptuous officials together with those of obscure working people to distribute free education among them."[2] Maestro Rafael provided boys with elementary schooling in his tobacco workshop for fifty-five years. Finally, when maestro Rafael was seventy-five, the Spanish colonial government recognized his labor and provided him with a monthly salary of $15. He initially rejected the salary but eventually accepted it. He used the funds to provide clothing and books for his poorer students and distributed the rest among the homeless in the streets of San Juan. Many of maestro Rafael's elite students left the island to attend university abroad. Nineteenth-century doctors, writers, lawyers, scientists, priests, and abolitionists such as José Julian Acosta, Román Baldorioty de Castro, Alejandro Tapia y Rivera, and Francisco del Valle Atiles attended maestro Rafael's school as children.

Former student Lorenzo Puente Acosta eulogized maestro Rafael in 1868 in a biography printed in pamphlet form.[3] This became one of the primary documents scholars, teachers, and writers reproduced as new generations revisited the legacy of maestro Rafael. In 1891 other former pupils wrote biographies of maestro Rafael's life as part of the ceremonies at the Ateneo Puertorriqueño held to commemorate Francisco Oller's oil painting of maestro Rafael. As part of that commemoration, the San Juan community also organized a three-day event in which they placed a plaque outside of maestro Rafael's *escuela-taller*, "school-workshop." The activities were attended by the San Juan Association of Teachers and other elite members of San Juan society, including writers, intellectuals, and journalists such as Federico Asenjo, Alejandro Tapia y Rivera, Salvador Brau, Manuel Fernández Juncos, José Daubón, and Sotero Figueroa. These authors, in turn, published their reflections of maestro Rafael in biographies, memoirs, and newspaper articles.

The 1890s narratives proposed the argument that through the multiracial and cross-class space he created in his school and by example, maestro Rafael planted

La escuela del maestro Cordero, Francisco Oller, 1891.

a seed of liberalism and equality in the minds of those students who returned to the island as adults and contributed to the abolitionist movement or fought for autonomism. Despite being "a son of the oppressed and degraded race," wrote Sotero Figueroa, "without hate in his heart, without curses on his lips, [maestro Rafael] raised the humble tribute of public instruction in the same capital where the governor resided, avenging himself of his hates and persecutions, teaching the sons of whites, whom he placed in admirable union with the blacks, to be learned and laborious, noble in word and deed, mild and humble."[4] Figueroa acknowledged that in colonial Spanish society, a freed black might have "hates and persecutions" against the white creole and peninsular elites and slave owners. Somehow, however, maestro Rafael had overcome those sentiments, and he spent his life generating class and racial harmony through his labor in the classroom. For these reasons, maestro Rafael's example, Figueroa argued, was "noble."

Although the authors celebrated maestro Rafael's understated commitment to the equal treatment of black and white, rich and poor, in Spanish colonial society, in their writings they reproduced their own deeply racist and classist assumptions about African-descended peoples in Puerto Rico. The writers highlighted how maestro Rafael was exceptional "for his race," a "good-natured black man" (*negro bondadoso*), and a "racial integrationist" (*integrador de razas*). In the earliest published eulogy (1868), Puente Acosta considered him a "brilliant exception" to "the miserable state of degradation and disregard that dragged down that unfortunate race."[5] Figueroa, another student, glorified maestro Rafael's successful life and example, considering that he was, after all, "branded with the stamp of degradation (black skin . . .)."[6] Creole elites did not expect African-descended peoples to value education, be dedicated to teaching or to Christianity, attempt to overcome poverty, earn a "respectable" living as skilled artisans, or show benevolence for the poor. These assumptions guided Puente Acosta's final assessment of maestro Rafael's labor: "Public instruction slumbered in the forgotten island the heavy sleep of death, [when] a poor black man, overwhelmed by the challenges of poverty and branded by the fatal mark [black skin] that characterizes his unfortunate class, was able to offer a surprising example of virtuousness, abnegation, and patriotism."[7]

This 1890s narrative about the exceptional example of maestro Rafael's practice constructed by liberal autonomists during the Spanish colonial period was rearticulated in the early twentieth century. The myth of racial harmony and the emblematic image of maestro Rafael allowed late nineteenth-century writers and early twentieth-century teachers to promote a romanticized narrative that was disassociated from the race relations that shaped nineteenth-century Puerto Rican history. Maestro Rafael, his sister, and his parents before him were not allowed to attend the racially segregated school for elite boys in San Juan. These conditions forced his parents to homeschool their children and open that space to other children of color denied public schooling. The practice of racial segregation in a nineteenth-century Caribbean slave society shaped the story of the Cordero family. Although in the early twentieth century the myth of racial harmony became a powerful tool employed by multiple sectors of the Puerto Rican creole elite to challenge US assertions of white supremacy and superiority, it was a mythic foundational story that was challenged by the material reality of the majority of the island's working class and nonwhite peoples. As Eileen Findlay, Luis Figueroa, and Ileana Rodríguez-Silva have argued, it was a myth that attempted to erase Puerto Rico's violent history of racial and class discrimination.[8]

These visions of maestro Rafael, published in 1868 and the 1890s, were reproduced in the writings of teachers and educators in the early twentieth century. In particular, Puerto Rican educators reproduced the brief biography of maestro Rafael written by former pupil José Daubón in new teacher training materials. In the 1920s two prominent Puerto Rican educators resurrected maestro Rafael's story. Gerardo Sellés Solá and Juan José Osuna collected and published documentary sources about the history of education during the Spanish colonial period. This publication represented the demands of a new generation of educators to acquire knowledge about the local history of teaching as a challenge to the assumption that this was an imported practice from the United States. *Lecturas históricas de la educación en Puerto Rico*, finally published in 1943, was one of the only teaching sources that reproduced pre-1898 historical documents, and in it Sellés Solá and Osuna included Daubón's 1891 biography of maestro Rafael. Daubón's interpretation of maestro Rafael's life and legacy has become a standard part of the narrative in publications about the history of education since the 1940s.[9]

Maestro Rafael's example is part of a broader foundational myth of nation building. He is remembered as the model teacher of the children of San Juan and as the teacher of elite children who left the island for university training abroad and returned radicalized as autonomist leaders or abolitionists. The twentieth-century narratives about maestro Rafael suggested that the main political ideology that guided emerging creole nationalist identities in late nineteenth- and early twentieth-century Puerto Rico—autonomism—was crystallized through the example of maestro Rafael's classroom.[10] Creole autonomist leadership, which was not succumbing to but negotiating with US colonial authority in the early twentieth century, the narrative suggests, had been initiated into literacy and socialized in the cross-class and multiracial space cultivated by the skilled artisan of African descent. In this interpretation, maestro Rafael is remembered for "overcoming his own economic and social limitations in order to provide the first schooling to the great men who forged nineteenth-century Puerto Rican society."[11]

However, maestro Rafael's example also supported the argument teachers and educators developed to challenge US assertions of authority over the colonial school project. He represented how local teachers intended, in the early twentieth century, to distinguish teachers' labor from the limitations and policies of the colonial state, whether it was the old Spanish or the new US version. Maestro Rafael's example spoke to how Puerto Rican educators were dedicated to providing children with access to education by any means necessary. Although an artisan and teacher with limited resources, he provided free instruction to poor children and accepted whatever donations the families of elite students offered. When he received a salary from the municipality or was honored with a monetary award, he used the money to buy books and distributed the rest among the homeless and beggars of San Juan. By not denying poor or rich access to his school, maestro Rafael generated a cross-class space for creole children. Despite the lack of support or recognition from the Spanish colonial state, maestro Rafael dedicated his life to the children. In maestro Rafael's example, teachers and educators could propose a history of patriotic labor—"that patriotic achievement" (*esa hazaña patriótica*)—that was carried out at the initiative of teachers, parents, and students, despite whatever limitations and policies the Spanish colonial state posed.[12] This relationship between local teacher and colonial state allowed early twentieth-century teachers and educators to demand recognition for the history of their labor throughout the nineteenth century and to establish a tradition of independence between their patriotic labor and the politics of the colonial state.

In addition, through the maestro Rafael example, teachers distinguished themselves from Americans on the grounds of race and morality. Teachers articulated a challenge to the US racial project in the colonies. They recognized that Americans were members of a white supremacist society that segregated schools by race in the mainland. Although the new public schools on the island were not segregated by race, Puerto Rican children sent to study in the United States on a fellowship were designated to attend African American industrial training schools or Native American boarding schools. The maestro Rafael example allowed teachers and educators to counter with the myth of racial harmony, to propose an alternative narrative about racial formation, by suggesting that local teachers were the product of generations of educators who reproduced and valued the tradition of working through race and class differences. This identity with racial harmony intended to condemn US racial practices of segregation while locating local teachers on a higher moral plane.

In these ways, the emblematic local teacher, best personified in maestro Rafael's image, was used to challenge the US racial project and to contest the location of Americans in the forging of a new colonial school project. Teachers and educators turned to maestro Rafael's story to relay their imagined alternative racial project and to locate public instruction at the core of a broader challenge to US colonialism. Specifically, by highlighting the morality and selflessness of the Puerto Rican educator as outside the control of the colonial state, maestro Rafael's story empowered teachers to challenge US interpretations of nineteenth-century Puerto Rican history, the negligent legacy of Spanish colonialism, and the authority and intentions of the new self-defined modern and benevolent US colonial state. His image also allowed teachers to lay claim to the political legacy of autonomist leadership in the late nineteenth century, a legacy carried forward in early twentieth-century debates.

Silencing Celestina

Gender and patriarchy also informed how local teachers used maestro Rafael's story. The martyred teacher was also a gendered image that glorified male teachers who were committed to the education of young boys. Appropriate gender roles, as defined by the *familia puertorriqueña* organizing framework, assumed the authority of male voices and leadership in public spaces. His authority extended to all members of the household, particularly women and minors. For the local teaching leadership, control over the school project was also a struggle to retain male privileges to labor outside the home, provide education to boys, and police and restrict women's right to education, access to public spaces, and labor.

Gender and patriarchy shaped practices in the colony and the metropole. US overseas expansion was an expression of turn-of-the-century masculine definitions of manhood.[13] US empire scholars, like Kristen Hoganson and Gail Bederman, argue that US expansion overseas, the acquisition of empire, and, particularly, engaging in war in the colonies were foreign-policy decisions deeply informed by a US national crisis in masculinity. Overseas expansion promised an opportunity to practice a new definition of masculine manhood. However, the Puerto Rican example suggests that US men, in the form of colonial authorities, did not limit their practices in masculinity to foreign policy and war. Consolidating authority over colonial schools was another venue through which US officials tested their ability to expand their own masculine authority and export definitions of gender roles. However, gendered ideologies and patriarchy were already deeply rooted frameworks in Puerto Rico, although defined differently from the bellicose and masculine US men. In the debate over the direction of colonial schools, teachers and educators (in the form of local and imperial men) also had to negotiate their right to establish, maintain, and redefine patriarchal authority.

Paul G. Miller, despite the "benevolent" imperial lens that shaped his interpretation, was not mistaken when he reported in *Historia de Puerto Rico* that women and people of color had been disproportionately denied the right to access public instruction. As Fernando Picó argued, nineteenth-century schools privileged boys and elites and reproduced clear class and racial differences in Puerto Rican society. Although women and people of color had less access to schools than elite white males, women—African-descended women, in particular—had generated a legacy of providing private instruction for girls. Salvador Brau was one of the few turn-of-the-century scholars who recognized the labor of female teachers and of African-descended women in particular. His acknowledgment, nevertheless, was mediated within a broader reflection of how maestro Rafael integrated both races in the classroom. Maestro Rafael's example, Brau argued, was also typical of "conduct practiced all over the island by women, some of them blacks or free coloreds, intellectual mothers of an entire generation of both sexes."[14]

The way the 1890s creole elite interpreted the image of the emblematic teacher denied and silenced the history of female teachers in the nineteenth century, but particularly the history of African-descended female teachers. Early twentieth-century historical narratives reproduced that silence. This silence is particularly apparent because maestro Rafael's biographies always included a brief but tangential reference to his sister, Celestina. The late nineteenth-century biographers did not explain that when he became a teacher at the age of twenty, maestro Rafael was following in the footsteps of his older sister. Born in 1787, Celestina, like maestro Rafael, was homeschooled. In 1802 she opened a school for girls in San Juan that serviced both blacks and poor whites. In the 1810s she acquired a license from the bishop "to impart a Christian education to poor and black girls."[15] Celestina appeared in the historical record on February 10, 1817, when she came before the meeting of the city council of San Juan to request financial assistance for her school. She appealed for funding before the council members, reminding them that for the past fifteen years she had taught 116 girls without receiving support from the municipality. Nevertheless, her request was denied. When her brother opened his school in 1820, he was already a cigarmaker by trade. As Jack and Irene Delano have argued, maestro Rafael was "following in her footsteps" when he opened his school for boys.[16]

When Celestina was acknowledged, her labor was presented as marginal and/or complementary to her brother's work. Carmen Gómez Tejera's and David Cruz López's early narrative, *La escuela puertorriqueña* (1970), for example, quotes at length Daubón's biography of maestro Rafael and then mentions, within parentheses in a footnote, that his sister ran five schools during her lifetime in San Juan. Some scholars have merely portrayed her as maestro Rafael's assistant in his school for boys, while still others have only narrated that later in life Celestina fell ill and became an additional burden and responsibility to the selfless maestro Rafael. Salvador Brau wrote that maestro Rafael refused to deposit his "poor wretched sister" in a house of charity, where she could be attended to, for she "lacked reason."[17] Only in the recent Delano and Delano publication (1994) is Celestina's history presented relatively independently of her brother's labor.[18]

When early twentieth-century teachers, intellectuals, and politicians celebrated maestro Rafael's example and canonized him as an emblematic teacher and foundational figure in nineteenth-century Puerto Rican history, they also chose to dismiss, silence, and diminish his sister's labor and the legacy of an African-descended

Celestina and maestro Rafael. In this illustration, Celestina is inserted into the traditional narrative and image of maestro Rafael, represented in the 1891 painting by Oller. Celestina is located in a central and active position in the classroom, engaging with students (Delano and Delano, *En busca del maestro Rafael Cordero*; reproduced with permission of the Estate of Irene and Jack Delano).

woman who spent a lifetime running private schools for girls in San Juan. Celestina's example was not centered in the narrative that male teachers reproduced in the early twentieth century. There was little interest in acknowledging black women's leadership in the early colonial school project. Black women's labor fell outside the cross-class, multiracial, fraternal narrative that creole elites and teachers used to challenge US colonial officials. Black women were not part of that alliance, for the racial harmony myth did not intend to overcome existing racial and gender hierarchies. Black women's labor, whether enslaved or freed, was normalized rather than exceptional. Neither elite Puerto Ricans nor US colonial officials recognized that labor or granted it value in the discursive struggle to establish authority over schools. Therefore, Celestina's story was not incorporated into the cross-class, multiracial, male alliance that was at the heart of the nation-building romance.

In the early twentieth century, as local teachers from multiple generations came together to challenge US authority over the new colonial school project,

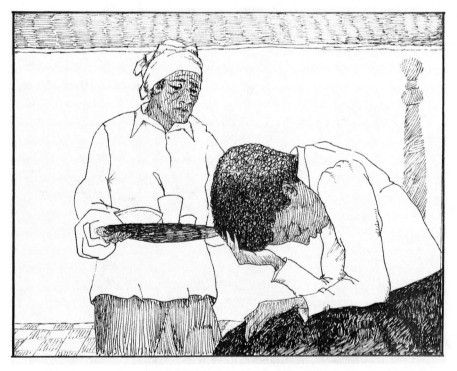

Celestina as burden to maestro Rafael (Delano and Delano, *En busca del maestro Rafael Cordero*; reproduced with permission of the Estate of Irene and Jack Delano).

they resurrected the narrative of maestro Rafael's selfless, moral, and patriotic labor, even as they silenced Celestina. Maestro Rafael's image became a symbol of resistance to US colonialism more broadly. It was located at the core of the island's foundational nation-building narrative of racial harmony. Maestro Rafael was credited with planting the seed of liberty and equality in the minds of generations of political leaders, particularly autonomists and abolitionists. He was an educator who, by providing an alternative to the US mainland practice of racial segregation, allowed teachers and educators to claim a higher location on a moral hierarchy. Although the symbol could be used to represent a unified front to challenge US colonial authority, it was also emblematic of the race, class, and gender hierarchies that elite teachers tried to reproduce in the face of changing cultural norms and definitions of tradition, progress, and modernity. Nevertheless, the conflicts within the teaching class—the generational conflict between the older leadership and new teachers, between men and women, between those from middle-class and working-class backgrounds—would reemerge throughout the first half of the twentieth century as teachers struggled to present a unified voice before the demands of the new US colonial officials (see chapter 3).

Teachers Mobilize

With the *maestro sufrido* image, teachers and educators proposed a discursive challenge to the new US authority, specifically US narratives about the legacy of nineteenth-century Spanish colonialism, the history of teachers' labor, and the alleged benevolence and superiority of the US school project. This discursive challenge was articulated through the competing ideology of racial formation at the turn of the century, an ideology that reproduced patriarchal authority over teachers, schools, and students. In addition to the discursive challenge, however, teachers were carrying forward the tradition and practice of professional resistance they had developed in the late nineteenth century.

Late nineteenth-century teachers, in fact, mobilized in defense of their professional rights and defended them before municipal school boards and the centralized Spanish colonial government. Rubén Maldonado Jiménez documented how teachers struggled against the politically repressive tactics of the Spanish colonial state and the partisan politics of members of school *juntas* (boards). Municipal school boards, responsible for hiring and appointing teachers to local schools, became one additional barrier for teachers demanding professional rights. At the turn of the century, teachers bore witness to change in colonial authority, to centralization and consolidation by US administrators, and to the increased partisanship of school boards. In the face of these challenges, Maldonado Jiménez argued, teachers were vocal and persistent in their pursuit of fair labor rights.[19] By the early twentieth century, teachers had begun to unionize by region—in San Juan, Ponce, and Mayagüez.

This tradition of forming alliances within the profession to challenge assaults from the colonial state and municipal school boards led to the founding of the islandwide Asociación de Maestros de Puerto Rico (AMPR, Association of Teachers of Puerto Rico). The union was founded in 1911 under the combined leadership of San Juan and Mayagüez regional teachers' unions.[20] As the public school system expanded and a new generation of teachers were trained and hired, the AMPR became the organization through which the teaching leadership sought to more effectively represent their professional demands before the commissioner of education, the Puerto Rican legislature, and municipal school boards.

Once the AMPR was founded, local branch representatives met during annual conventions held in late December. Teachers elected at the municipal level attended the conventions, contributed to committee meetings, elected the AMPR board of directors, approved or rejected amendments to their constitution, and negotiated an annual list of *acuerdos* (demands). During the three to four days the convention met, committees were elected and called to meetings organized by topic (home economics, agriculture, and physical education) and/or occupation (teachers, principals, and inspectors). The convention produced amendments to the AMPR constitution as well as a list of *acuerdos* to be presented before the commissioner of education and the legislature. The annual *acuerdos* addressed a series of concerns. In addition to professional demands regarding salaries, appointments, and tenure, teachers proposed demands to the colonial government regarding the future of home economics instruction, the welfare of children in rural schools, and the organization of civics and history textbooks.

The AMPR was an important organization for the profession. Despite important ideological and generational divisions within the teaching force, negotiation with the US colonial state required a unified front. The AMPR became the venue through which teachers channeled their goals—professional demands as well as ideological visions for schools and children. And through the support of the majority of its members, the AMPR, as an early version of a civil service labor union, was empowered to negotiate the stated interests of the rank and file with colonial administrators—the commissioner of education and the island legislature. While the AMPR represented this unified voice when it negotiated with colonial officials, it was also a fragmented organization. The teaching profession underwent deep transformations in the early years of the twentieth century.

Those elected to the AMPR board of directors were university-trained individuals who came from families of elite or middle-class social standing within their

regional communities. I characterize the leadership of the AMPR as "elite teachers." Their backgrounds were not necessarily typical of the majority of the teaching force. They were older, had more professional training, and were connected
to regional elite families. Some rose to the leadership of the teaching profession
through the colonial Department of Education (DE). Their class and professional
training set them apart from the younger teachers. These differences became
more pronounced in the 1920s and 1930s as the teaching force changed. Elite
teachers authored and produced the majority of sources in the AMPR archives,
newspapers, and education journals. In the sources, their perspectives and opinions are more prominent than those of nonelite teachers. I refer to them as elite
teachers, therefore, in order to maintain a distinction between the opinions and
experiences of the elite of the teaching profession and the rank and file.

Francisco Vincenty is an example of the vocal leadership of the teaching profession in the early twentieth century. Vincenty's life story, for example, was typical
of those who rose to the leadership of the AMPR through the late 1920s. Vincenty
was fifty-eight years old when he was elected president of the organization in 1917.
Originally from rural Mayagüez, Vincenty attended primary school in Maricao
and earned a bachelor's degree from the Colegio San Juan, where he was a student
of Rafael Janer y Soler. He studied pharmacy and acquired the title of *licenciado
en Farmacia.* He alternated between teaching Latin and Spanish and practicing
pharmacy in San Juan, Jayuya, and Mayagüez. Immediately before the 1898 US
invasion, Vincenty was practicing pharmacy and owned and directed the private
school known as the Liceo de Mayagüez. After the US occupation, he and other
educators were required to take annual exams that certified them to teach in the
new colonial schools. After taking his exams, Vincenty began working as the principal of the Mayagüez schools, a position from which he retired in order to direct
a private school, the Instituto Municipal de Mayagüez, founded by the Puerto
Rican educator Eugenio María de Hostos. Over the next fifteen years, Vincenty returned to teaching and administrative work in Mayagüez, Cabo Rojo, and Caguas
and finally became a lawyer in 1913. He had nurtured a career in public and private education when, in 1917, he was elected to the presidency of the AMPR.[21]

Vincenty represented those who became islandwide leaders of the AMPR and
the teaching profession. They were members of prominent regional families.
They were intellectuals, men privileged with education and professional training,
from landowning families. They had chosen not to pursue the traditional profession of the elite (medicine or law) and instead dedicated themselves to public
service, particularly education. This was the history and experience of the early
leadership of the AMPR. Their class and training informed the organization's
political and social positions vis-à-vis the colonial DE and US colonialism.

Vincenty's generation of educators, with the arrival of the Americans, found they had lost some authority over the direction of the new US colonial schools. In turn, they created alternative venues through which to present their opinions about policy and through which to negotiate their visions with colonial authorities. The leadership of regional teachers' unions, which came together in the islandwide AMPR, represented these newly displaced educators. These educators reemerged as the vocal leadership of a new generation of public school teachers. In the 1910s the AMPR provided that generation of educators with a venue through which to establish their prominent voice and moral authority over the direction of schools. However, Vincenty and other elite teachers who assumed the right to speak on behalf of their profession found that they had to negotiate their visions not only with US colonial officials but with the new, younger generation of teachers joining the profession.

The first twenty years, between 1900 and 1920, the primary challenge for the colonial DE was expansion and growth. From 1910 to 1920 the number of classrooms tripled, and the number of teachers doubled (table 1). A growing number of educated, middle-class students responded to the call to fill the new teaching positions in the expanding school system. In the early years, urban cities and towns received more attention and resources than rural areas. Addressing rural communities, however, became a priority as more and more rural schools were founded to service children and communities. By 1921 2,100 rural classrooms had been founded.[22]

By the 1920s, teaching had become a predominantly female profession. Seventy percent of all teachers were female (table 2). However, there were some regional variations. In San Juan, a larger percentage than average of women was employed in the profession (88 percent). This higher percentage was likely due to the concentration of foreign-born female teachers in the city, US women recruited to the island through policies of US commissioners of education. San Juan also had a higher concentration of modern school buildings (graded and

TABLE 1. Schools, teachers, and students, 1910–1940

Year	Number of government-owned schoolrooms	Number of teachers	Public school enrollment
1910	522	1,623	95,342
1920	1,422	3,220	176,617
1930	3,273	4,451	221,189
1940	4,048	6,294	286,098

Source: Osuna, *A History of Education*, table 6, 628.

TABLE 2. Teachers by gender, 1920 and 1930

	1920	1930
Male	1,106	1,456
Female	2,636	4,254

Sources: United States Bureau of the Census, *Fourteenth Census*, table 39, 1303; United States Bureau of the Census, *Fifteenth Census*, table 4, 188.

built of concrete) and secondary schools. Ponce, the island's "second capital," meanwhile, had a higher concentration of male teachers (23 percent) than San Juan (12 percent).

Academic debates over the accuracy of racial classifications in national census records in Latin America and the Caribbean are rich and extensive. Deciding how an individual should be racially classified on a census form is one of the most socially constructed processes. It is also a beacon for academic debate, particularly because of the assumption that the process of collecting census data can be scientific and objective. In Latin America and the Caribbean, the social construction of race allows for occupation to influence racial categories and vice versa.[23] A professional who was of an intermediate racial category (such as a light-skinned mulatto) might have been enumerated as white instead of black. In addition, racial classification can be influenced by the identity of the enumerator. Although individuals reported their race, enumerators filled out the census form. Puerto Rican censuses of the early twentieth century can be particularly challenging to read and interpret because of the colonial encounter. The US Census Bureau applied its standards and definitions to the colonial and multiracial Caribbean population. These are factors to keep in mind as we try to draw information from the records.

Race and gender statistics for Ponce and San Juan suggest some variations between the regions (tables 3 and 4). In both urban centers, the majority of teachers were categorized as native white women. In San Juan, black men and women were a small percentage of all teachers. About 14 percent of all male teachers were black. The same percentage of all female teachers was categorized as black. However, in

TABLE 3. Ponce schoolteachers, 1920

	Native white	Black*	Foreign-born white
Male	39	15	7
Female	164	25	14

Source: United States Bureau of the Census, *Fourteenth Census*, table 37, 1299.

* The census uses the term "Negro" in English.

TABLE 4. San Juan schoolteachers, 1920

	Native white	Black*	Foreign-born white
Male	29	7	7
Female	256	54	69

Source: United States Bureau of the Census, *Fourteenth Census*, table 38, 1301.
* The census uses the term "Negro" in English.

Ponce, about 25 percent of all male teachers were black. The composition of teachers in San Juan and Ponce was predominantly white and female. However, San Juan had a high concentration of US female teachers, while Ponce had a relatively high representation of black male teachers.

The shifts and transformations in the field of education in the early twentieth century were also informed by generational changes within the teaching profession. As the writings of the older AMPR leadership in the 1910s and 1920s suggest (see the next section), all teachers witnessed important transitions in education—control by Spanish versus US colonial administrations, Catholic versus secular instruction, sexually segregated versus coeducational classrooms, a majority-male to a majority-female profession. Political views, class identities, and racial ideologies also clashed between and within generations. Finally, "modern" versus "traditional" pedagogy introduced changes to the curriculum.

The 1920 census records some of the generational differences emerging within the profession. Teachers in 1920 were divided. About half of all teachers (1,949) recorded in the census were born at the turn of the century. Those born in the late nineteenth century, between 1876 and 1895, composed the second largest group of teachers (42 percent), while the eldest group (ages forty-five to sixty-four) was only about 5 percent of the total. Census records also document that the younger the teacher's age group, the higher the percentage of women. For example, 76 percent of all teachers within the sixteen to twenty-four age range were women. In the twenty-five to forty-four age group, 64 percent were women, while in the forty-five to sixty-four age group, 60 percent were women. This gender pattern changes slightly for teachers sixty-five years and older. In that range, a larger percentage (72 percent) than the average was female. This might suggest that older female teachers worked in the classroom later in life than men (see table 5).

The younger generation of teachers born at the turn of the century received their elementary and secondary instruction during the early years of US colonial schools. Teachers born in the late nineteenth century might have been informed by late nineteenth-century creole ideologies and then balanced those with the

TABLE 5. Teachers by gender and age, 1920

	Age 16–24	Age 25–44	Age 45–64	Age 65 and above
Male	467	550	80	8
Female	1,482	1,010	123	21

Source: United States Bureau of the Census, *Fourteenth Census*, table 39, 1303.

influence of US colonialism at the turn of the century. It was the elders, teachers in their late forties and fifties, who had the most professional experience as teachers from the late nineteenth century. They also represented the elected leadership of the AMPR in the first two decades of the twentieth century.

The gender transformation of the teaching force, however, was not reflected in the hierarchy and organization of the AMPR leadership. Although teaching became increasingly female-dominant, the elected president and public face of the AMPR continued to be male. While women joined public service occupations in unprecedented numbers in the early twentieth century, the patriarchal framework continued to be reproduced at every level of the Department of Education as well as within the directorship of the AMPR.

Meanwhile, the social background of the teaching force did not undergo a significant transformation but rather a reinforcement of its middle-class roots. The social origin of the majority of teachers represented a range of occupations that can be categorized as an intermediate or middling group. The intermediate group included a combination of white- and blue-collar occupations, such as farmers who owned their land, merchants, and skilled artisans. At the opposite margins of the intermediate group were "professionals" who traditionally composed the elite (doctors, surgeons, and lawyers) and "laborers" at the bottom of the social hierarchy (non-property-owning agricultural and industrial wageworkers).

In the late nineteenth century, the coffee planter class was at the pinnacle of its economic, political, and cultural influence. However, the coffee elite suffered the displacement of its social status in the early twentieth century as investments and growth in the colonial economy shifted away from coffee production toward modern sugar plantations and *centrales* (mills). A range of occupations satisfied the demands of a primarily agricultural economy and its increasingly export-oriented growth. Meanwhile, the export economy generated an increase in service-oriented occupations. As the bureaucracy of the colonial government grew, the range and number of civil service occupations multiplied.[24]

A survey of 1920 census data suggests that the majority of teachers came from families whose head of household was employed in a range of occupations that fell primarily within the middle sector of the colonial economy.[25] For example, the majority of occupations held by heads of household in which a teacher was a relative or a spouse included farmers (18.9 percent), merchants (14.1 percent), and civil servants (13 percent).[26] Within the sample that included teachers, most of the heads of households enumerated as farmers were in the coffee industry, and the rest were distributed among farms that produced varied fruits and vegetables, tobacco, and sugar. Most merchants traded in foods, small goods, and provisions (*pulpería, mercería, víveres, o provisiones*), while the second largest group of merchants traded in tobacco. Blue-collar households represented a range of skilled workers and artisans. For example, the majority of teachers in blue-collar households were related or married to a head enumerated as a seamstress, tobacco worker in a factory, carpenter, or shoemaker. The rest of the blue-collar occupations included a variety of skilled workers, such as bakers, mechanics, hatmakers, silversmiths, and painters. The census data suggest that the teaching force absorbed the labor provided by the children or spouses of the socially descending and displaced coffee planter class in an increasingly sugar-centered, export-market, colonial economy as well as the children of aspiring artisans.[27]

The 1910s and 1920s teaching force united under the leadership of the AMPR at a time of great change. The older generation carried forward their experiences under the Spanish colonial government in the late nineteenth century. They emerged as the leading voice of the profession. They were elite teachers and acted as the representatives of all local teachers. That generation, defined by their class and gender privilege in the colonial society, saw the AMPR as the organization through which they could promote their professional demands before the new US colonial authority and all its agents—the commissioner of education and the legislature. The AMPR leadership, however, had to contend with a new, younger generation of teachers who came into the profession in increasing numbers. The new teachers brought with them a different perspective, for they had been trained and educated within the US colonial framework. In addition, most of the new teachers were women.

Despite the transformations in the teaching force, the AMPR leadership tried to speak in a united voice. Their writings, petitions, speeches, and conferences spoke to broad intentions. First, they sought to firmly establish the boundaries and parameters of their profession. Second, they intended to channel the energy of new teachers into the primary social agenda of the AMPR—nurturing the relationship between the home, school, and country. This vision was complex, for it represented teachers' intentions for their students, defined by progress and modernity. It imagined the regeneration of the citizenry, a transformation that only teachers, as modern actors, could lead.

Hogar, Escuela, Patria (Home, School, Country)

Nancy Leys Stepan and scholars of race, science, and eugenics in Latin America identified a common concern of late nineteenth- and early twentieth-century national elites.[28] Intellectuals, politicians, professionals, and others questioned how they could "create out of their heterogeneous populations a new and purified homogeneity on which true 'nationhood' could be created." Different social contexts in each country, or regions within countries, allowed for an interpretation of social eugenics that lent itself to imagining the regeneration, or uplift, of populations. Eugenic ideas were combined with national definitions and identities, especially after World War I and in the 1930s. Eugenic visions, particularly neo-Lamarckian hereditary definitions, "in which no sharp boundaries between nature and nurture were drawn," informed the "history of medicine, family, maternity, population, criminology, public health, and social welfare." Improving the health of the individual was part of the process of addressing the health of the nation and the "quality" of its citizens.[29]

Puerto Rican teachers in the early twentieth century, like educators in Brazil, Mexico, and Argentina, proposed their own interpretations of social eugenics.[30] In their speeches, petitions, and letters to newspapers and legislators, they advocated policies they believed could lead to the regeneration of "the nation." They emphasized the relationship between home, school, and country.[31] The root of the problem, they explained, was found in the home. Teachers critiqued the alleged failures of rural and urban parents, specifically the nonelite. Informed by modern pedagogy, teachers questioned parents' abilities to create healthy and nurturing home environments in which children could thrive. Within this line of argument, schools were that much more urgent given the failure of homes. Teachers, informed by modern methods of instruction, could educate children where parents could not. Teachers could contribute to the regeneration of the *pueblo* (people) through the teaching of home economics, physical education, and rural agriculture. Children, then, as they brought home lessons from schools, could serve as a model for parents. Children could effect change in contemporary and future homes, leading to the potential transformation of communities and neighborhoods. In this way, together, teachers and students could build a healthier, modern, and more progressive *patria*.

Teachers articulated a relationship between home, school, and *patria* that was a national vision. Teachers were contributing to the formation of national identities in the early twentieth century. The fact that the national project was crafted and promoted within a colonial school system, that a national vision for Puerto Rico (the *patria*) was imagined as part of, but not independent from, the US empire was not exceptional nor paradoxical. Rather, it was typical of the history of island politics. Elites had proposed definitions of emerging national identities since the nineteenth century, identities that were imagined within and in relation to the Spanish empire.[32] These were reinterpreted as more liberal and progressive in association with the US empire. In the 1910s and 1920s Puerto Rican teachers also articulated a vision for schools that was typical of liberal autonomist defini-tions of national identities, visions that could be promoted within the colonial school system. This, however, required a careful balance. Teachers promoted national identities that did not mean to subvert the authority of the US colonial administration, for when they crossed that boundary, when in the 1930s they promoted nationalist ideas that challenged colonialism and imagined political sovereignty, they were quickly reprimanded.[33]

Addressing the home, school, and *patria* became a priority. In the late 1910s and 1920s teachers envisioned that the potentially healthy and modern *patria*

Directiva de la Asociación Local de Maestros
Presidente Honorario .....Santiago Negroni. Presidente efectivo......Vicente Soltero. Vice-Presidente......
Charles E. Miner. Secretaria......Elvira Vicente. Tesorera......María C de Toro. Vocales..... Paz López de
Victoria, Esther Roura y Juanita Ortiz.

"Directiva de la Asociación Local de Maestros" (The advisory board of the local teachers' association), 1925. Santiago Negroni, honorary president of the Yauco association, was the author of the *hogar, escuela, patria* speech printed in the *PRSR* (Masini et al., *Historia ilustrada de Yauco*).

of Puerto Rico was being undermined by the allegedly palatable "degeneracy" of homes and the *raza*. In this relationship, the term *raza* was a reference to "the people," *la raza*, of the island, a national *raza*. The concept of *raza* was informed by but different from the concept of race. US census records reported that Puerto Rico's population at the turn of the century was 62 percent white (native and foreign-born) and 38 percent nonwhite (32 percent mulatto and 6 percent black).[34] These census categories of race (white, mulatto, black) are socially constructed.[35] They are particularly slippery when a foreign government (the United States) defines categories of race, informed by its history of race relations and law, and applies them to a colonial territory (Puerto Rico). Puerto Rican society had its own history with those categories.[36] Two different yet complementary systems of racial classification overlapped during census enumeration. Region further complicated the reported percentages of racial categories. The populations of the coast and the highland mountains were shaped by the history of export commodity production (sugar, coffee, tobacco) and its labor systems (free and enslaved). Urban and rural populations, which required different occupations in port towns versus agricultural farming, shaped the distribution of black, mulatto, and white populations as well.[37] At the moment of enumeration, class biases informed how the enumerator defined his or her subject's race. Finally, census records silence how individuals defined their own identity.

Keeping these factors in mind, we can, nevertheless, propose that teachers were informed by both race and *raza*. Teachers in urban and rural settings, in the coasts and in the highlands, wrote about the degeneracy of the student population. This vision of degeneracy was informed by interpretations of race as a biological category—comments on racial mixture, miscegenation, and hybridity in student populations. At the same time, those critiques were presented and informed by the language of science and environment—disease, poverty, illiteracy, ignorance.

There was, however, an additional layer. When teachers used the term *raza* to refer to the "national body" of Puerto Ricans, they were also responding to the context of empire. They were claiming a heritage different from that of the imperial Americans. Use of the terms *raza* and *race* was intended to distinguish a Puerto Rican "community" from the foreign and occupying Americans, who were stereotyped as Anglo-Saxon, Protestant, and English-speaking, despite the heterogeneity of Americans on the island and in the United States. The colonial encounter, therefore, heightened elite local claims to a Hispanic, Catholic, and Spanish-speaking heritage. This was one of multiple frameworks (Latin versus Anglo-Saxon) that shaped local discourses on race and served to further homogenize teachers' interpretations of *raza*. *Raza* became a national term to define

Puerto Rican children in opposition to US visions. At the same time, however, it silenced more complex discussions of racial heterogeneity within the student population and the teaching force, for children and teachers in urban Ponce and Guayama did not look the same as children and teachers in the rural schools of Yauco and Utuado.

In the home/school/*patria* trilogy, proposing the reconstruction of the home first required addressing the alleged degeneracy of the *raza*. Discourses about the state of children's bodies became a primary location for identifying degeneracy. Elite teachers like Gerardo Sellés Solá proposed that children's unhealthy or dysgenic state was the result of the environment to which they were exposed in homes and streets. Discussions about the state of children's bodies were, therefore, contributions to a debate over the health of the *raza* and the nation. Sellés Solá, president of the AMPR in the 1920s, made this connection explicit in his proposal for expanding access to physical education courses. His intention was to justify the expansion of physical education classes, to make them accessible to all students, not just elite children in urban high schools. He proposed that physical education might be an effective method for "the emerging enterprise of the regeneration of the *patria*."[38]

Sellés Solá was thirty-three years old when he was elected president of the AMPR at the 1921 annual convention, held in Arecibo. A native of Caguas, he represented the generation of teachers who received their elementary education during the late Spanish colonial period. In 1902, at the age of sixteen, Sellés Solá graduated from the one-year rural teacher training course offered through the newly founded University of Puerto Rico and was certified to teach by the Department of Education. In many ways, his career as an educator was typical of many of his generation. Although he began as a rural teacher, he quickly moved to urban schools and eventually became an administrator, a school inspector for the DE. The 1920s teaching leadership was composed of individuals who entered the teaching profession early in the US colonial period and then rose into administrative positions and became leaders by the 1920s. The education Sellés Solá acquired, however, distinguished him from others. A recurring concern of US colonial administrators was the lack of education the majority of teachers held. Sellés Solá, however, earned a BA in education in 1926 and an MA in 1930. His MA thesis, which examined the political history of Spanish-language instruction in the first thirty years of the twentieth century, became a core reading in the history of education.[39]

Sellés Solá embraced the challenge of addressing the health of the student body. His intention was to "modernize" the curriculum through the expansion of physical education in urban and rural schools. The physical health of students, he argued, "is considered of secondary importance." Instead, he proposed that it was as important as the teaching of reading, writing, and arithmetic. This was an interpretation of the post–World War I theory of modern education that promoted the balanced development of a child's mind, body, and soul. As AMPR president, Sellés Solá proposed his argument for the overhaul of physical education in a *carta circular* that was distributed to all teachers. With it, he also intended to address municipal school authorities. He demanded that all educators become aware of what surrounded them: children who were physically "abnormal" and in an "alarming" state of health. He highlighted the "cataclysmic" conditions of physical degeneracy among the children of Puerto Rico and called for action.

Sellés Solá proposed that a core goal of public instruction was the formation of healthy, moral, and intelligent citizens. He was alarmed at the reportedly "cataclysmic levels of physical degeneracy" within the student body, which ultimately challenged teachers' broader intention of forming citizens. "We are on the verge of a cataclysm of physical degeneration, or we are in full-fledged cataclysm, and yet we remain serene, not looking for means to resolve the problem. . . . No one seems moved by the presence of such physically abnormal children. So many feeble children, with weak lungs, deaf, with rotten teeth, poor vision, and abnormal height and weight!"[40] Sellés Solá identified these to be markers of "degeneracy," but they were preventable and, more important, reversible through the modern practice of physical education and other methods. Physical education was just one modern method that could contribute to the sanitation of home and public spaces with the goal to regenerate the child. This was an interpretation of "preventive" eugenics.[41]

For Sellés Solá, racial degeneracy was due to a combination of factors. On the one hand, it was the legacy of a history of ignorance, illiteracy, and poverty. On the other, it was compounded by neglect, tradition, and isolation. Children without access to schools, he feared, were engaged in behaviors that were both symptoms and causes of racial degeneracy, such as public drinking, gambling, and prostitution: "Hundreds of children advance toward the field of immorality and crime for all the well-known reasons: poverty, ignorance, overpopulation, prostitution, alcoholism, *concubinaje*, and so on." The spectacle of "children who smoke, children who gamble, teenage boys who stay up all night, young women who have barely reached normal height and whose pale faces sport makeup that disguises the shortage of red blood cells," Sellés Solá lamented, could be corrected. "Down with indolent youth who smoke, who age prematurely, who lack vitality and energy, whose bodies are unhealthy, and whose spirits are unhealthy too! Down with young women who are mystical and woeful, who know nothing of exercise, of sun or fresh air! Let's have healthy and strong youth who see no limits to their aspirations, because the power of their physical, mental and moral force is unlimited!"[42] Sellés Solá wanted to leave that "traditional" history and behavior in the past and move forward with modern methods.

Youth reformatories came under scrutiny in the early 1920s as journalists reported on the abuses and neglect children faced in punitive institutions.[43] Reformatories, therefore, were not the preferred choice for Sellés Solá, who was guided by the liberal methods of modern education. Instead, he promoted founding the Bureau of Home Extension so that teachers could be authorized to "go into homes" and teach families "how to live."[44] In 1922 he addressed the legislature and shared the *acuerdos* approved by teachers at the annual convention. He spoke of the emerging awareness of child delinquency in urban spaces and proposed that legislators support mandatory attendance laws. As the voice of the AMPR, he demanded that politicians give due attention to the "enormous problem of children who are being initiated into perversity."[45] Otherwise, he asked, "What will become of them?"[46]

> They occupy posts at roadside games and are regular clients in the public billiard halls, where they are drawn so as to be exploited and where they continually receive the most impure and corruptive example. I know a place in Puerto Rico where a group of boys shoot craps from the early hours of the evening to the break of dawn the following day, sometimes accompanied by men, professional dice players. And these boys, filthy, ragged, emaciated, do not attend school. If only a means could be found to bring them to school![47]

Dysgenic behaviors were not limited to urban spaces. They were also a rural problem. However, in the *campo* (countryside) the main concern was resources. Sellés Solá advocated the founding of public parks in rural areas where children could spend time in organized play, outdoors, under the direction and guidance of physical education teachers: "The peasant masses are hungry for amusement and pastimes. When lawful diversions and outdoor games become popular, we will slowly see the disappearance of cockfights, of games in street intersections, and other pastimes that so contribute to their demoralization and impoverishment."[48] Teachers had the power (knowledge) with which to introduce appropriate leisure activities and help create healthy (sanitized) environments: "One of the major causes contributing to our youth's deficient development is the lack of exercise and outdoor play. Our youth, our girls, and our boys, must play. Playing is joy. Playing allows unconstructive worries to be forgotten; it foments health and destroys vice."[49]

Sellés Solá's speeches, lectures, and presentations in the early 1920s force-fully proposed that teachers had the obligation, through public instruction, to help improve the conditions under which the *raza* was degenerating. This was a patriotic call in service to the nation and future generations. Dysgenic behaviors, Sellés Solá warned, could only further weaken the race by producing degener-ate offspring: "This weak, lifeless youth is a precursor to disgraced homes, sick and degenerate offspring. Such are the sad consequences of complete negligence toward the study and treatment of such ills, for the love of our children, for the good feelings we all hold in our hearts."[50] Through teacher supervision and pro-motion of healthy physical education, he believed a new generation of healthy and vibrant youth could replace the current degenerate one and, in time, produce a healthier *patria*: "Let us raise strong generations, proud of this condition and inclined to conserve it, giving them a pure and moral life, and an adequate mental cultivation. Let us form the perfect home, the happy home. Our *patria* will thus become great thanks to the health, the purity, the intelligence, and the hard work of its sons."[51]

Why were schoolchildren unhealthy, unfit, and degenerate? Teachers argued that these problems were a reflection of conditions in the home. José González Ginorio, president of the AMPR in 1919 and elected honorary president in 1921, was especially critical of the state of homes. Like Sellés Solá, González Ginorio stood apart from the teaching rank and file. He began his career as a teacher but distinguished himself through academic and professional achievements, especially as the author of Spanish-language instruction textbooks. In the 1910s and 1920s the Spanish language was taught in island schools using the "Ginorio method."[52] In the 1920s he rose to the highest administrative positions within the DE as the general superintendent of schools.

In 1917 González Ginorio wrote a series of articles on the value and promises of "domestic education" for Puerto Rican homes. He addressed his articles, pub-lished in *La revista escolar de Puerto Rico/Porto Rico School Review* (*PRSR*), to parents and teachers. In these articles González Ginorio introduced "a new sys-tem of rational domestic instruction" as a method of modern pedagogy. His arti-cles did not call for funding to hire home economics teachers and to create a home economics curriculum.[53] In 1917 his intention was to work within the existing relationship of home and school, to assess the current conditions of parenting in homes, and to suggest modern ways to improve them. The key, he argued, was the connection between home and school. The school was simply an exten-sion of the home. Mothers and teachers must work together to generate harmony and consistency in the rearing of children and modern citizens: "When the child arrives at school, the educational labor of the home is not concluded. No. At that moment the school enters into a pact with the home, and both commit to working in harmony. They complement each other. School is an extension of the home."[54] In this vision, González Ginorio assumed that the formation of a child and future citizen required a coalition between, specifically, mother and teacher. The father was absent.

González Ginorio's assessments of the state of homes were rarely complimentary. He was concerned with parenting methods. He believed parents had the ability to nurture or destroy a child's character. Unfortunately, he feared, the harshness and inconsistency that parents used to correct children's behavior at home caused more harm than good: "In spite of the tender love that all parents feel for their children . . . in their noble eagerness to give them the best possible education, they follow educative methods or practices that can easily destroy forever the probability of happiness and success that all children have. And, most unfortunate of all, such parents do not realize the evil they are doing to their children."[55] Children's behavior in schools, therefore, was a reflection of parenting and the environment of the home: "Without fear of equivocations, the troubles of which almost all children are accused—disobedience, willfulness, daring, and so on—are a product of the poor or deficient education that they have received at home."[56] Teachers and schools, in the end, were forced to correct children's behaviors.

While González Ginorio called for a harmonious and collaborative relationship between home and school, it was a relationship he imagined would come in the future. At the moment, he argued, the core of the problem was parents and homes. The solution was teachers and schools: "The home and the school are brothers. Let it be the link of love that joins those sacred institutions. And tell me, what strange power will be able to destroy that which the natural love of a mother and the spiritual love of a teacher have made? Let the Home be the shield of the School. Only then will the School be the salvation of the Home."[57] This was the promise of schools. They could transform allegedly failed homes. Reconstruct the home, and you transform a generation. González Ginorio promised that this was the path to the "regeneration of our people [*pueblo*]."[58]

Teachers identified themselves as primary actors responsible for cultivating an effective relationship between home, school, and *patria*. In the 1910s and 1920s, as the teaching profession continued to grow and expand, the AMPR solicited essays from teachers that contributed to the definition of their duties and responsibilities to the *patria* through the school. In particular, at the annual conventions in December, the AMPR held a literary contest (a *certamen*), and a panel of judges selected winners. The *certamen* topics revolved around defining the profession, clarifying teachers' duties and responsibilities, and suggesting useful ways for teachers to collaborate with parents to overcome obstacles to progress. The essays, authors, and judges were contributing to the process of defining teachers' identities and commitments to students, communities, and the *patria*. The winning essays were published in the *PRSR* and distributed widely among teachers throughout the island. One teacher in particular, Lorenza Brunet del Valle, rose above the rest. She won the annual *certamen* at least four times between 1917 and 1925. Brunet del Valle, who was born in 1883, and her brother, Carlos, were teachers in Ponce in the 1910s and 1920s. Brunet del Valle, although younger than Sellés Solá, was of the same generation and committed to the promises of modern education for the "future and progress of our *patria*."[59]

Brunet del Valle's essays defined the role of schools in the home/school/*patria* trilogy. They also reflected the paternalist lens through which some elite teachers viewed their students. The distance teachers established—based on intellectual, moral, and class differences—was often most clear when they described their responsibilities to the "uplift" of rural students, parents, and communities. In their descriptions they appeared overwhelmed when they imagined the responsibilities of teachers and schools for the regeneration of rural children. It was, according to Brunet del Valle, the teachers' duty nonetheless. "The teacher," she explained, "is called to bring to fruition the very noble task of enlightening the peasant masses, of leading them out of the thick fog of ignorance in which they live." Brunet del Valle imagined the peasantry as a people living in the past, in traditional ways. They were a contemporary obstacle to the progress of the *patria*. Nevertheless, the teacher, armed with the knowledge of modern education practices, could transform and regenerate the individual and community. Teachers could "bring the newspaper and the book to our countryside, along with hygienic rules and modern agricultural methods in order to rouse those sleeping souls." A teacher's patriotic labor could "take them out of the apathy in which they live, lighting a ray of enthusiasm in their hearts, and interest for those material things that can be useful." Brunet del Valle, an urban teacher, believed rural teachers had a special duty above all others. Theirs was a "labor of love, patriotism, and faith."[60]

What was the *patria* Sellés Solá, González Ginorio, and Brunet del Valle spoke of? How did they define the concepts of country, nation, and empire? *Nuestra patria*—"our country"—was Puerto Rico. In speeches, lectures, and essays, teachers addressed their partners—other teachers, educators, and legislators—in the struggle to rebuild the *patria*. In the 1910s and 1920s their use of the concept of *patria* was informed by the assumption that they were in conversations with the people of Puerto Rico as a national community, or a people who shared a common history, language, and values. Rarely did they mention the "biological" (racial) heritage of the community other than in references to "Latin" culture and heritages. Instead, they spoke of the potential regeneration of the *raza*. Their expressions of national identity were also rooted in the geography and physical boundaries of the island. The struggle was to build links across regions—from Mayagüez to San Juan to Ponce to Juncos—and to address the needs of both rural and urban communities. At great expense, elected local AMPR leaders traveled once a year to their central conference. By doing so, they participated in the process of articulating their commitment to the *patria* of Puerto Rico. When they spoke of the *patria*, they assumed a shared knowledge of language, territory, and community.

For Puerto Rican educators in the 1910s and 1920s, imagining a national community was an extension and rearticulation of the political projects that emerged in the second half of the nineteenth century. They were not advocating a nationalist vision that required the founding of a politically sovereign state. Instead, their visions were within the parameters of existing autonomist political ideologies. They imagined the *patria* could continue to evolve, strengthen, be uplifted. This was not contradicted by maintaining a *temporary* relationship with an empire. Autonomists had called for increased local authority and control under the Spanish colonial state in the late nineteenth century. They initially imagined that a relationship with the self-defined liberal, progressive, and modern United States could only lead to more liberal ideas and developments for the island. Teachers were not arguing that there was a contradiction in nurturing the *patria* while maintaining a temporary relationship with the United States.

Therefore, in December 1919, when González Ginorio addressed teachers in attendance at the annual convention in San Juan, he was free (without fear of repression from US colonial authorities) to call on others to commit to the task of "regenerating our people." He asked teachers to recognize their "saintly mission" in the name of the community and the *patria*: "The educational problem of a country . . . should be addressed everywhere: in schools, homes, streets, places of recreation, the press; there where a member of society dwells, the city and the countryside, the plains and the mountains. Such is the duty that, conscious of its mission, the Association of Teachers of Puerto Rico accepts."[61] Teachers, as members of the AMPR, would contribute to the regeneration of the *patria*. In the 1910s and 1920s this was imagined to be a process that could be undertaken in collaboration, rather than in conflict, with US colonial officials.

In fact, Puerto Rican and US educators spoke across the boundaries of language and empire. They worked together to implement a colonial school system that could address those concerns—the home/school/*patria* trilogy—that were a priority to both teachers and US colonial officials. The vision of rebuilding the home, centering the school and teacher in the community, and contributing to the *patria* was not entirely foreign to US educators. US liberal educators saw potential in Puerto Rican students, potential educators were not sure they could identify in other colonial subjects, particularly Cubans and Filipinos. These differences were as much informed by the armed revolutionary practices of these groups as they were by the racial and cultural characterizations of Puerto Ricans. The allegedly whiter, more benevolent, docile, and receptive Puerto Ricans were imagined to be a good test for Americanization practices.[62] This was a test US liberal educators imagined could be more successful in Puerto Rico, in the tradition of Hawaii, than in other colonies.

The writings and declarations of the AMPR leadership acknowledged that Puerto Ricans were a people currently under the "protection" of a larger nation, but they never conceded that this was a permanent relationship or that Puerto Rico would be "absorbed" within the United States. The island's colonial relationship to the United States was not foreign to the older leadership. In the late nineteenth century, teachers struggled for recognition before a Spanish colonial state. In the early twentieth century, they reorganized and carried forward that struggle, but now before the US colonial state. The change in imperial authority created a different impetus for public education, but it did not undermine the teaching leadership's vision that the island and its people were a community and culture different from those of the colonizer.

In the tradition of autonomist politics and with the intention to lay claims to their intermediate position in the colonial hierarchy, therefore, the AMPR membership voted in support of a "resolution of Gratitude and Loyalty to the President and Congress of the United States." In response to the US Congress's approval of the Jones Act in March 1917, which granted US citizenship to all Puerto Ricans born on the island, the AMPR expressed its "appreciation and gratitude . . . for this signal recognition of the capacity and right of the people of Porto Rico to enjoy *a larger measure of self-government and full citizenship*." Teachers, who were emerging from the repression of a declining Spanish colonial state, imagined Puerto Rico's right to "a more liberal form of government" as part of the modern US empire.[63]

This interpretation of the promises of US colonialism for schools and students, however, did not negate the grave disagreements between elite teachers and US administrators. In fact, they disagreed over the content of the curriculum, the language of instruction, and the political allegiance teachers were expected to instill in their students. After the Jones Act, the policies of the US colonial Department of Education changed. The DE more aggressively promoted the Americanization of students, the creation of "tropical Yankees," and instruction in the English language. During this transition, the AMPR leadership claimed their location within the colonial hierarchy. This negotiated position, the choice to locate themselves within the colonial hierarchy rather than in direct opposition to it, was a rational choice for the older leadership of the AMPR, since they were seeking the most direct and effective way to control how the colonial school project would evolve in the early twentieth century. Negotiating imperial policies guaranteed them as much autonomy as they could secure within the new US colonial state.

Nevertheless, the AMPR leadership's method of negotiating imperialism was equally informed by the repression they faced when they directly challenged US colonialism. Teachers faced very real restrictions on public expression. They were civil servants of a colonial state. US officials were unforgiving of open expressions of radical nationalism or critiques of US colonialism. Those teachers or education students who stepped outside of the narrative were penalized, decertified, fired, blacklisted, and pushed out of public schools and into private practice.[64] US education officials were particularly intolerant of anticolonial expression in schools, for they imagined education to be the primary ideological tool for reproducing support for US colonialism. Teachers, therefore, who worked within the colonial framework as employees of the Department of Education were aware of the restrictions imposed on them regarding critiques of US colonialism.

The subordinated position of teachers in the politically charged early twentieth century was evident in the process by which elite teachers sought to define the parameters of their profession. In an act of self-censure, Sellés Solá clarified that the AMPR membership should not intervene in political debates. The late 1910s and 1920s were years of dynamic political debate and contestation between political parties and US colonial authorities regarding colonialism, autonomism, and citizenship.[65] In 1921 Sellés Solá distributed a letter to local association members highlighting the professional character of their union. In fact, political censure of teachers was law. School law no. 52 denied teachers the right to advocate for a particular political party or candidate; the penalty was the loss of their teaching license. Sellés Solá's position was that teachers must show that "the Association of Teachers of Puerto Rico is not a political party, nor does it wish to intervene in political disputes." Sellés Solá and the AMPR moved away from building solidarity with trade unions and toward strengthening their relationship with other elite professional organizations, such as associations of doctors, dentists, and lawyers. "Nor is the Association of Teachers of Puerto Rico a purely economic organization; it is essentially a professional association. This is how we understand the association, and working from this perspective, we will better uplift ourselves and surround ourselves with greater prestige before all the country's social classes."[66] This professional distinction was part of the process by which teachers increasingly disassociated themselves from the organized working class of the 1910s and 1920s and from the children of working families in their classrooms, children upon whom teachers located symptoms of racial degeneracy. However, this was also a response to the intolerance and repression of US officials. Therefore, there were limits to the strategy pursued by elite teachers, the intention to promote their visions within the US colonial framework rather than in opposition to it. Promoting the relationship between home, school, and *patria* required teachers to employ nonpartisan policies and temper anticolonial critiques.

The promise of the regeneration of the *patria* was not an ideology unique to teachers. It was precisely the vision that Rosendo Matienzo Cintrón proposed in the early twentieth century. Matienzo Cintrón was a political leader who advocated for the unification of Puerto Rican political leadership in the interest of regeneration, or the cultivation of a Puerto Rican personality. He warned against physical degeneration and supported the regeneration of the *raza*. At the same time, Matienzo Cintrón advocated for regeneration *within* the process of Americanization, which he conceptualized as liberal, modern, and progressive. Americanization, however, should not become a practice of imperialism. He vehemently opposed Americanization when it meant the reproduction of empire, when it embodied the process of imperial formations, when it generated exemptions from basic definitions of republicanism and democracy to allow for colonial relationships and impositions. Matienzo Cintrón's definitions of regeneration and Americanization were emblematic of autonomist ideology—they were proliberalism and modernity but anticolonial. This was the ideology that also informed the founding of the Partido Unión, a liberal reform party under the leadership of Luis Muñoz Rivera and José de Diego in the 1910s.[67] While this vision of regeneration, which was at the core of autonomist ideology and the reproduction of colonialism in the early twentieth century, was not unique to the teaching leadership, it is important to recognize that teachers fervently advocated for these concepts as well, for they were the daily transmitters of cultural norms to students and parents. This vision of regeneration was complementary to Matienzo Cintrón's vision and to the ideology that guided the liberal Partido Unión. However, it also became the dominant ideology of important intermediate actors—teachers—in the colonial hierarchy.

The documents teachers produced—letters, speeches, lectures, petitions, *acuerdos*—in the 1910s and 1920s spoke directly to how the home/school/*patria* trilogy informed their visions for Puerto Rico's schools. The trilogy was a popular interpretation of social eugenics. It promised the regeneration of the *raza* and the cultivation of a healthy, modern, and progressive *patria*. The way teachers articulated the promises of the trilogy, however, did not allow for an acknowledgment of the economic structures that shaped the material conditions of urban and rural workers. In these early years, teachers located symptoms of degeneracy in the individual, on student bodies, in failed parenting, and in homes. They were not calling for a revolution—for the transformation of political and economic structures—that could allow for the material improvement of families and students. Although national visions informed by the home/school/*patria* trilogy were not revolutionary, they were significant nonetheless. For these were the ideas that led to the reform of curriculum in the 1930s in order to better address the daily needs of students through physical education, home economics, and agricultural economics.

chapter 3

Citizenship, Gender, and Schools

In 1917 the US Congress approved legislation for Puerto Rico and other territories that embodied the practices of "imperial formations," providing another
example for how the United States as a modern empire "blurred genres of rule
and partial sovereignties" as it "created new subjects . . . under uncertain domains
of jurisdiction and ad hoc exemptions from the law on the basis of race and cultural differences."[1] World War I reminded US legislators of the geopolitical value
of Puerto Rico to the United States in the Caribbean. In March 1917 the US Congress approved the Jones Act, which replaced the Foraker Act as the island's colonial constitution. The Jones Act did not fundamentally alter the colonial terms
of the Puerto Rican–US relationship as established by the Foraker Act in 1900.
Instead, although it provided some reforms, it reinforced Puerto Rico's status as an
unincorporated colonial territory. In a controversial move, the Jones Act granted
US citizenship to all persons born on the island. In April 1917 the US Congress
declared war against Germany and entered World War I. A month later, the US
Congress approved a new Selective Service Law, requiring obligatory military
service by all men age twenty-one to thirty. Puerto Rican men, as US citizens,
were obligated to register for military service according to the Selective Service
Law.[2] Puerto Rican men were recruited into the newly founded colonial military
regiment (the Porto Rico Regiment) and deployed to guard the Panama Canal
for the duration of the war.

The 1920s education debates sought clarification of the definitions and obligations of this new colonial citizenship. This apparent contradiction—granting
US citizenship to those born on a colonial territory—generated great criticism
and opposition from the vocal leadership of the island's political parties. When it

was approved, the Jones Act caused grave disillusionment among the political leadership, including Rosendo Matienzo Cintrón, Luis Muñoz Rivera, José de Diego, and José Celso Barbosa. While the leaders of political parties maintained opposing opinions regarding the practices of US colonialism in Puerto Rico, none expected that the United States, as a self-defined liberal democracy, would grant US citizenship to Puerto Ricans at the same time that it denied fundamental colonial reform and consolidated the island's unincorporated status. Historians César Ayala and Rafael Bernabe argue that in response to the new colonial parameters that the Jones Act established, political parties from 1917 forward reorganized into a politics of colonial reform. "With the demise of the Partido de la Independencia," the political party founded in 1912 that advocated for the independence of Puerto Rico, "Puerto Rican politics . . . came to be dominated by the clash of versions of colonial reformism, which included the accommodation of the Partido Unión to the limits of the relation of nonincorporation with the U.S., the collaboration of the new pro-Statehood Partido Republicano with U.S. colonial rule, and the colonial reformist drift of the Partido Socialista."[3] The year 1917, therefore, marked a historical shift toward the politics of colonial reformism, embodied in the new colonial citizenship and the Porto Rican Regiment's participation in World War I.

The colonial reformist politics of the 1920s were also informed by a cultural debate over the process of cultivating a Puerto Rican identity and personality. Liberal leaders linked the promises of regeneration with the formation of national identities. Rosendo Matienzo Cintrón, for example, argued that the "essence of a Puerto Rican identity" already existed and only needed to be cultivated. Proannexationist Republicans like José Celso Barbosa, meanwhile, did not recognize a burgeoning national identity and instead argued that "the true Puerto Rican identity would be created through the process of Americanization itself."[4] The debate over the practice of Americanization in the 1920s required defining the parameters of colonial citizenship, identifying the space for promoting the uniqueness of Puerto Rican identities and practices within the limits of the colonial framework established by the Jones Act. Public schools were at the center of the process of negotiating colonial reformist politics. Puerto Rican teachers and administrators consciously contributed to debates over the promises of colonial reformism and citizenship.

Colonial reformism and the cultural debates, in addition, were shaped by bourgeois women's public appeals for moral reforms in the 1920s. Women's participation in the public sector grew as more working-class women became seamstresses, laundresses, hatmakers, fruit canners, and *tabaqueras* and as middle-class women joined the teaching and nursing professions. Radical working-class leaders like

Luisa Capetillo and Juana Colón called for the eradication of patriarchy in public and private spaces. Women workers led labor strikes and challenged political and labor leaders' assumptions about women's appropriate roles in Puerto Rican society.[5] In addition, a more moderate group of middle-class women emerged as the leading voice of the 1920s moral reform movement.[6] Middle-class women's advocacy represented the ideology of "social feminism," which imagined ways of improving women's "influence and autonomy" within the home, community, and society.[7] Social feminists advocated for women to become better mothers and to more effectively complement the husband in the home. An ideology that accepted assumed biological differences between men and women, social feminism nevertheless intended to advance women's roles as a requirement of a modern and liberal society. In the 1920s social feminists called for the moral reform of working-class families and advocated for the right of literate women to vote. In their struggle to demand the franchise for their gender, and particularly their class, they reproduced their vision of social feminism. Teachers occupied a prominent role in the leadership and membership of social feminists, suffragists, and moral reformers. Through the suffragist campaign, middle-class feminist visions of moral reform, patriarchy, and gender also demanded further clarification of the definition of colonial citizen.

In the 1920s working-class students faced multiple challenges. The decade witnessed growth in the professions that employed large concentrations of child labor—tobacco, sugar, and needlework. At the same time, unemployment and seasonal unemployment, in particular, rose. Rural workers, displaced from agricultural work and in search of city jobs, migrated to urban areas at higher rates. Migrants lived in overcrowded housing and labored in congested work spaces. The lack of circulation in *talleres* (workshops), particularly tobacco, shoe, textile, and bakeries, facilitated the spread of tuberculosis among workers. Labor struggled against working and living conditions that contributed to the rise of preventable diseases like malaria, diarrhea, tuberculosis, and anemia. In the face of these material conditions, workers mobilized into labor unions (e.g., Federación Libre de Trabajadores) and political parties (e.g., Partido Socialista) in the 1920s, demanding improvements in labor and housing. Ultimately, throughout the decade, laborers became increasingly disillusioned with the conservative reformism of their leadership. In the meantime, working-class parents and students became targets of middle-class reformers. Teachers, in their quest to fulfill their professional duty to create modern citizens, imagined the regeneration of working-class families but especially sought to reorganize the practices of husbands and wives through teachers' particular visions of modern gender norms.

For teachers in the 1920s, the politics of colonial reform, cultural debates, and moral reform were not simply academic exercises. These debates were at the core of teachers' daily practice in the classroom. The challenge of defining the new colonial citizenship took center stage. Creating citizens was teachers' primary responsibility. Now that the permanency of Puerto Rico's colonial status within the US empire was more clearly established through the Jones Act and the acquisition of US citizenship, how would this political framework shape colonial schools? What were the rights and responsibilities of this new form of colonial citizenship? How would it affect the teachers' broader citizenship-building agenda? And, more precisely, how would teachers contribute to the definition of colonial citizenship? In the tradition of autonomist politics, teachers found ways to define the new colonial citizenship while also affirming a Puerto Rican identity within the parameters of US colonialism.

In the 1920s school debates, one of the principal methods for defining the promises and limits of the new colonial citizenship was through debates over gender and patriarchy. Teachers articulated their citizenship-building project, which was grounded on the relationship between home, school, and *patria* and the practice of modern education, by defining gender roles and modern patriarchy within Puerto Rican society. The 1920s debates among teachers highlighted three lines of argument. First, teachers who were liberal reformers found ways to embrace what they saw as progressive, liberal, and regenerative in the redefined colonial relationship, the new colonial citizenship, and modern education. Teachers imagined that the young men who joined the Porto Rican Regiment and the young girls who were introduced to coed physical education classes were engaging in regenerative opportunities granted by a liberal and modern colonial government. Second, educators who were radical reformers found greater promise than ever in the regeneration of Puerto Rican families through the process of Americanization. In the tradition of proannexationist ideology, Commissioner Juan B. Huyke, for example, believed that the modern and scientific practices that undergirded Americanization ideology in the 1920s promised to instruct working-class mothers in healthy and eugenic mothering practices. In effect, Americanization could help liberate the contemporary child from allegedly "backward" mothering practices. Third, conservative educators and parents rejected some of the gender reforms promoted by liberal reformers and tried to reimpose what they considered more traditional norms. Liberal teachers faced a conservative backlash. The conservative critique not only targeted the modern education of young girls but also criticized a new generation of female teachers.

In the 1920s, therefore, education debates reflected a broader anxiety over changing gender norms. The island's emerging women's social movement challenged the assumed authority of the older generation of male teachers and the dominance of patriarchy within the teaching profession. Working-class women

unapologetically claimed their rights in public spaces as labor organizers and suffragists. Middle-class women swelled professional ranks. In addition to teaching,
they emerged as leaders in social work and nursing.[8] As women organized and
claimed public spaces, educators debated what they feared were newly emerging
gender crises: men's masculinity during World War I, physical education instruction for boys and girls, and the example set by women as teachers of rural schools.
These moments of crisis allowed for a broadening of the definition of appropriate roles for women in the 1920s. Nevertheless, the debates highlighted the limits
of incorporating new gender roles for women and served to reinforce patriarchy
within the profession.

The 1920s debates over education and schools, therefore, highlight the competing visions of colonial citizenship and gender. They also allow us to examine how teachers, as intermediate actors in the colonial hierarchy, contributed
to the definition of colonial citizenship for all Puerto Ricans. This was a definition that, in the tradition of autonomist ideology and practice in the early twentieth century, affirmed the uniqueness, difference, and promise of a Puerto Rican
identity within the limits and boundaries of US colonialism. The contribution of
this chapter, therefore, is to show how teachers—as historical actors other than
elite intellectuals and politicians—also contributed to early twentieth-century
conversations about the new colonial citizenship granted in 1917. This chapter also notes that at the core of the definition of the new colonial citizen and
the modern school lay the contested definitions of gender, families, and homes.
Through the debates over the citizenship-building project of schools in 1920s
Puerto Rico, from the location of the colony, and as they questioned traditional
gender norms, teachers were making their contribution to the practice of "imperial formations."

ILLITERACY, MASCULINITY, AND WAR

Illiteracy was at the core of debates over the right to exercise the franchise, capacity for US citizenship, and potential for self-government. Puerto Rico's illiteracy
rate in 1899 was 80 percent. For US colonial officials, high illiteracy rates helped
legitimize the founding of US colonialism. Both US colonial officials and elite
Puerto Rican politicians questioned the capacity of illiterates to fully participate
in government.[9] When universal male suffrage was reinstated in 1904, Puerto
Rican elites feared losing control over the colonial government to the interests
of the working class.[10] The proannexation Partido Republicano proposed that,
once illiteracy was reduced to 29 percent, it would move forward with a petition
for incorporation into the US federation of states. The liberal Partido Unión

characterized illiteracy as a "social evil." Although bourgeois female suffragists in the 1920s demanded the right to vote for their gender, they were divided over whether to support this right for illiterate women.[11] Literacy was a privilege of the elite, despite the rapid growth in colonial schools and the new access education granted to girls and the working class more broadly in the early 1900s and 1910s.[12] Adult men and women were the least served by colonial schools.

The debates over literacy as a measure of capacity for citizenship, as a stepping stone toward self-government, and as a measure of the progress, modernity, and civilization of Puerto Rico took center stage between 1917 and 1919. When newspapers reported that the majority of men who volunteered to join the Porto Rican Regiment during World War I were rejected due to illiteracy, a crisis ensued.[13] The 1910 census reported that the island's illiteracy rate had dropped to 65 percent, but in 1917 a larger percentage of rural adult men who had registered for the draft had been rejected.[14] If the majority of adult men were, in fact, illiterate and failed to meet that basic requirement of citizenship, teachers asked, how could they fulfill the duties of the newly granted US citizenship? Literacy and military service were duties, not privileges, of citizenship. What did these military rejection rates imply about literacy in Puerto Rico? Were illiteracy rates higher than had been reported? Was public school attendance a privilege for children that excluded adults? Was there a regional division? In 1910 79 percent of Puerto Ricans lived in rural areas. Had the colonial Department of Education, by founding most schools in urban centers, failed to address the demands for public instruction where it was most urgently needed—the countryside? The illiteracy rates among men who volunteered to join the Porto Rican Regiment brought to light the limited reach of public schools in 1917. When Puerto Ricans were granted US citizenship, colonial officials, teachers, and parents demanded urgent attention to teaching literacy. The crisis surrounding adult men's capacity for citizenship that the military rejections generated became a practice in defining colonial citizenship in the late 1910s.

Before the war, the successes and failures of the colonial Department of Education in Puerto Rico were measured first and foremost by illiteracy rates.[15] Colonial administrators had proposed the argument that literacy through English-language instruction had to be intensified in order to create US citizens out of colonial subjects. Assistant Commissioner of Education Carey Hickle proudly declared that in 1917, now that the Jones Act had been approved, "the chief business of the school is to produce . . . good citizens."[16] US colonial officials saw the path to literacy and to fulfilling requirements of citizenship through English-language instruction. For them, the English language and literacy were at the core of definitions of US citizenship. While the education scholarship has condemned commissioners for their English-language policies, in fact, in the 1910s and 1920s they were careful to balance English- and Spanish-language instruction. The intention was to promote English while "conserving" Spanish.[17] This approach assumed that Spanish would remain important on the island but subordinate to English. Nevertheless, the teaching of English to a Spanish-speaking people in an unincorporated colonial territory was a practice in further consolidating the colonial relationship between the island and the United States and reinforcing the assumed superiority of Americans over Puerto Ricans.

Improving literacy rates, however, meant many more things within Puerto Rican debates. First, illiteracy rates allowed teachers to critique what they perceived to be the failure of the US colonial Department of Education to satisfy the popular demands of the *pueblo* for education. The colonial government had not been able to expand quickly enough. It needed to build more schools and train and hire more teachers to educate more children! Newspaper articles declared: "To acquire success what is needed is money, money, and money. Schools, schools, and more schools."[18] Attaining literacy and access to education was not an imperial imposition. Instead, it was demanded by parents and students. Sadly, the US colonial Department of Education, many complained, nineteen years after the United States invaded and occupied the island, had failed to meet that demand.[19] This was a critique of the capacity of the colonial government to fulfill the declared promises of "benevolent imperialism."

Second, some used low literacy rates to condemn what they saw as the US colonial administrators' misguided imperial mission in Puerto Rico. The emphasis on using English as the language of instruction, as part of the grander Americanization vision, was wasting valuable time. Most children only attended school for three years. This was too short an amount of time to waste on teaching English when teachers could be teaching literacy in Spanish in addition to more practical topics like home economics, hygiene, agriculture, and so on.[20] The US colonial officials' unrealistic prioritization of English-language instruction had in the end failed to at least teach literacy, and, therefore, it had undermined Puerto Rican students' path toward citizenship.[21] These critiques of the work of the colonial Department of Education, nevertheless, were also a practice in reinforcing Puerto Rico's colonial relationship to the United States, for by advocating for the intensification and expansion of schools, teachers and parents were also contributing to the consolidation of a colonial school project that would further incorporate Puerto Ricans as second-class citizens of the US empire.

Nevertheless, local calls for improved literacy were not always tied to US colonialism. Some educators and parents demanded the eradication of illiteracy in the name of the progress and modernity of Puerto Rico's "civilization." José C.

Díaz, Comerío's school board president, argued that it was "time for us to fight to erase that stigma [illiteracy] that belittles us to civilized nations."[22] For the good of the *patria*, teachers demanded the intense cultivation of culture and dignity, which began with the acquisition of literacy. Díaz concluded: "We would be sinning for lacking patriotism, if we did not fight to extirpate the evil that harms us and that presents us to the world with such a high percentage of illiterates like a country that lacks true and ample culture."[23] Carlos Rivera Ufret, secretary of the AMPR, rivaled Díaz's patriotism when he called on teachers and other literate persons to "demonstrate to the illiterate the necessity of becoming instructed not only for their own well-being but in order to contribute by giving a more honorable seal and pride to our race and our beloved land."[24] Teachers wanted to generate pride in representations of Puerto Rican men abroad to the imagined audience of modern and scientific educators in the United States, Europe, and Latin America. This was a reflection of teachers' vision of self (the *magisterio*) as modern and cosmopolitan, mediated through the shame and embarrassment over the "degeneracy" of working-class adult illiterates.

Three months after granting Puerto Ricans US citizenship in 1917, the United States entered the great world war. The US military called on men to join the US Army through the segregated Porto Rican Regiment and to "do their bit."[25] Military service was a crucible. Puerto Rican men, categorized as colonial subjects for the past eighteen years, had just been granted a restricted form of US citizenship and were called to demonstrate their commitment to the empire by serving in the military during wartime. This was an important moment for the intensification of autonomist ideology on the island, for choosing to participate in military service in a colonial regiment reinforced the island's subordinate relationship to the United States. It was, at the same time, an opportunity to assert the capacity of Puerto Rican men for citizenship: 236,000 men registered for the draft; out of these, 18,000 men were accepted and served. "More than one-half of the teaching force [entered] into the service of the United States as either officers or soldiers."[26]

A crisis in the definitions of masculinity and citizenship ensued when the public learned that 75 percent of the volunteers had been rejected from Camp Las Casas not only for failing to meet the US Army's literacy requirements but also for failing to meet its physical standards. The rejection of so many adult men, particularly rural men, because they failed to pass their physicals generated a new category in public debates about the definition of colonial citizenship: "physical illiteracy."[27] The military recruits were doubly illiterate when they failed to meet both literacy and physical requirements. The spectacle of physical illiterates had two immediate consequences: a debate over the most effective ways to

"Hermanos Irizarry" (The Irizarry brothers), 1925. The caption reads: "Yauco holds the honor of being the only town on the island that offered the US Army four officers who were brothers during the great world war. They are here today to serve in whatever emergency may arise. Their ranks are Luis Antonio Irizarry, Lieutenant Colonel of the National Guard and the Reserve; Eustaquio Irizarry, First Lieutenant of the Reserve; Plinio Irizarry, Second Lieutenant of the Reserve; Eustasio Irizarry, Second Lieutenant of the Reserve." The two eldest brothers were teachers at the time they participated in World War I. In 1917 Luis Antonio was the supervisor of schools in Aguadilla and served as captain. Eustaquio was an English graded teacher in Yauco and a second lieutenant. The youngest brother, Eustasio, was enrolled as a student in Yauco's "Continuation School" when he went off to war as a lieutenant (Masini et al., *Historia ilustrada de Yauco*; "Roll of Honor: Schoolmen of Porto Rico in the Military Service," *PRSR* 3, no. 1 [September 1918]: 41–50).

reconstruct the Puerto Rican "man" and a popular movement in support of literacy campaigns.[28] The concern about overcoming the physical illiteracy of adult men, in particular, also reflected the gendered construction of the category of "citizen" in the 1910s and 1920s.

The concept of the physical illiteracy of the male military volunteer touched on existing anxieties in Puerto Rican debates over the island's "culture," levels of degeneracy, and limits of modernity. Teachers saw in the military rejection rates an opportunity to advance their agenda for citizenship building by focusing on penetrating the *campo* (rural areas) as intensely as possible. The physical illiterates represented everything teachers were trying to overcome through modern education. They encapsulated the worst effects of "traditionalism" within rural communities and the Spanish colonial heritage of neglect of the countryside. The *masas ignorantes* (ignorant masses) were slowing down the island's ability to catapult into modernity and fully embrace progress. Military rejection rates confirmed how the physical state of Puerto Rican men was "degenerate." Here was proof that the tropical climate and the isolation of the highlands forced the degeneration of the mythic founding "Latin race."

The concept of physical illiteracy, in fact, complemented teachers' already existing assumptions about rural communities. The isolation of rural society, from the urban teacher's perspective, generated little value for literacy, schooling, and modern forms of parenting and homemaking.[29] Genaro Concepción, who was providing an update in the *PRSR* on the "war work" activities of teachers in Luquillo and Fajardo, offered a sympathetic yet paternalistic reflection on the *jíbaros*' condition:

> He lives today as his ancestors did many years ago; as innocent as a child, with complete lack of knowledge of events that occur outside of his island, stuck to the land that he irrigates with sweat, and like the pariah of the Middle Ages, he has not an inch in which to dig his tomb; . . . he lives in a miserable *bohío* that looks more like a big bird's nest rather than human housing, his children barefoot, hungry, and ragged. And the reward for a long-suffering and laborious life? When he reaches old age he finds he must go to the towns to beg for public charity so as not to die of hunger and destitution.[30]

Sadly, teachers argued, *jíbaros* were a contemporary representation of the past with little to contribute to the modern nation-building and citizenship-building efforts of Puerto Rico's liberal progressives.

Thankfully, educators like Concepción argued, the physical illiteracy of *jíbaros* was the result of their environment—the highlands, the home, the farm—and was therefore subject to change and regeneration. The war, US citizenship, and military service could be the catalyst for that change. The war, therefore, was a great opportunity for *jíbaro* men to evolve. Through military training, *jíbaros* could be exposed to methods, practices, and experiences they would not otherwise have experienced:

> In the Puerto Rican countryside an unexpected transformation is taking place that is completely altering the destiny of our *jíbaros*. What once was tranquility and apathy today is activity and concerted effort; what once was submission and weakness is now patriotism and courageousness. . . . It seems that a new Messiah has spoken in the ear of our *jíbaro* the magic words *surge et ambula* [rise and move forward], and to the enchantment of that solemn order he shakes off the traditionalism that weighs on his conscience, like an immense lead slab, and presents himself to America as a new man capable of all sacrifices and renunciations. What magic wand has caused this resurrection? War.[31]

In the meantime, those men who had not been accepted into military service were also being pulled out of the backwater of rural areas, Concepción reported, as they were being asked to contribute to the intensified food production efforts during the war. Finally, once the war was over, military recruits could return to the island and serve as models of labor and leadership to those *jíbaros* left behind.[32] For Concepción this was a great opportunity for regeneration, the regeneration of local men who contributed military service to the US empire.

Teachers imagined that reversing the illiteracy of rural adults, however, required intense effort and support from the entire community. They called on the legislature, politicians, and even US colonial officials to support their initiatives by funding literacy campaigns.[33] After all, adult rural illiterate men, educators reminded legislators, had the right to vote in insular elections. Literacy was at the core of the right to vote, of the rights of citizenship, of the immediate direction of local politics.

Teachers offered a series of proposals for urgently and systematically attacking the "social evil" of illiteracy and demanded that legislators and the colonial Department of Education support them. More rural schools should be founded and more teachers trained and hired. But in addition, new legislation must allow for compulsory school attendance for children, harsh penalties for parents who kept children out of school, and mandatory night school attendance for adult illiterates. Luis García Casanova, winning author of the 1918 AMPR annual literary contest, argued that the legislature should fund a "school police force" responsible for conducting a census of illiterate adult men ages seventeen to fifty. The men could then be forced to attend night school. The school police could also enforce children's compulsory school attendance during the day and persecute those parents who took children out of school to labor in the fields or factories.[34]

In this early 1917 literacy campaign, teachers designated rural parents and land-owners as equally culpable for illiteracy in rural areas. While they called on the colonial state to legislate mandatory school attendance for children and adults, and they imagined rural landowners were hindering literacy by forcing children to work in the fields instead of attending school, teachers did not offer a broader critique of the island's colonial economy: agricultural production for export, the expansion of light manufacturing, and the corresponding processes of the prole-tarianization and loss of land for small farmers.[35] Teachers were more critical of the parents who pulled children out of schools than of the rural elite who hired them. When teachers did offer a critique of the rural elite, they called for reform of specific child labor practices rather than of colonialism more broadly.[36] The exception to this conservative critique of colonial economics was José Padín. During his brief appointment as assistant commissioner of education in 1917, he offered a critique of US colonialism, the granting of US citizenship, and the labor practices that reinforced colonialism and reproduced dire living conditions for the working class.[37] However, this was likely the type of explicit critique that school-teachers would have been censured for sharing publicly.

Teachers were not alone in their mission. Island legislators also proposed a series of projects to support literacy campaigns in 1919. They were guided by the fear that the 1920 census might document little progress in literacy for adult men, particularly now that they had acquired US citizenship.[38] And reducing literacy was a concern that the colonial reformist leadership of the Partido Unión, Partido Republicano, and Partido Socialista shared in the late 1910s. Fear of the illiteracy of adult men in the age of universal male suffrage demanded forming difficult alliances and coalitions in the late 1910s and 1920s.[39] Three legislators proposed a bill to found a Universidad Popular, or People's University, which could con-tribute to the specific goal of teaching literacy while also offering conferences and lectures by local political leaders and educators on contemporary matters.[40] Other legislative proposals requested $20,000 to be distributed as cash prizes for teachers and students who taught literacy in their spare time.[41] A call was made to fund a Liga de Instrucción para Analfabetos (League for the Education of Illiter-ates) to combat the "army of illiterates . . . crucifying our land with its ignorance."[42] These proposals resonated with teachers' initiatives. Educators like Carlos Rivera Ufret called on eighth-grade graduates, "as proof of civic responsibility and . . . interest in . . . our people . . . and gratitude to our *patria*," to take the initiative to establish night schools and teach adults literacy. "It is worth us making the sacri-fice for the good of our poor class and for the pride of our country!"[43]

The initiatives proposed by teachers, legislators, and concerned community members imagined the regeneration of the large number of physical illiterates that came to light during the recruitment efforts of World War I. In their proposals, historical actors engaged in two interconnected conversations. As they proposed ways to support literacy campaigns "to teach them [*jíbaros*, adult male illiterates] how to live as men and as citizens," they were at the same time further inscribing themselves and their initiatives in support of the colonial form of US citizenship they had just been granted.[44] Overcoming illiteracy and regenerating the physicality of rural men were at the heart of local intentions to create healthier and more "cultured" male citizens. Teachers identified this to be a minimal requirement of citizenship, a marker of progress, culture, and civility among modern nations. The teachers' campaign, however, lacked a critique of the colonial limitations of the franchise and of the colonial and subordinate relationship that military volunteers reproduced through military service. The 1917–19 literacy debates, nevertheless, allowed teachers to promote the regeneration of adult men, for the good of Puerto Rico, within the limits of US colonialism.

GENDER AND PHYSICAL EDUCATION

The spectacle of the physical illiteracy of Puerto Rican men during the World War I registration campaign, in fact, generated long-term consequences for the colonial school curriculum. In addition to the more immediate demands for literacy campaigns, it led to a transformation in the definition and practice of physical education.[45] Organized athletics and sports, especially baseball, had been part of high school sports culture, particularly in larger urban towns. However, as awareness emerged in the 1920s of the "presence of so many physically abnormal children" and the fear of a "cataclysm of physical degeneration" of students' bodies, teachers began to advocate for the expansion of physical education for all students.[46] The transition to a "modern" version of physical education was imagined to be a requirement for establishing a "foundation for citizenship." Modern physical education, with its intention to create healthy citizens, was meant to reach beyond select athletes to the general student body and to be equally accessible to both boys and girls. While educators agreed about the value of creating "perfect citizens" in Puerto Rico, the coeducation aspect raised some reservations.[47] Should young girls be allowed to take physical education classes, where they might be wearing athletic clothing, alongside boys, in the outdoors, under the sun? The debate over how much access to grant girls became a conversation about the limits of modern school practices in colonial schools. In the 1920s, as educators debated the transition from athletics to physical education for the "good of the *patria*" and with the intention to create citizens, they were also engaging in the process of defining the limits of the "modern girl" and "proper motherhood."

The physical education movement was not embraced with the same urgency and enthusiasm as the literacy campaign of the late 1910s. The educators who advocated more aggressively for physical education, who employed a neo-Lamarckian eugenic discourse, and who closely linked physical health and forming "perfect citizens" were particularly represented within the leadership of the 1920s teaching profession. In the 1920s a new generation of men, after working as teachers and attaining higher education and training in the 1910s, moved into administrative and leadership positions within the colonial Department of Education. They became principals of municipal high schools, supervisors of school districts, and directors of departments. Many had been long-term members or leaders of the AMPR in the late 1910s. It was this group of educators—Gerardo Sellés Solá, Pedro Gil, Julio Fiol Negrón, and Carlos V. Urrutia—who began to replace US educators in the Department of Education. The department became increasingly controlled by local educators, although it was under the leadership of Juan B. Huyke, a commissioner who was adamantly pro-Americanization and pro-English. The core elite of Puerto Rican educators assumed leadership of the physical education campaign in the 1920s. As they did so, they often considered the average young teacher and parents as constituencies they had to educate about the value of physical education and the urgency of this project for Puerto Rico.

The transition from athletics to physical education after the war was, first, about definitions of citizenship. Yes, physical illiterates had raised the alarm about the alleged "degeneracy" in the majority of the adult population. More importantly, however, they had generated closer scrutiny of the health and hygiene of students. In 1920 Pedro Gil, the principal and athletic director of Yauco High School, appealed for a commitment to physical education on behalf of all teachers: "We witnessed half of our young men rejected during the first recruitment due to physical incapacity. [It] renders them incapable of carrying out military duties and denies them the first obligation of all citizens—defense of country. Are we educators to stand by and remain undaunted and immutable before such a terrible reality? . . . Are we pretending to create a citizenry [*pretendemos levantar un pueblo*] out of this anemic and scrawny *raza*, one that is prepared to stand proudly among civilized nations?"[48] The "weakness" of "our *raza*," represented in students' bodies, had to be overcome in the interest of creating healthy and robust citizens for the *patria*. The health of the body was the foundation for the development of moral and intellectual abilities. Gil concluded: "We have the moral obligation to mold the future generation: . . . we must not forget for an instant physical education, the foundation on which rests the rules of order that will make our men strong so they may assume the fight in defense of the holy principles of *universal democracy.*"[49]

Student bodies not only represented the physical weakness of the *raza*. They were also emblematic of social conditions that the middle-class teaching profession feared and defined as working-class practices. These social behaviors, in addition to the physical bodies, were targeted for rehabilitation in the 1920s. Physical education courses, like the literacy campaigns, were intended as a cure for the imagined debilitating and corruptive examples children might have been exposed to in both their homes and public streets. Newspapers reported increases in juvenile delinquency, lamented the spectacle of street children, and questioned children's participation in games that incorporated gambling (dice, dominoes, horseracing, cockfighting, and even baseball).[50] The physical and moral instruction students received in physical education courses, teachers argued, would help students overcome those negative environmental influences, which could, in neo-Lamarckian logic, otherwise prove corruptive for future generations.

Prewar athletic traditions, as a result, were characterized as *decadente*, generating decay—traditional, elitist, and individualistic. The more physically fit students were chosen to participate on high school and semiprofessional teams. They became the "privileged" elite few who received attention and resources from coaches. Municipal teams met once a year to compete in the Insular Annual Interscholastic Athletic meet.[51] It was there, teachers argued, that observers could best identify the stark differences between the few elite athletes and the majority of students: "While we see teams of strong, robust children full of life and happiness who have been mentored into the sport . . . we forget about the physically weak, scrawny, diseased youth." In the stands, the children's "quiet weeping" fell on deaf ears as the children witnessed the "wheel of progress" leaving them behind.[52]

In addition, traditional "recreation" was feared to be organized around gambling. Horseracing and cockfighting, in particular, were defined as corrupting and immoral for young children.[53] Elite teachers identified these activities as part of a colonial Spanish heritage that was failing to contribute to the contemporary push for the regeneration of the citizenry. Physical education, as a counterpoint to the traditional Spanish popular practices, was part of a modern health and hygiene campaign. It was meant to be healthy, progressive, inclusive, and popular and to generate a sense of community. Advocating for modern physical education, therefore, required teachers to negotiate Spanish and US heritages, influences, and visions.

US educators who came to the island to evaluate the state of athletics, physical education, and leisure activities in the 1920s identified local traditional games as the worst examples of Spanish elitism and gambling.[54] They juxtaposed these

Spanish practices with the best American ones, defined as democratic, inclusive, modern, and progressive. Helen V. Bary's assessment of the island's "child welfare" celebrated that schools were transitioning away from Spanish games. Children were benefiting from the "transition from the old tradition of Spanish aristocracy to that of American democracy—of universal participation and responsibility to community life."[55] US educators' definitions of appropriate physical education curricula were exported from Columbia University to US colonies. Visiting faculty from the United States traveled and shared experiences across Puerto Rico and the Philippines, and they brought physical education course books with them. The regeneration of colonial students through physical education was part of a broader 1920s US imperial project.

In Puerto Rico, meanwhile, teachers offered more nuanced characterizations of physical education. Yes, it was considered foundational for creating modern citizens. And while the citizens they were creating were of a colonial type, teachers were explicit that they were advocating the creation of well-rounded citizens for the good of their *patria* and their country, which in the 1920s they identified to be Puerto Rico, not the United States. Ismael Ramos, a physical education teacher from Mayagüez, reported, "One of my life dreams had always been to have the opportunity of offering the youth of my country, this little Island, the means of acquiring a well-developed body which may serve as a basis for future generations, for every learned person knows that the mind cannot attain its fullest development in all its activities unless it is within a well-developed body."[56] The potential for witnessing progress and achieving modernity, as seen through the healthy regeneration of students' bodies, therefore, was not a simple exercise of teachers embracing Americanization practices. Instead, it was a deliberate negotiation of the aspects of modern education theory that they identified as important for the regeneration of Puerto Rico's students, for the good of the country. This was an example of autonomist ideology in practice, as teachers chose to advocate for physical education within colonial schools as a modern practice that was particularly relevant to local conditions.

How did teachers intend to implement physical education and its broader citizenship-building goals? The primary goal was to make it accessible to the majority of the students. First, teachers advocated the training and hiring of instructors specially trained in physical education and for making it a mandatory course.[57] Baseball and track-and-field coaches, educators feared, were invested in the success of their semiprofessional teams at the expense of teaching greater lessons, like sportsmanship. And as the director of the new Physical Education Department explained, educators feared that many *maestras inexpertas* (inexperienced teachers) simply lacked training and preparation to effectively teach physical education.[58]

As a result of the elite teachers' campaign for the expansion of physical education and the support and collaboration of the colonial Department of Education, a new generation of physical education instructors was trained, hired, and deployed throughout the public schools. The Department of Education hired ten physical education instructors in the 1920s, but only one was female.[59] Those who were recruited and trained as physical education instructors epitomized the ideal modern man—athlete, veteran, teacher. The Faberllé brothers best exemplified this example. Before the war, they were famous athletes. Ciqui and Fabito Faberllé were two of the four most well known baseball players of the time; the group was known as *los cuatro jinetes del beisbol* (the four leaders of baseball).[60] During the war they served in the Porto Rican Regiment and were members of the regiment's baseball team. After the war they were recruited into the physical education training program at the University of Puerto Rico. They represented the best example of intellectual, moral, and physical development.[61] This idealized modern man was imagined to be capable of leading the physical illiterate out of the past into the present through the teaching of physical education.

Advocating for mandatory physical education, however, was greater than the physical education classes themselves. It was about applying neo-Lamarckian eugenic ideology in support of the sanitation and hygiene of public spaces and the home. Teachers called for the founding of public parks where students could play "healthy" games under the supervision of teachers.[62] The curriculum should also provide for organized leisure activities. The modern methods of physical education, which included supervised outdoor play, were meant to replace the unsupervised time children spent in public spaces, which Sellés Solá and others feared exposed children to "social vices" (gambling, drinking, smoking, and prostitution) and led potentially to the degeneration of future generations of the *raza*: "Let us raise strong generations, proud of this condition and inclined to conserve it, giving them a pure and moral life, and an adequate mental cultivation. Let us form the perfect home, the happy home. Our *patria* will thus become great thanks to the health, purity, intelligence, and hard work of its sons."[63]

While literacy campaigns generated popular support, parents proved less than enthusiastic about the modern practice of physical education. Elite teachers expected parents to contribute to the physical education movement in multiple ways. The propertied classes should donate plots of land to be developed into public parks or athletic fields. The less-wealthy parents, at the very least, should support teachers' efforts to expose their children to modern methods of sports and recreation. However, elite teachers were hard-pressed to understand why all parents were not enthusiastic about physical education. Some teachers even lacked empathy for those parents who asked for their children to be excused from physical education classes because their participation was wearing down the children's clothing and shoes. Carlos Urrutia, a leading member of the AMPR recently appointed to the newly created position of superintendent of physical education in 1921, considered this a small sacrifice: "Who cares if they break a pair of shoes? That is insignificant. The health and happiness of the family make up for such small losses."[64] In his fervor for physical education, Urrutia failed to understand the economic challenges working-class parents faced in the 1920s. They struggled to provide clothing for their children so that they could attend school.[65]

In particular, educators were dismissive of those they identified as "conservative parents," characterized as "incredulous" and from a "past era" who opposed the modernization and diversification of school curriculum. These parents were particularly concerned about girls' access to physical education. When parents wrote notes to teachers requesting that their daughters be exempted from physical education classes, teachers sometimes assumed that parents did so because of their "traditional" and "conservative" thinking about girls' and women's roles.[66] Parents were concerned about coed physical education classes in high schools. They were not interested in having their girls running around public plazas and playgrounds under the glaring sun. For some educators, it was these conservative parents' traditional characterization of women's role in the community and family that had to be overcome. While Puerto Rican educators experienced "some difficulties" in their campaign to expand physical education, they felt particularly challenged by the "old customs and traditions of the people, who expect for their girls, not the sturdy, hardy type of Anglo-Saxon womanhood, but rather a medieval type of girl, light-skinned, sweet, delicate, brittle, romantic, and highly sensitive."[67]

Elite teachers identified this conflict and resistance as parental misunderstandings about traditional versus modern definitions of "proper womanhood." Teachers countered conservative parents by deploying the 1920s ideology of social feminism. Julio Fiol Negrón, the new supervisor of physical education in 1928, argued in support of girls' right to physical education. Girls "have a right to the sports and amusements of the world just as they have a share in the tears and toils of life." On the one hand, girls had to develop their health and strength in order to succeed in their future occupations. More women than ever were employed outside the home. As "a rival of man in the world's work . . . the occasions for her to use physical strength have multiplied, whether she be in a room facing fifty pupils, or typewriting, selling, curing, giving legal advice, or laboring in field or factory." These labors required physical strength and "vigor." On the other hand, he reproduced the biological differences between men and women. Girls also had the right to develop healthy bodies to prepare them to fulfill their "earthly mission in this world, bearing and rearing children." Elite educators like Fiol Negrón defined women's appropriate roles in public and private spaces within the modern patriarchy of early twentieth-century Puerto Rico and argued that they too were "entitled to the privileges of a complete education." Girls' rights to physical education, their right to overcome conservative parents' apprehension about modern girls' practices in colonial schools, were rationalized within the parameters of local patriarchy. The visions for the modern girl were neither a US imposition nor revolutionary. They were, nevertheless, social feminist visions about the new requirements for a modern and liberal Puerto Rico.

In the 1920s the directors of the newly founded Department of Physical Education oversaw its expansion through the hiring of specialized teachers and the broadening of the curriculum. A special section was created in the education journal (PRSR) to promote the activities and goals of physical education in the classroom. The intention of the articles and the images published in the section was to educate teachers on the value of physical education and to suggest the best methods through which to promote it. The images published in the PRSR, with the intention to promote physical education for girls, suggest how educators struggled to balance appropriate practices that supported their definition of the new, modern schoolgirl. Some of the images were typical of those that might have represented US physical education classes in the 1920s—high school girls wearing knee-length shorts or skirts and kneesocks, running track, stretching in organized rows, or playing basketball. Other images, however, represented island-specific interpretations of acceptable female domesticity promoted through schools.

For example, in the November 1926 edition, teacher Generosa Fernández wrote an article introducing the US-based organization founded in 1912 known as the Girl Scouts. In the article, Fernández defined the intention of the organization to be threefold: to introduce girls to natural and healthy outdoor activities that help develop body and mind; to provide them with the skills to become responsible homemakers; and to serve the community. The goals of the Girl Scouts fit perfectly within the social feminist vision that women could be educated to become more efficient and modern in their homemaking and civic duties. However, the image that accompanied Fernández's article highlighted a more traditional interpretation of appropriate activities for young girls as they were promoted through physical education coursework in 1920s Puerto Rico. It was a photograph of the young women who were members of the Future Mothers' League in the Juncos public schools. The Girl Scouts' mission was progressive, as it imagined women's civic duties in the community and the practice of physical activity in the outdoors. The acceptable local version of women's clubs, however, emphasized training young girls in the required skills for their primary responsibility as mothers.[68]

A second popular image in the physical education section of the *PRSR* presented children engaged in folk dance. Elizabeth Lutes, an instructor of "natural dancing," promoted teaching dance to children as a form of physical and intellectual expression: "Dancing does not mean only that one is able to move in time to music. It means a finer understanding of emotional expression, a free, uninhibited use of the intellect." Dancing was an "intellectual activity worthy of a prominent place in physical education."[69] It was also acceptable within local schools, for it complemented local views that women were more delicate, refined, and artistic than men. Folk dancing, in particular, was a method that helped local girls develop their feminine, rather than feminist, characteristics. The folk dances taught in schools in the 1920s originated from Europe rather than the island or the Caribbean region. The photograph that accompanied Lutes's natural dance article captured the work of a first-grade teacher from Carolina, Esperanza Cuín. Cuín's class posed for a photograph that exhibited their mastery over a French minuet.

By the late 1920s, elite teachers could proudly report that, after their campaigns in local communities, parents were fortunately beginning to "awaken." They were

Schoolchildren dancing a minuet in Carolina, Puerto Rico, 1927 (Elizabeth Lutes, "Natural Dancing," *PRSR 11*, no. 9 [May 1927]: 39–41).

no longer, through their conservative and traditional biases, inhibiting the progress of colonial schools. Young girls as well as boys would reap the benefits of modern physical education with the support of their enlightened parents: "Parents and teachers are today in agreement that the school cannot generate character, that is, cannot fulfill the essential goal of education, as long as we are not instilling in the child the habits of play and physical development, disciplining his will, molding good hearts and perfect citizens."[70]

Building from the momentum for "regeneration" that came from the World War I rejection rates, teachers linked physical education, modern practices, and citizenship building. Teachers imagined that fulfilling the requirements of colonial citizenship required a gendered reconstruction of boys and girls through the schools. Overcoming physical illiteracy, while initially focused on adult men's alleged degenerate physical bodies and illiteracy, also meant redefining women's roles in schools and modern society. If women were to carry out their complementary roles as wife/mother/educator, then teachers also had to address girls' physical illiteracy. Regenerating girls' health, exposing them to modern methods of physical education, leisure, and recreation above and beyond the reservations of conservative parents, was one way teachers could generate modern colonial citizens in the 1920s.

Maestras inexpertas (Inexperienced Teachers)

As educators continued to define the parameters of the newly granted colonial citizenship in the 1920s, they also raised questions about the promises and limits of women as teachers. Urrutia's brief reference to the problems of the *maestras inexpertas* affecting the success of physical education was only the tip of the iceberg. Definitions of women's practices and contributions were meant to establish the boundaries of progress and modernity in the school project and beyond. In the 1920s the male leadership of the teaching profession assumed the authority to define colonial citizenship and the goal of regenerating the *raza*. Literacy, hygiene, and schools were increasingly identified as core elements in the creation of modern, yet colonial, citizens.

The 1920s, however, was also a moment when large gender and generational shifts within the teaching profession were becoming increasingly evident. The number of classrooms expanded, the total number of children attending schools grew, and a new, younger generation of teachers joined the force. They were a combination of eighth-grade or high school graduates who qualified to teach in rural schools and graduates of the University of Puerto Rico certified to teach special topics in urban high schools. Since 1898, more women and more nonelite students in general gained access to public instruction than they had in the late nineteenth century. Twenty years later, as the department grew and as the people's demand to access public instruction multiplied, these young women, many from intermediate class backgrounds, became the majority of the teaching profession. In 1920 70.4 percent of all teachers were female. By 1930 the percentage had grown to 74.5.

Despite these demographic changes within the ranks, the AMPR leadership in the 1920s was solidly older and male. Women ran and organized several of the committees within the AMPR, and a few women—like Beatriz Lasalle and Carlota Matienzo—were elected to the board of directors.[71] Nevertheless, as a professional organization, the public leadership of the AMPR in the 1920s reproduced a fundamentally patriarchal order. An older male leadership claimed their authority to define the political and ideological direction of the AMPR. On the one hand, they promoted policies such as physical education that were defined as modern and progressive, for they were intended to be democratic, popular, and inclusive of all students, including women. On the other hand, there was a limit to the leadership's celebration of modern gender norms. This limit was most explicit when they reflected on the labor of young female teachers in the classroom. In the background, informing the conservative positions of the AMPR leadership, was the dramatic emergence of women in public spaces as labor leaders and suffragists.

Older male educators feared that young female teachers might simultaneously undermine the creation of strong male citizens and provide a negative example for other women. Female teachers were critical for the reconstruction of the home and mother and were imagined to be the best examples for working-class and rural girls to model themselves after. They were, therefore, at the heart of the intentions of modern home economics instruction. But female teachers were also assigned to teach outside of that topic. Often a female teacher was the sole teacher appointed to attend to a new rural school. In that capacity, reservations emerged about the inherent limits of women's contributions, as teachers, to the citizenship-building project. Female teachers could mold the modern homemaker, but mold the modern man? These reservations highlighted the gendered definition of a modern citizen within the teaching profession. They also spoke to the generational differences within it.

Several crises in the late 1910s, including illiteracy rates and military rejections, forced the reassessment of the colonial Department of Education's strategies in the 1920s. Teachers called for the department to address the communities with the greatest needs—rural communities. The early and rapid growth of the colonial department in the first twenty years focused on cities—the building of modern concrete schools to replace wooden schoolhouses and the construction of modern high schools in the larger and more populous municipalities. But the 1917 reports had been particularly negative about rural men. That the majority of military volunteers were rural adult men might have reflected the rural-to-urban migration of the time. In 1920 Puerto Rico was 78 percent rural. Leading educators declared that rural children, the rural home, and rural communities should receive the urgent attention of teachers. The 1919 AMPR president, José González Ginorio, called on teachers to awaken to the urgency of rural education: "Inspire yourselves in the Association so that you can carry out the holy mission that has been entrusted to you: the education of the Puerto Rican peasant. Your task is the hardest, most important, the biggest, the most difficult, the only one that truly involves all types of sacrifices, the most humble for being the most ignored, but the only one that will truly determine the regeneration of our people."[72]

This was the combination of events that raised the question of the appropriate roles of female teachers in modern rural schools. Rural students required the focused attention of modern teachers for their reconstruction and regeneration— for them to overcome the alleged physical and intellectual illiteracy of the countryside. The building of rural schools intensified in the 1920s. But more young women than men were entering the teaching profession. More women, then, were in charge of rural schools. Could the citizenship-building project be carried out successfully if it was left in the hands of these young women? Did young urban women have the ability, strength, capacity, and commitment to undertake the challenges of rural schools? Or were female teachers, ultimately, undermining the process by which young boys became modern men? Alternatively, were female teachers, because of the assumed biological limitations of their sex, losing their femininity through their labor in this public space and, therefore, providing a bad example for rural girls? Although the AMPR membership supported women's suffrage—one of the more vocal political movements in 1920s Puerto Rico—the male leadership of the AMPR and other older male teachers, nevertheless, expressed these concerns.[73]

Parents and teachers were disappointed with the colonial Department of Education and what they saw as the slow progress of schools and literacy. Theirs was a critique about the allegedly benevolent imperial intentions of the colonial department. Meanwhile, the department leadership—Commissioner Paul G. Miller and Assistant Commissioner Carey Hickle—disagreed with the popular complaints. While they were also unhappy with the measured progress of colonial schools, they staunchly stood behind the policies and practices of the colonial administration in the face of public critiques. Therefore, US administrators identified the new teachers, "young and immature boys and girls," who were running the newly founded rural schools as the problem. Hickle was concerned that this new generation did not represent the "right kind of teacher." He feared they were a young cohort "with wrong ideas and false hopes" and with professional qualifi- cations that were "little short of alarming." "The inexperienced boys and girls" were "city born and reared and received their education in urban schools." The new rural teachers lacked knowledge of the specific conditions and needs of rural communities and, therefore, would prove to be "an obstacle in the way of rural progress." Finally, Hickle questioned the new generation's commitment to a rural uplift campaign. He saw them as members of the 1920s' untrained, surplus labor force. Their intention was not to help in the regeneration of the countryside but simply to gain access to a civil service profession, even if it required teaching in a rural school.[74] Within the year, they would apply for a transfer to an urban school and return to the city. Miller was concerned about the 730 changes of teachers in rural areas in 1917.[75] That year, in response to the popular critiques, illiteracy rates, and its own assessment of new teachers, the colonial department collaborated with the University of Puerto Rico and the College of Agricultural and Mechanic Arts (CAAM) in a new initiative focused on the intensive training of a new generation of rural teachers.[76]

The AMPR had historically staunchly defended all teachers before any cri- tiques, especially when they came from the colonial Department of Education. This time, however, the AMPR leadership's response highlighted the emerging generational division within the teaching class as well as the willingness to cri- tique women's labor. AMPR president Francisco Vincenty, in a December 1918 speech at the teachers' annual convention, identified the multiple factors chal- lenging the success of rural schools: the bad roads that limited teachers' access to schools and students; the poverty, ignorance, and illiteracy of parents; and the shortage of housing for rural teachers. These and many other reasons were slow- ing down progress. But additionally, he conceded that the new rural teachers were failing to meet expectations. The majority of the new rural teachers were young women.[77] Only fourteen of the seventy-three rural teachers who graduated from the new 1917 rural teacher training institutes were male.[78]

Isaac del Rosario, a senior educator, identified the new, young, female teachers as the root of the problem. Del Rosario, like many others, argued that commit- ment to rural schools was the greatest labor to be undertaken for the progress of the *patria*. Rural teachers chose to take on the noble mission of "reconstructing the social body of our country."[79] Proudly, del Rosario had been one of the first rural schoolteachers of the early 1900s. And he, more than others, could attest to the personal sacrifice rural teachers undertook. Rural work required overcoming physical and material challenges: bad roads, one-room wooden schoolhouses with few resources, the uninterest of rural parents. But through his hard work and commitment, despite the challenges it posed for the happiness of his own nuclear family, del Rosario argued, he persevered for the good of the *patria*. Over the years he came to realize, however, that rural families were less willing to host new rural teachers, which meant that rural teachers were forced to commute from urban centers, making the process that much more difficult. Del Rosario suggested that the rural parents' resistance was due to the behavior of the new, young, inexperienced, female teachers. They were *muy señoritas* in their expectations of the host family, making demands for better accommodations, meals, and service. Rather than offering a broader critique of the economic hardship of rural landowners in the 1920s, del Rosario argued that the parents' resistance was generated from the behavior of the *señoritas*.[80] They were not prepared to succeed in the modern rural school because of the privilege of being raised in cities, because of their sex, and because of their middle-class background. The rural school project demanded more commitment and dedication to the students, countryside, and *patria* than these young women could offer. They proved a challenge and potential impediment to the success of the rural school project.

Women suffragists in the 1920s, as they worked to secure the vote for women when it was denied them by the island legislature, faced severe criticism for stepping outside of the ideal role of women in the modern Puerto Rican patriarchy— the role of wife/mother/educator. They were derided for forcing the issue of women's suffrage, especially for strategically reaching beyond the island legislature and seeking direct support for their cause from US politicians. In addition, some questioned why women, expected to be gentle and delicate, were asking to be allowed access to the "dirty" public sphere of politics. Their participation in this public space might prove corruptive to their femininity. This was also precisely the type of critique women as teachers received within the broader debate over rural schools and citizenship building. Significantly, however, female teachers received these critiques from fellow teachers, particularly older male educators who struggled to imagine what type of contribution young female teachers could really offer to the reconstruction of rural men.

The winning essay of the 1917 AMPR literary contest proposed ways to fix "the rural school problem." The author, working within a modern education ideology that imagined the interconnectedness of body and mind, also offered a critique of women as teachers. Like del Rosario and others had argued before him, M. Benítez Flores highlighted that running a rural school was a physically and mentally demanding job that required teachers to manage a school with little resources and to create relationships with uninterested rural parents. But, unlike the others, Benítez Flores was particularly concerned with how the labor and practice of teaching forced a type of "degeneration" of a woman's body, personality, and mind. He proposed that the demands of teaching took a physical toll on women's bodies that led to negative changes in personality. He approximated that after six years of teaching, women began to lose their compassion and beauty. Some even became mean-spirited or lost all their energy, which led to further psychological deterioration.[81] This author assumed that women's role in Puerto Rican society was to represent the beauty and qualities of their sex, to complement their husbands, to nurture their children. Women's labor outside the home produced a less-feminine, less-sane version of this ideal woman. These were some of the challenges that woman as teacher posed to the AMPR citizenship-building project. Female teachers in rural schools were feared to more likely emasculate men and set bad examples for young girls than to promote the goal of creating modern citizens.

While male educators considered the possibility that young women put in the position to lead rural men would be potentially dangerous for citizenship building and emasculating for boys and men, the woman's role that was celebrated was the one that was imagined within the limits of social feminism. The social feminist view, which María de Fátima Barceló Miller defined as the ideology that imagined a liberal and modern Puerto Rico that required improvement and advancement in women's position in society, was the one rewarded by the AMPR leadership. Several leaders of the women's suffragist movement, including Ana Roque de Duprey, Mercedes Solá, Ana López de Vélez, Isabel Andreu, Beatriz Lasalle, Carmen Gómez, and Carlota Matienzo, were teachers.[82] The social feminist ideology dominated ideas about women's work and contributions to the classroom with the intention of regenerating the rural mother and wife.

In addition, one particularly prolific teacher who promoted the social feminist ideology within the AMPR was *ponceña* Lorenza Brunet del Valle. She was a prolific promoter of the modern ideology concept in the late 1910s. She embraced a gendered definition of citizen, advocating for the reconstruction of the modern man through education: "The ideal of the modern school . . . is to take the weak and imperfect boy . . . and transform him into a strong man, moral and vigorous of body and spirit, guided by reason, sustained by a controlled and educated will."[83] Young girls should be taught to complement their male partners. A young girl's primary responsibility was to be a "conscious collaborator with a man in his social mission."[84]

While the primary goal of the school was to help generate this modern man, who must "contribute to the progress of his *patria*," Brunet del Valle also identified how women might make a difference in rural schools: "A great number of rural teachers are women gifted in the labors appropriate to their sex, the domestic sciences. How much good they might offer the poor and ignorant rural women!"[85] Brunet del Valle envisioned rural teachers contributing to the reconstruction of wives and mothers by undertaking a series of projects outside of regular school hours. On Saturday mornings the teacher could offer "simple and easy" lessons in sewing techniques or nutrition. Weekday afternoons she could host reading circles, during which the teacher read to the mothers, choosing selections that were "within reach of their intelligence." Finally, the teacher could organize community gatherings and simple parties with the intention of "raising the spirit of the simple and ignorant" country folk.[86] These were unique contributions that female teachers could offer the rural school project. Brunet del Valle imagined that they were skills and practices that most female teachers had already mastered because of their sex. She was not advocating for a home economics curriculum but rather for Puerto Rican women to deploy the skills they "naturally" brought with them to rural schools. In this way, women could go above and beyond the call of duty to fulfill the goal of the modern school: "to create the perfect citizen—a conscious patriot who will contribute to the progress of his and her *patria*, to the improvement of social welfare, and to the sustenance and advancement of that democracy [the United States] of which he is also a part."[87]

Brunet del Valle was particularly mindful that the teachers' practice in rural schools should be adapted to the limited capacities of rural families. Rural girls and women might be illiterate, traditional, and poor examples of mothers and housekeepers, but the modern female teacher could help change that. Rural men, meanwhile, could be regenerated as well. The target was rebuilding the home, helping rural girls become better wives and mothers, helping young boys become better husbands and providers. It was this social feminist ideology, which fundamentally reproduced gender-specific roles within the modern Puerto Rican patriarchy, that the AMPR leadership rewarded and welcomed. It did not threaten patriarchy; instead, as it advocated for improving women's conditions and opportunities, it served to reproduce patriarchy for the benefit of all. Through these conversations, teachers were proposing the gender-specific definitions of colonial citizenship in the late 1910s and 1920s. Social feminist ideology was modern and liberal in how it imagined the potential regeneration and modernization of the citizenry. It was politically reformist and gender conservative in its reproduction of the colonial framework and modern patriarchy.

CONCLUSION

In August 1922 a parent from the municipality of Mayagüez wrote an anonymous letter to the island governor. The letter suggested that the author had acquired a basic level of literacy, although most words were spelled phonetically, and there was little punctuation. The parent was concerned about the person recently appointed by the commissioner of education to the position of inspector of schools in the parent's municipality. Commissioner Juan B. Huyke, the parent wrote, "did not realize what he had done when he appointed such an immoral man to be inspector." The parent was particularly concerned about the new appointment because his daughters attended the Mayagüez schools.

The parent challenged the morality of the inspector based on his treatment of women teachers and young girls. The inspector's history spoke to the ways he violated the honor of his wife, teachers, and other young working-class girls. The parent reported that the inspector had taken a teacher as a lover, impregnated her, and moved her to his home in Bayamón, which he shared with his wife. He ultimately divorced his wife and married his lover. But, in addition, he had also "dishonored" the daughter of a *zapatero* (cobbler) and had a child with his wife's young cousin, who resided in his home. When the inspector worked as an assistant in Mayagüez, the parent reported, he would lock himself in a classroom with a teacher in the school. How could this inspector, "such an immoral man," have the right to supervise anyone in the public schools?[88]

The Mayagüez parent, as he wrote this letter of complaint to the governor, was claiming for himself and his daughters the honor and respectability that middle-class teachers had denied him. His letter of complaint, professing the immorality of the school inspector, challenged the underlying assumption in the 1920s writings by educators—that children should be rescued from parents who failed to provide moral examples. In this example, it was the parent who claimed morality, who defended the honor of the young girls and teachers, and who questioned the character and capacity of the school administrator. The parent challenged the decisions made by the commissioner of education for the benefit of children in Mayagüez. Teachers and educators were imagining carrying out a modern and progressive citizenship-building project where they could rebuild the foundations of honorable men and women in cities and the countryside. The subjects of reconstruction, however, maintained their own critiques about the qualities and morality of those educators who assumed authority over those subjects' homes and children. They demanded educators to be mindful and held accountable for their participation in activities that undermined the morality and honor of communities.

Gender constructions were at the core of the 1920s education debates. Teachers and educators proposed ways to generate modern and progressive colonial citizens through public schools. Boys and girls, men and women became targets of ambitious middle-class teachers. At the same time, the teaching profession underwent a demographic and generational transformation. The older genera-tion of male teachers struggled to retain their authority over the citizenship-building project as they witnessed the feminization of the profession. The debate over the acceptable practices of women as teachers, of the limits of women teach-ers' contribution to the citizenship-building project, exposed the limits of the older male teaching leadership's vision for colonial reform through public schools. The anonymous parent from Mayagüez, meanwhile, reminded teachers and poli-ticians that parents too were holding teachers accountable when they crossed the boundaries of respectability and honor.

The late 1910s and 1920s provided historical moments of crises and contradic-tions. The highly contested definition of colonial citizenship emerged and cre-ated a space where gender ideologies and practices required further clarification. Generational differences highlighted the boundaries of the social constructions of gender, patriarchy, and citizenship. Negotiating the new definition of colonial citizenship within the new imperial framework required balancing definitions of tradition and modernity. Teachers elected aspects of the Spanish and Puerto Rican heritages and practices to retain if they were not considered too "backward" and "traditional." Teachers redefined modern practices as progressive Puerto Rican initiatives rather than as US impositions. This process of negotiating the defini-tion of colonial citizenship, the intention of schools, and the reconstruction of gender roles was carefully worked out within the limits of the colonial framework established by the Jones Act. Through these debates and practices, teachers as intermediate actors contributed to the process of reproducing and consolidating "imperial formations."

chapter 4

Testing for Citizenship
in the Diaspora

The Puerto Rican diaspora of the early twentieth century was a product of US imperial practices in the Caribbean and the Pacific. The new colonial relationship between Puerto Rico and the United States facilitated the immigration of Puerto Rican labor to the metropole, to Hawaii, Florida, and throughout the Northeast.[1] Although the "great migration" of Puerto Ricans to the United States was a historical phenomenon of the 1950s and 1960s, the early twentieth-century migration and the Northeast diaspora were also important for 1930s constructions of "national" identities in Puerto Rico and the United States. There were approximately 53,000 Puerto Ricans in the United States in 1930, a tenfold increase from the 1,500 just twenty years earlier. As the diaspora grew, it became a prism through which historical actors, in both the United States and Puerto Rico, would more clearly define "national" characteristics and qualifications for citizenship.

In late 1935 the Chamber of Commerce of the State of New York (CCSNY) published the results of a study conducted on Puerto Rican children in the city of New York.[2] The Chamber of Commerce's Special Committee on Immigration and Naturalization initiated the study and contracted a small team of social scientists who conducted the tests and analyzed the results. The study and the special committee's assessments were essentially negative and derogatory. The psychologists (C. P. Armstrong, E. M. Achilles, and M. J. Sacks) concluded that Puerto Rican children in the city's public schools were, in comparison to other student groups, intellectually inferior. They suggested that Puerto Rican children be tracked into vocational programs for fear that the students' potential disaffection with academic instruction might push them toward their "natural proclivities"—delinquency and criminality. The leading researcher, Armstrong, feared that Puerto Rico was sending to the United States the most intellectually inferior members of its population.

The chairman of the special committee, John B. Trevor, in turn, would recommend, for fear of "grave consequences," that Puerto Rican migration to the United States be restricted as soon as possible. He addressed the hearings then taking place in the US Congress, which were assessing whether Puerto Rico might be placed on the path to statehood, recommending that the congressmen take that political option off the table immediately. Trevor warned the congressman that, "inasmuch as a grant of statehood can never be rescinded, the investigation conducted . . . certainly suggests that the proposition to incorporate Puerto Rico as a State in the Federal Union should be held in abeyance."[3] He implied that the political policies of US empire could have unforeseen consequences for the quality of immigrants to be incorporated into the US national body.

The 1935 study highlighted how local actors in the United States contributed to the construction of national boundaries, calling for a reconsideration of US imperial expansion and narrowing the definition of citizen. While the 1920s witnessed the height of immigration restriction debates, immigration restrictionists and racial eugenicists came together through the CCSNY committee on immigration and naturalization to continue to pursue their agenda in the 1930s. The Puerto Rican diaspora had grown throughout the early twentieth century. In the face of the 1930s economic crisis, however, many migrants returned to the island. Despite the rate of return migration, the 1930s economic crisis heightened the immigration restrictionists' anxieties over the "Puerto Rican problem" in the city, a problem emblematic of broader anti-immigration movements targeted against non-Anglo-Saxon communities in the United States.[4] Although Puerto Ricans became US citizens in 1917, Trevor and Armstrong targeted the Puerto Rican diaspora through the language of immigration restriction. The goal of the study, therefore, was not only to advocate for the restriction of immigrants into the United States but specifically to justify denying a group of US citizens access to the US mainland because of their "racial difference" and "national origins."[5]

The targeting of the Puerto Rican diaspora in New York City in 1935 demonstrates how local actors in both the United States and Puerto Rico expected to inform US congressional debates over imperial legislation. The mid-1930s were particularly significant legislative years for US colonies, as they marked the approval of the 1935 Tydings-McDuffie Act and the drafting of the 1936 Tydings Bill. The 1935 act, also known as the Philippines Independence Bill, set the archipelago on a ten-year path toward independence. In the Puerto Rican example, 1936 stands out as the year that marked the height of radical nationalist activity and labor struggles. A casualty of this political unrest was an American, the chief of police of Puerto Rico, Col. Francis Riggs. In retaliation for his death, Riggs's powerful friend, the Maryland senator Millard Tydings, chairman of the Territories and Insular Affairs Committee in the US Congress, proposed the Tydings Bill, which supported an island plebiscite on independence. Scholars have characterized the 1936 bill as punitive legislation meant to punish Puerto Rico for the murder of the US colonel. If 1935 and 1936 were years when the US Congress supported legislation that proposed the independence of the Philippines and Puerto Rico, why was the chairman of the special committee in New York anxiously addressing US congressmen whom he feared were seriously considering statehood for Puerto Rico? Placing the CCSNY research within a broader comparative analysis of the persecution of non-Anglo-Saxon communities in the United States in the 1930s helps address this apparent contradiction.

The study of Puerto Rican children in New York City brought together different actors (immigration restrictionists and racial eugenicists) and ideologies (racial difference, national origin, colonial peoples, imperial spaces, and national identities) at a decisive economic and political moment in the United States and Puerto Rico. In the United States, for immigration restrictionists and racial eugenicists like Trevor and Armstrong, the Puerto Rican diaspora represented the material dangers of the expansion of US empire in the Caribbean. Puerto Rican migration into New York challenged the nationalist agenda these US actors had carried forward from the 1920s. An analysis of the 1935 study, therefore, highlights the relationship between race, migration, and empire in the early twentieth century, as the coalition of US immigration restrictionists and racial eugenicists felt threatened by and targeted the migration of Caribbean colonial peoples.

In Puerto Rico the 1930s also marked a vital moment in conversations over the construction of national and cultural identities. Therefore, the Armstrong study received a strong response from a representative of the Puerto Rican elite and professional classes, the assistant commissioner of education, Pedro Cebollero. As proposed in chapters 2 and 3, in the early twentieth century, teachers and educators collaborated in the promotion of a citizenship-building project with the intention to regenerate the Puerto Rican "race" through neo-Lamarckian eugenic practices and behaviors. In the tradition of turn-of-the-century Latin American elites and intellectuals, Puerto Rican intermediate actors (teachers and educators) embraced and rearticulated the racial logic of regenerating the body by improving the environment through public sanitation campaigns, personal hygiene instruction, and reconstruction of healthy homes and families. These scientific practices, according to neo-Lamarckian eugenics, could regenerate and improve the individual and, by extension, the "national race." This 1920s neo-Lamarckian interpretation of the values of education and sanitation was rearticulated through the 1930 debates over the new definitions of Puerto Rican national identity.

The 1935 study of Puerto Rican children in New York City challenged and undermined the island-based educators' carefully crafted vision. The new 1930s debates over Puerto Rican identity embraced Hispanic heritage and cultivated a Latin identity that inverted US definitions of Anglo-Saxon supremacy. Cebollero's response to the study, therefore, represented the broader struggle of Puerto Rican elites, professionals, and educators who demanded recognition of their claims to a scientific, modern, and progressive location within the island's social hierarchy. Cebollero provided a careful and methodical rejection of the 1935 study, in the process demonstrating how race and class differences were critical to the construction of a Puerto Rican national identity. For as Cebollero dismissed the study, he paradoxically reinscribed the imagined race and class differences *between* the diaspora and the island as well as the value of race and class hierarchies *within* Puerto Rico. Scholars have argued that early twentieth-century Puerto Rican national identities were constructed vis-à-vis Americans as the "other."[6] I suggest that, in addition, Puerto Rican intellectuals constructed a national identity in opposition to the diaspora as the "other." The diaspora's racial and class composition would situate it outside of the island's imagined national boundaries as early as the 1930s.[7]

The following analysis of the 1935 study, therefore, highlights these parallel and interconnected conversations about race, national identity, and citizenship. Both groups—US racial eugenicists and immigration restrictionists and Puerto Rican educators and professionals—were engaged in the process of articulating and defining their respective "national" identities. These national identities, however, were deeply informed by the broader framework of US empire, embodied in the Puerto Rican diaspora. The diaspora posed a grave challenge for US racial eugenicists and immigration restrictionists who wanted to defend the imagined boundaries of the US nation, which they feared were endangered with the immigration of US colonial peoples. Meanwhile, the diaspora would undermine the Puerto Rican elite's new definition of a modern and progressive national identity, for it symbolized both the colonial relationship between the island and mainland and the class and racial characteristics that the Puerto Rican elite denied existed within the island's imagined national boundaries. Responses to the 1935 study revealed how the diaspora of the 1930s became a prism through which racist and elitist definitions of "national identity" and citizenship were constructed.

RACE, MIGRATION, AND EMPIRE: THE HISTORICAL CONTEXT

The context under which the 1935 study emerged contributes to our understanding of the politics of race and empire, the collaboration between immigration restrictionists and racial eugenicists, and the history of the early twentieth-century

Caribbean diaspora. The 1930s were years when colonial peoples in the mainland United States were negotiating their rights to access labor markets, years when US citizens of non-Anglo-Saxon descent were targeted for deportation and colonial peoples for decolonization.[8] These were also years when immigration restrictionists who had collaborated with racial eugenicists struggled to maintain an agenda they proposed in the 1920s and that became policy in the 1924 Immigration Act. The growing community of Caribbean and other colonial peoples in the United States challenged the foundation of the 1920s immigration reform— the national origins and racial exclusion arguments. The practice of an expanding US empire in the Caribbean and the proposed policies of colonial reformers would undermine the goals and intentions of the immigration restrictionists and eugenicists in the 1930s.

Situating the historical actors who initiated the 1935 study of Puerto Rican children in the city of New York within the broader history of early twentieth-century immigration debates allows us to recover the politics of race, migration, and empire. The leadership of the special committee and the members of the Chamber of Commerce crafted a close collaboration with psychologists and researchers. Their relationship represented the political alliance between immigration restrictionists and racial eugenicists. Both groups wanted to maintain their influence in the immigration restriction movement that reemerged in the 1930s after the Great Depression.

John B. Trevor, the chairman of the special committee, was transparent about the anxiety that guided the study: the expansion of US empire would be accompanied by the unrestricted migration of colonial peoples from the islands to the mainland. The incremental expansion of US empire, negotiated in the US Congress and Supreme Court, was undermining the carefully constructed exclusionist and restrictive immigration policies proposed by immigration restrictionists and racial eugenicists, embodied in the 1924 Immigration Act. Trevor alerted the Chamber of Commerce members: "An agitation now on foot to include Puerto Rico as a State in the Federal Union suggested that an investigation of the quality of immigration received from Puerto Rico would be a valuable contribution to our knowledge."[9] The study intended to document that failing to regulate and limit the migration of Caribbean peoples into the US mainland would prove a dangerous gamble. Trevor explained that the study's conclusions suggested that "a serious local condition not only exists at present in New York City as a result of the admission of Puerto Ricans, but also the introduction of this element portends the development of grave consequences, unless steps are taken to check the inflow of surplus populations from our dependencies in the Caribbean."[10]

Trevor's interest in assessing the "quality" of Puerto Rican migration to New York City represented the confluence of a series of events and relationships. A year before the US Congress supported the punitive, pro-independence Tydings Bill, the Committee on the Territories of the House of Representatives held hearings on a bill "to enable the people of Puerto Rico to form a constitution and state government and be admitted into the Union on an equal footing with the States."[11] In 1934 Puerto Rico's resident commissioner, Santiago Iglesias, introduced H.R. 1394. Although the House Committee on the Territories held hearings on the status bill in May and June 1935, it did not make it out of committee.[12]

To document his opposition to both the statehood bill and Puerto Rican migration to New York, Trevor thought to produce a study of the "quality" of Puerto Rican migration in the tradition of the racial eugenics studies previously supported by the CCSNY special committee. The special committee had recently published a "comprehensive study" on immigration control by the well-known eugenicist Harry H. Laughlin.[13] The 1934 Laughlin study included an appendix by Dr. Clairette P. Armstrong, a psychologist of the Children's Court of the City of New York, which reported the results of psychological examinations on children of immigrants. Armstrong became the lead researcher of the Puerto Rican children's study.[14]

The immigration restrictionists and racial eugenicists who composed the special committee had also been central actors in the crafting and framing of the Johnson-Reed Immigration Act of 1924. The nation's first comprehensive immigration restriction law, the act created numerical limits, known as "racial quotas," for immigration into the United States according to "national origin." In her analysis of the regimes of immigration restriction that emerged in the 1920s, historian Mae M. Ngai argued that the 1924 Act consolidated two important features of immigration restriction: "first, the invention and codification of new racial concepts—'national origins' and 'racial ineligibility to citizenship'—and second, the articulation of a new nation-state territoriality based on border control and deportation policy. . . . [C]onsidered together, these features of restriction put European and non-European immigrant groups on different trajectories of racial formation, with different prospects for full membership in the nation."[15] The act established the criteria that defined races and national origins, criteria used to evaluate the restriction of immigration from those groups considered racially ineligible for citizenship. Historian Roger Daniels reminds students of US history that subdivision "d" of section 11 of the 1924 act excluded "any immigrants from the New World and their descendants; any Asians or their descendants; the descendants of 'slave immigrants'; and the descendants of 'American aborigines.'"[16]

Trevor, in particular, had a distinguished history as a leading immigration restrictionists who had contributed to the definitions of national origins and racial quotas incorporated in the 1924 act.[17] In the 1920s Trevor was the head of "an immigration-restriction coalition of patriotic orders and societies." In March 1924 Trevor "submitted a proposal for quotas based on 'national origins' to the Senate Immigration Committee," and in May the US "Congress passed the new immigration act based on Trevor's concept of national origins quotas."[18] In addition, in the 1920s Laughlin, the lead researcher of the 1934 CCSNY immigration control study, was a leading eugenicist who worked with the US Congress House Committee on Immigration, supplying "data on 'degeneracy' and social 'inadequacy' (crime, insanity, feeblemindedness) showing the alleged racial inferiority and unassimilability of southern and eastern Europeans."[19] Historians consider Laughlin "the eugenist with the greatest influence on immigration policy during the 1920s."[20] He was the research director at the Eugenics Institute at Cold Springs Harbor, New York, founded by Charles Davenport. Davenport was a leading US eugenicist who promoted the ideology of biological determinism and positive race breeding and opposed social and environmental reform.[21]

In the 1930s the CCSNY provided the platform and funding for immigration restrictionists and racial eugenicists. The organization brought together politically connected immigration restrictionists and eugenicists like Trevor, Laughlin, and Armstrong. The CCSNY served a similar purpose to other immigration exclusion groups on the US West Coast, like the California Joint Immigration Committee, which advocated for the exclusion of the Japanese from US national territory.[22] The actors who conducted the 1935 study of Puerto Rican children and the ideologies that informed their research questions were building on their historical participation in the early twentieth-century policy debates that justified immigration restriction on the grounds of racial exclusion and incapacity for citizenship.

In addition, Trevor's concerns about Puerto Ricans' alleged intellectual incapacity and fundamental racial ineligibility for citizenship and statehood were framed within a particular anxiety over a broader Caribbean migration to New York due to the expanding US empire in the region. Trevor specifically warned against the consequences from "the inflow of surplus populations from our dependencies in the Caribbean."[23] While Trevor's and Armstrong's prior support for restrictionist legislation and scientific studies was targeted at eastern European immigrants, the 1930s concern was specific to Caribbean migration. The history of Caribbean migration and the growth and diversity of the Caribbean diaspora in the US Northeast in the early twentieth century provide context for understanding Trevor's and Armstrong's concern with Puerto Ricans specifically as well as

Caribbeans more broadly. It seems there were many reasons for Trevor, Armstrong, and their Special Committee on Immigration and Naturalization to worry that their goal of restricting non-Anglo-Saxon immigration would be challenged by the growth of the Caribbean diaspora. While Puerto Rican migrants in the 1935 study were characterized as a voiceless and weak group dependent on the state for assistance, welfare, and direction, in fact, the Caribbean community of New York City was known for its political radicalism both at home and in the diaspora.

Historian Winston James carefully documented the new scale of migration from the Caribbean to the United States between 1899 and 1937. Originating from the Caribbean islands and Central America, almost 150,000 black Caribbeans traveled to the United States in the early twentieth century. The majority migrated to New York State, but particularly New York City, where by 1930 almost a quarter of black Harlem was of Caribbean origin.[24] As part of this broader Caribbean migration, the number of Puerto Ricans in the United States had grown from 1,513 in 1910 to 53,000 by 1930. Armstrong, citing the 1925 Columbia University study of Puerto Rico's public schools, warned that "the Puerto Rican colony in New York City already rates as the second largest Puerto Rican city in the world."[25]

Since the 1890s, Caribbean migrants in New York City had represented a broad spectrum of radical thought and practice, ranging from revolutionary socialism to black nationalism. Harlem, New York City, and the Northeast bore witness to the radical leadership of Hubert Harrison, Richard B. Moore, and Marcus Garvey. In addition, Cuban and Puerto Rican anticolonial revolutionaries exiled from the islands established fund-raising and intellectual bases from New York City and Tampa to contribute to the goal of liberating the islands from US imperial rule.[26]

Meanwhile, in the Puerto Rico of the 1930s, anticolonial nationalism was accompanied by the militant demands of the working class. Since 1898 a growing portion of the island laborers had been employed in the sugarcane fields of the modern *centrales*, owned by US corporations and Puerto Rican businessmen, a core component of America's "sugar kingdom."[27] The 1930s crisis highlighted Puerto Rico's dependence on US markets for sugar and tobacco. Like the economies of other countries that were primarily agricultural producers and exporters, Puerto Rico's economy suffered. Workers organized and went on strike, challenging their employers and the colonial state to provide jobs and wages as unemployment surged and wages quickly declined. At the same time, intellectuals and middle-class sectors mobilized under the leadership of the anticolonial nationalist Pedro Albizu Campos. The militant supporters of the Nationalist Party, combined with the organized strikes and demands of the working class, characterized 1930s radical politics within Puerto Rico.[28]

Trevor and Armstrong wanted to restrict the immigration of these radical Caribbeans, some of whom were US citizens (Puerto Ricans and US Virgin Islanders)
and others of whom sought the protection of their own imperial embassies in the
United States. While the political radicalism of the Caribbean and the diaspora
was evident, the researchers chose to employ the language of racial eugenics
to construct the imagined inferiority of the colonial migrant group. Immigration restrictionists and racial eugenicists like Trevor and Armstrong, represented
through institutions like the CCSNY, sought the support of their congressmen
in Washington, DC, to limit as quickly as possible the migration of these radical,
black, foreign, and/or colonial migrants. The contradictions of race and empire
had come home.

Within the Caribbean colonial context, Trevor and Armstrong were also react-
ing to the colonial reform policies of the early 1930s. In Puerto Rico, colonial
reformers and social scientists early began to establish the relationship between
overpopulation, economic development, and immigration. When Armstrong
stated the "reasons for research," the first justification established validity by referencing the alleged social and economic burden of the Puerto Rican community:
"According to teachers, social workers, relief investigators, probation officers and
others, the difficult adjustment of Puerto Ricans in New York City has become a
serious problem."[29] While Armstrong began by referencing the alleged anxiety of
local police, social workers, and teachers, the 1930s fears of Puerto Rican poverty
and presence on welfare rolls were also bolstered by the colonial reform studies
conducted on the island.

Referencing the 1930s Brookings Institution report selectively to present the
overpopulation theory as an explanation for the economic hardship on the island
instead of the economic structures that defined the colonial relationship between
island and mainland, Armstrong pondered the potential growth of the Puerto
Rican community in the United States: "Since the population of Puerto Rico is
said to increase with jungle fecundity, the States, particularly New York, are in
line to receive large increments of population from the Island."[30] She turned to
the 1925 Columbia University study, which ultimately contradicted the Armstrong
study conclusions about the intelligence of Puerto Rican children, to warn that
New York City was already "the second largest Puerto Rican city in the world."[31]
The 1930 study by Samuel J. Crumbine, sponsored by the Russell Sage Foundation, documented the island's population density and confirmed, for Armstrong,
that "overpopulation is serious in Puerto Rico."[32] The neo-Malthusian thesis about
overpopulation and economic poverty shaped these studies. Armstrong feared
that colonial reformers were seriously entertaining immigration of "surplus"
laborers to the United States as a practical remedy. "The high Puerto Rican birth

rate, which many consider the crux of their economic difficulties, and over-crowding, offers a serious economic problem. Commissions investigating Puerto Rico have suggested as one way to economic betterment and reduction of population, emigration of skilled or unskilled labor to the States."[33]

The 1920s and 1930s studies provided a logic that racial eugenicists like Armstrong could engage. She drew out the now familiar argument from these studies: consensual unions, illegitimacy, and the young age distribution of the population were at the root of the island's 1930s economic crisis. Together, these forces would generate the reasoning that supported increased migration to New York. The Russell Sage Foundation study established, "as have others," that "for ages, illegitimacy has been one of the great social evils of the Island." The census confirmed the "illegality" or the foundation of disorganized family units: "The 1920 census shows that one-third of the marriages were illegal or so-called consensual, making for loose home ties and the easy and frequent abandonment of children, of whom there are so many thousands on the Island."[34] These illegal and disorganized families generated a young population, a "surplus" of children. "According to the United States standard of estimated age distribution in 1926, Puerto Rico had 174,654 children too many." Armstrong feared that the "jungle fecundity" of tropical Puerto Ricans was uncontrollable, as she was perplexed at how "the near-starvation food resources seem not to check reproduction." And this was why, Armstrong feared, migration to New York City was an attractive solution for colonial reformers: "These figures illustrate how Puerto Rico could well be an inexhaustible source of population supply for a complacent mainland."[35]

Armstrong's argument, pulled together from colonial reform studies, represented what Laura Briggs has defined as a "North American version" of "exclusive nationalism": "A contrasting ideal of nationalism [to *independentista* nationalism] was the North American version that sought protection for the (white, U.S.) nation from too many of 'them'—working-class and/or dark-skinned people. It was an exclusive nationalism derived from 'hard' eugenics, which feared the reproduction of the lower classes, Puerto Ricans in general, and, indeed, all non-'Nordics.'"[36] The overpopulation thesis that emerged in the 1920s and was well established by the 1930s blamed the island's economic conditions on the reproduction rates of working-class families. The island's export-agriculture economy, the modernization of the sugar industry, the colonial trade patterns with US and European markets—these economic and colonial relationships were not considered. While in Puerto Rico *independentista* (pro-independence) nationalists, overpopulation theorists, local and imperial feminists, and liberal professionals engaged in debates over the national project through women's bodies, the 1935 Armstrong study documented that, early in the twentieth century, the Puerto Rican diaspora of

New York City, not just the island population, was attacked and targeted by immigration restrictionists and eugenicists. A generation before the culture of poverty theorists analyzed "the Puerto Rican problem" in the city, immigration restrictionists and racial eugenicists had already identified the diaspora as a model case study.

The 1935 study of Puerto Rican children in New York City reminds US and Puerto Rican historians that the diaspora was at the center of historical debates over immigration control, scientific racism, and national identities within the broader territorial space of US empire. The study and the conversation it generated speak to how the diaspora in the Northeast has historically contributed to the construction and consolidation of national identities that were dependent on the articulation of racial difference. These national identities, however, were being simultaneously constructed by both US immigration restrictionists and racial eugenicists as well as Puerto Rican cultural nationalists of the 1930s. The contradictions of empire—Puerto Rico defined as a colonial territory of the United States that was "domestic in a foreign sense," Puerto Ricans as colonial subjects granted a limited version of US citizenship, the Puerto Rican diaspora depicted as a criminal and degenerate community of foreigners polluting a local "national" space (New York) by immigration restrictionists and racial eugenicists—informed identities emerging in both the island and the mainland.

"You Cannot Make a Silk Purse Out of a Sow's Ear": The Armstrong Study

Two overlapping intentions guided the 1935 Armstrong study. First, through the modern methods of eugenic scientific testing, the researchers carefully "racialized" the Puerto Rican diaspora. Second, within the logic of immigration restrictionists, they constructed Puerto Rican children in the United States as foreigners who were potentially "polluting" and threatening the eugenically healthy community of US citizens. The study created a picture of Puerto Rican children's alleged inferior intelligence, understood to be a product of their "confused" racial heritage and the island's legacy of consensual unions. Armstrong constructed this description of the Puerto Rican diaspora through a comparison to other US non-Anglo-Saxon groups (Native Americans and African Americans) as well as in conversation with comparative eugenics research on colonial peoples in the US empire (Hawaii). The imagined threatening eugenic heritage of the Puerto Rican diaspora was then extended to all residents of the island of Puerto Rico.

The brief study was fundamentally a practice in applying the modern methods of analysis of racial eugenicists and psychologists in the 1930s. Armstrong and her team of researchers gave the students the "short scale of the Army Individual Performance tests" and the verbal "Otis Test of general ability." This combination of tests was intended to measure the students' reactions to both concrete situations and a "verbal education." The researchers chose a public school where they believed the student enrollment included a "large and representative sampling of Puerto Ricans": Public School 57 at 115th Street near Lexington Avenue in New York City in East Harlem; "indeed many of our subjects had siblings in nearby public schools."[37] In the early twentieth century, along with growth in other boroughs and neighborhoods in the city, the Puerto Rican community began to concentrate in the East Harlem neighborhood, also known as Spanish Harlem or *el barrio*.[38]

Armstrong's study constructed and engaged its subjects—Puerto Rican students—as a group of "foreign immigrants." The test results could then be used to reflect more broadly on the racial eugenicists' and immigration restrictionists' arguments about the inferiority of foreigners in comparison to "native" (read "Anglo-Saxon") Americans. The test results of the Puerto Rican students would then be compared by age levels to control groups composed of "native" schoolchildren. The researchers examined 240 Puerto Rican children ranging in age from nine to sixteen in the fourth through sixth grades as well those in the non-English-speaking class. The control groups were from children examined in 1928 from PS 6 on the Upper East Side and PS 166 on the Upper West Side in New York City and rural schoolchildren in northern Westchester County, New York.

What did the student scores and the comparison with the control groups suggest? For Armstrong, the test results were clear. The Army Individual Performance tests provided "statistical evidence that this random sampling of Puerto Rican children in New York were very inferior to unselected public schoolchildren here in ability to react to concrete situations. . . . Only 16 percent of the Puerto Ricans reached the average of the control group, 19 percent were above and 65 percent below the average."[39] The Otis Test of general ability generated IQ scores from which the researchers concluded: "Their inferiority to the control group is marked and they are far below the average child in the States in native ability. . . . Only 6 percent of the Puerto Ricans reached the average of the control group. 14 percent were above and 80 percent below." Armstrong concluded: "Psychological examinations administered to a random sampling of Puerto Rican school children in New York City . . . demonstrate a marked and serious inferiority in native ability to public school children here. But few bright or even average Puerto Ricans were found."[40]

Armstrong concluded from these test results that Puerto Rican children in PS 57 were intellectually inferior to native schoolchildren. From this conclusion she would extrapolate and make recommendations about the Puerto Rican community in the United States more broadly, suggesting concerns about the "family mentality" of those on the island as well. How would the researchers explain the discrepancy between the Puerto Rican children's and the control groups' test scores? They looked for explanations in the supplemental family information they had gathered. The researchers wanted to understand the unique characteristics of the Puerto Rican community and collected information on family organization, class, and race, descriptions that spoke to other comparative "race psychology" studies within the tradition of racial eugenicists in the 1920s.

Armstrong's description of the community began with the most pertinent information to the broader argument of the study: immigration restriction. Researchers wanted to establish that the study subjects represented both US-born children of Puerto Rican parents and "foreign-born" (in Puerto Rico) children who migrated to the United States. One-third of the students reported being born in New York City, over a third had lived in the United States for six years or longer, and the remainder had lived in the United States for five years or less.[41] By establishing this distinction within the group, researchers then argued that the test results spoke to characteristics they believed were inherent in the Puerto Rican "national group," regardless of whether they had been born in the United States to Puerto Rican parents or were "foreign-born" in Puerto Rico but raised in the United States. Did granting students access to public instruction affect the performance of the group, despite the students' location of birth or their years of residence in the United States? Armstrong doubted that it would.

Second to foreign-born and length of stay in the United States was concern over the "illegal" and "disorganized" families of Puerto Ricans, which, according to the colonial reform studies that Armstrong cited, were allegedly at the root of the overpopulation and poverty of the island. However, the study results contradicted the assumption of disorganized families. The dominant family unit of the children under study was the nuclear family: "Slightly over two-thirds of the Puerto Rican children were living with both parents, the remainder lived with mothers alone, a very few with fathers and a few with other relatives." Occupation information was not collected, and the only sentence referencing employment remains unclear: "Over half said they were on relief, home or work."[42] Were over half the parents on relief? Or were half of the children able to report whether their parents were on relief, at home, or at work? The intention of the study, however, as Trevor's introduction suggested, was not to establish the occupational history of the family but rather to point out that the subjects of study were foreigners "on relief" and an economic burden on the state.

For eugenicists, clearly defining the "racial" heritage of the subject was important, for it was believed to be linked to a series of academic and social behaviors (feeblemindedness, criminality, delinquency). For "hard" eugenicists like Armstrong, racial mixture was problematic, for it potentially combined the worst qualities and behaviors of each "race."[43] However, the Puerto Rican students in New York and the racial heritage of those on the island did not easily fit into the racial definitions and hierarchies that guided the other studies published by the Special Committee on Immigration and Naturalization or the guidelines set forth by the Davenport eugenics school.

Armstrong defined Puerto Ricans as a racial hybrid and described the "color" of the students instead: "As to color: 58 were recognizable Negro, 91 white and 91 uncertain, with indications of Negro antecedents."[44] Relying on her observation of the students in combination with a reading of the post-1898 histories of the island published in the United States, Armstrong concluded that the Puerto Rican "race" was really the result of generations of racial mixture.[45] Indigenous native heritage was minimal, while "Negro" heritage was dominant: "The trace of Indian tribes many generations removed is almost lost but in marked contrast the Negro has been an important factor in the development of the island whose population in 1899 nearly a million, was 62 percent white and 38 percent colored." For support and explanation, she referred to L. S. Rowe's 1904 study, *The United States and Puerto Rico*. Quoting Rowe: "'In no other part of the world has there been such a mixture of blood' as in Puerto Rico and the 'entire gamut has been run from the aboriginal Caribs to the culture of Western civilization.'" The "racial" legacy of Puerto Rico, Armstrong explained, was due to the class organization of the island, where "the land-owning class is largely Spanish, the peasants in the coastal plain of Negro extraction with many admixtures and the jibaros, the mountain peasants, of Spanish descent with admixtures of Indian and Negro."[46] Armstrong's description of Puerto Rican "racial" heritage was slippery and contradictory. She simultaneously incorporated the categories of "color," "race," "national origin," and "civilization" to compose a description of her subjects of study that could fit the categories of analysis in "race psychology."

Armstrong's study, guided by the science of racial eugenics and framed by the goal of immigration restriction, looked for an explanation of the Puerto Rican students' performance in their racial heritage, their allegedly broken families, and their "retardation" by school age. Her summary of the study recommendations betrayed the political agenda that framed the pseudoscientific method of psychological tests in 1935. Fundamentally, Armstrong suggested that the study results confirmed the intellectual inferiority not just of the Puerto Rican children but of immigrants in general. And she supported a recommendation and practice that was familiar in debates over public education for African American and Native American children. Although the study was framed as a question of foreign immigration, the solution for the Puerto Rican example was found in the practice of separate curriculums for non-Anglo-Saxon groups. African American industrial training schools and the curriculum of Native American boarding schools reflected liberal educators' belief in the late nineteenth and early twentieth centuries that the groups required manual, rather than academic, instruction. This type of education would help develop the strengths of each community and allow students to seek "proper" forms of employment, such as domestic service for Native American and African American women.[47] Armstrong concluded: "The evidence indicates that the majority of Puerto Rican children here are so low in intelligence that they require education of a simplified, manual sort, preferably industrial, for they cannot adjust in a school system emphasizing the three R's."[48] The Puerto Rican case study served to reinforce the relationship between race, class, and education in US debates.

Armstrong was also particularly concerned about the scale of age-grade retardation of Puerto Rican children. She was guided by the assumption that this retardation fostered and cultivated the children's alleged "criminal tendencies." Her use of the descriptor "retarded" meant that for many students, their age did not correspond to their grade level. She began the conclusion: "Puerto Ricans are adding greatly to the already tremendous problem of intellectually subnormal school retardates of alien parentage, whence are recruited most delinquents and criminals." Placing older students in an earlier class grade highlighted, for Armstrong, the futility of offering academic instruction to such children. "Attempts to force such pupils into school grades for which they are not fitted . . . are all equally cruel to children, sufficiently poignant to give them a reckless disregard, even contempt for laws they flout, via truancy and other delinquency." The children's failure in the classroom, their "reckless disregard" for appropriate behavior in schools, combined with their low test scores, Armstrong argued, supported Trevor's position for immigration restriction: "Indeed the majority of the Puerto Rican children examined betray a family mentality which should not be permitted admission here, further to deteriorate standards already so seriously impaired by mass immigration of the lowest levels of populations of many nations." Immigration restriction, especially of those communities (Puerto Ricans and eastern Europeans) that betrayed behaviors such as "truancy and other delinquency," would better serve the interests of all students: "Most Puerto Rican children here cannot be assimilated in the existing type of civilization and they are helping to turn the tide back to a lower stage of progress."[49]

Armstrong supported her study conclusions and recommendations by referencing a second "race psychology" study of a comparative US colonial example. Dr. S. D. Porteus and Dr. Marjorie E. Babcock conducted a comparative study in "race psychology" of the different "races" that composed Hawaii's population. The 1928 study, *Temperament and Race*, was carried out through the Psychological and Psychopathic Clinic of the University of Hawaii and analyzed the history of Hawaiians, Chinese, Japanese, Portuguese, and Filipinos in Hawaii.[50] Porteus and Babcock compared each "race's" performance on their scale of "social analysis," "brain development," "mentality," and "psychosynergic traits," from which the authors then compiled a conclusion about each group's "racial implications." While the authors dedicated a separate chapter for each group in their "Historical Survey of Races in Hawaii," they did not develop a chapter specific to the "Porto Ricans." Instead, Puerto Ricans were discussed in comparison to other groups, often Filipinos.[51]

Porteus and Babcock grounded their comparative study on the primary value of race: "When a man has stated his race he has stated one of the most significant and important facts about himself, important in its bearing on his physical make-up, his personality, and his spiritual and mental outlook."[52] Armstrong used Porteus and Babcock to support her conclusions that the intelligence of Puerto Ricans was comparatively lower than other foreign "races" in the United States, in addition to native groups: "Porteus and Babcock, when comparing the various national groups in Hawaii, found all were inferior to California children in native ability but that the Puerto Ricans were the most inferior not only in intelligence but in nearly every social trait." Intelligence and delinquency in foreign immigrants in US colonial territories were interconnected: "They were lowest in age-grade standards[,] and court records showed much delinquency, with more Puerto Ricans in jail than any other national group, though they were nearly the smallest group."[53]

Porteus and Babcock characterized the Puerto Ricans who migrated to Hawaii in 1900 as members of the lowest "class" of Puerto Rico's population. In Armstrong's words, "These authors conclude that Puerto Ricans in Hawaii, who had come from the most undesirable strata, had made a hapless attempt to adjust to a cultural level, to a standard of morals and to a set of national habits far higher than theirs and so were the worst timber for citizenship of all the migrants."[54] The Porteus and Babcock study supported Armstrong's contention that Puerto Ricans were likely "racially ineligible" for citizenship. Porteus and Babcock questioned whether the second generation of Puerto Ricans in Hawaii would show much improvement over the first: "It will be interesting to see whether the second generation will continue to display the defects of character of the first. If so it will be a strong proof of the old adage that 'you cannot make a silk purse out of a sow's ear.' The evidence already points that way."[55] Armstrong's 1935 study, published as the language, logic, and method of racial eugenics was declining within scientific

FILIPINO GROUP

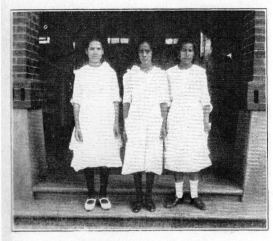

PORTO RICAN GROUP

Racial types, 1926. Porteus and Babcock presented photographs of each of the "racial types" they studied in Hawaii. The photograph of the "Porto Rican Group" shared a page with the "Filipino Group." They wrote: "Porto Ricans and Filipinos vie with one another for the invidious distinction of being last on the list in almost all traits" (Porteus and Babcock, *Temperament and Race*, 324).

circles, sought support from race psychology studies published at the height of scientific racism in the United States a decade earlier. The Porteus and Babcock study was presented to support Armstrong's test results but also, more significantly, to reinforce its political arguments regarding race, citizenship, and empire: Puerto Rican migration should be restricted; Puerto Ricans will make bad citizens; Puerto Rico's colonial government was taking advantage of US immigration policies.

The contradictory goal that guided the Armstrong study—immigration restriction of Puerto Ricans, that is, restricting the mobility of US citizens from a colonial territory to the US mainland—resurfaced in the conclusion. The state of New York, Armstrong restated, could not be expected to carry the burden: "How many more Puerto Ricans can New York support at public expense and how long and with what unfortunate modifications of existing social institutions?"[56] In their study Porteus and Babcock stated simply that it was "a matter of common report that the Porto Rican government embraced the opportunity of sending many of its undesirables as immigrants to Hawaii."[57] Was the Puerto Rican government replicating the earlier Hawaii migration strategy to New York in the 1930s? Armstrong asked: "Is this New York group of Puerto Ricans representative of children in Puerto Rico? Does Puerto Rico export to New York mostly her lowest strata and worst mental levels?"[58]

Whether or not Puerto Rican migrants in New York were representative of those on the island, Armstrong concluded by strongly reminding her readers that the solution proposed in the 1930s Puerto Rican colonial reform studies—immigration of laborers—was misguided: "It can be concluded that migration to New York offers no satisfactory, fundamental or permanent solution of the difficulties of Puerto Rico or New York and only seriously complicates matters all around."[59] She believed her study documented that there might be certain characteristics intrinsic in the heritage of Puerto Ricans that could not be improved through social services like public instruction: "It is evident that the serious problems of Puerto Rico cannot be solved by emigration of semi- or unskilled labor to New York, particularly in view of unemployment here, mandatory education and the existing standards. Such emigration results in placing many in most anomalous and unhappy situations, with dire results to unfortunate children and to education aiming at progress."[60]

Armstrong's study carefully crafted an argument—rich in contradictions—that brought together the political goals of racial eugenicists and immigration restrictionists in the years following the Great Depression. Applying the methods and logic of racial eugenicists, measuring intellectual capacity through Army Individual Performance and IQ tests, comparing the results to other "native" control groups, Armstrong argued that Puerto Rican intelligence was comparatively inferior. Intellectual inferiority laid the foundation for the argument that as a "national" and "racial" group, Puerto Ricans were the "worst timber for citizenship." The comparative colonial example could only provide further support for that conclusion. Researchers in both New York and Hawaii implied that the Puerto Rican government was relieving itself of its "undesirables" and "lowest strata" through migration. At the same time, they suggested that the Puerto Rican migrants, in fact, demonstrated some of the "family mentality" inherent in Puerto Ricans as a "national group" and/or "race." Armstrong maintained the argument that the subjects of study were "foreigners" to remind her readers and particularly the US congressmen holding hearings in Washington, DC, that scientific evidence supported the position that Puerto Rican migration should be restricted and Puerto Rico's colonial status not expanded in the path toward "incorporation into the Union." Racial eugenicists and immigration restrictionists worked together to warn US congressmen against the "grave consequences" of expanding US empire in the Caribbean. For the researchers, then, the alleged inferior intelligence, blackness, tendencies toward criminality, and disorganized families were enough evidence and justification for curtailing Puerto Rican migration to the United States.

Additionally, in the brief Armstrong study, the early twentieth-century Puerto Rican diaspora discursively underwent multiple levels of racialization. First, Puerto Ricans were racialized as a hybrid group. The dominant characteristics and foundation of the community, nevertheless, were found to be "Negro." Second, the blackness of the Puerto Rican community was consolidated in the researchers' fear of black Caribbean migration. They chose to study Puerto Rican children in Spanish Harlem. Puerto Ricans in the city shared housing, schools, and neighborhoods with the heart of the "New Negro" community of Harlem. Their spatial location defined the broader radical Caribbean community of New York. Third, in addition to the construction of Puerto Ricans as foreign immigrants from the Caribbean, they were feared to be a colonial problem. Test scores and family mentalities, therefore, were compared to other "racial" groups in Hawaii. The Hawaii study, as a source of comparison and support for Armstrong, represented the link between the acquisition of overseas territories, the expansion of empire, and the fear over how new colonial peoples were constructing a "new citizenship" and "new nation"; as Babcock and Porteus lamented, "It is perhaps more proper to speak not of the Americanization of the alien but of the alienization of America."[61] The 1920s racial eugenics literature provided comparative analyses of "national" groups within US imperial spaces, and Puerto Ricans were evaluated not only in comparison to "native" control groups but also in comparison to Hawaii's colonial groups. Fourth, Puerto Rican students were also understood to be relatively familiar to other "domestic" non-Anglo-Saxon groups. Armstrong could recommend that Puerto Ricans follow the tradition of African American industrial training schools in the Southeast and Native American boarding schools throughout the United States. Fifth, Armstrong, in the tradition of racial eugenicists and immigration restrictionists, sought to erase Puerto Ricans' US citizenship and to minimize the island's colonial relationship to the United States. This was an additional form of racializing Puerto Ricans as a non-Anglo-Saxon group in the tradition of the 1930s anti-immigration, deportation, and decolonization campaigns that targeted Filipinos and Mexican Americans on the US West Coast. In the end, within one study, as the researchers sought supporting evidence and constructed arguments to establish their position (immigration restriction of the comparatively inferior group of Puerto Ricans), they defined the Puerto Rican diaspora (and all Puerto Ricans by extension) as a community of non-Anglo-Saxon, racially hybrid, but predominantly black foreigners and colonial subjects from the Caribbean. The example of the Puerto Rican diaspora, as constructed in the 1935 study, provides a case study that highlights how the 1930s relationship between race and empire emerged and was constructed through the layering of multiple and contradictory discourses about race, science, migration, citizenship, and nation.

"Porto-Rican Boy," 1926 (Porteus and Babcock, *Temperament and Race*, 208). Armstrong described the "race" of Puerto Ricans: "The trace of Indian tribes many generations removed is almost lost but in marked contrast the Negro has been an important factor in the development of the island" (Armstrong, Achilles, and Sacks, *Report*, 5).

"Unwarranted," "Groundless," and "Inadequate": Cebollero Responds

The 1935 Chamber of Commerce of the State of New York publication was outrageous in its derogatory and racist characterization of Puerto Ricans and willfully ignorant of the colonial relationship between Puerto Rico and the United States, so much so that it was met with a "classic" response—editorials and letters challenging and denouncing the study appeared in newspapers on the island and in New York. Politicians, labor leaders, feminists, and other intellectuals in early twentieth-century Puerto Rico cultivated a diverse and active newspaper culture where they debated multiple events, policies, and ideologies. A derogatory study of Puerto Ricans in New York would understandably generate a reaction from the cosmopolitan intellectuals and politicians who were widely read and daily debated the values, dangers, and implications of contemporary news. However, the response to the 1935 study was different from the everyday newspaper debates on the island, for in addition to the letters to the editors of newspapers, the second-in-command of Puerto Rico's Department of Education also drafted an "official" denouncement of the study. The response prepared by Pedro Cebollero, the assistant commissioner of education, was published in the island's monthly education journal, *La revista escolar de Puerto Rico/Porto Rico School Review*, and printed in pamphlet form by the Department of Education.[62]

Why would the local 1935 New York study warrant such a response—an "official" one from a leading education administrator in Puerto Rico? And this was a response that was not a simple dismissal of the study but rather a methodical and substantive discussion and refutation of its arguments as well. Cebollero rejected the study's "fallacy of reasoning" and "illogical inferences": first, that migration of Puerto Ricans into the US mainland could be restricted; second, that the quality of a "race" or "national" group could be evaluated through an immigrant population in the United States. He devalued the "ineffective," "useless," and "absurd" intentions guiding the study by dismissing them "as pardonable because after all the committee members are not scientists but just Chamber of Commerce members." However, he condemned the psychologists for "also fall[ing] under the spell of the delusion suffered by the Chamber of Commerce members."[63] Cebollero rejected the study's assumption that the sample might be representative of all Puerto Ricans on the island, challenging its characterization of Puerto Ricans on the basis of race, class, and mental capacity: "To accept—as the researchers have accepted—that a sampling which is 76 per cent colored, over 50 per cent on relief, and 47 percent retarded is representative of Puerto Ricans is, to say the least, unbelievable."[64] He also challenged and dismissed the researchers' methods—sample size, tests conducted, language employed, and support sought from the Porteus and Babcock study. He turned to the 1925 Columbia University study, a comprehensive study of Puerto Rico's public school system, to refute the 1935 study results by challenging the arguments based on racial psychology and intelligence tests.

Why did the modest 1935 study warrant any reaction at all? Cebollero's response, his rejection of the study's intentions, methods, and arguments, was more than a simple academic exercise. Puerto Rican identity—particularly its 1930s interpretations of "race," class, and modernity—was at stake. First, Cebollero's refutation spoke to how he defined his own position in Puerto Rico's colonial social hierarchy—as a member of the liberal elite, an intellectual, a modern educator. It also reflected his "national" ideology in the 1930s as an administrator of a colonial school system that represented a new generation of educators who were challenging the practice of Americanization and its legacy of censure of nationalism within the public school system. Cebollero's response contributes to our understanding of how liberal intellectuals engaged the concepts of race, nation, and colonialism in the 1930s and how students, schools, and public education were at the heart of this debate.

In addition, the way Cebollero crafted his rejection of the study reflected one of the ways Puerto Rican intellectuals and intermediate actors constructed their own characterization of the early twentieth-century diaspora in conversation with the 1930s debates over race and nation. The diaspora was clearly present in Puerto Rican "national" debates. Cebollero's response was establishing the historical construction of difference between diaspora and nation as early as the 1930s. He demonstrates how "racial" and "national" differences were fundamental to the construction of "authentic," island-based, Puerto Rican identities. Finally, Cebollero's response highlighted how both supporters and opponents of US empire in the Caribbean generated a contradictory logic that highlighted the existing racial and class hierarchies. Part of the urgency of the 1930s national identity debates was an awareness of the economic and political limitations within the US imperial framework. For both the Puerto Rican and US examples, national identities were interconnected and constructed within the broader imperial framework.

An analysis of Cebollero's reaction to the 1935 study, then, allows us to examine the construction of national identities, the reproduction of empire, and the centrality of race and class within both processes. These processes, in particular, were negotiated through the construction of the Puerto Rican diaspora as the emblematic "other"—it was an identity vis-à-vis which Cebollero could define what Puerto Ricans on the island were not. Puerto Rican identity in the early twentieth century, therefore, was not simply constructed in opposition to the Anglo-Saxon, North American *Americanos.*[65] It was also constructed in opposition to those characteristics that social scientists and educators (both US and Puerto Rican) discursively imposed on the diaspora in the United States.

"We Cannot Warrant Their Authenticity"

Cebollero's discussion about the "representativeness" and "sampling" of the 1935 study allows for an analysis of two interconnected intentions: first, the practice of constructing "difference" between island and diaspora, and second, the process by which elite educators of the 1930s generation chose to define themselves as cosmopolitan and informed by modern science.

Racial and national difference sits at the core of generational conversations that imagine a grave cultural difference between Puerto Ricans on the island and those in the diaspora. These debates over authenticity and national identity are often examined through the academic and literary discussions about the 1950s great migration of Puerto Rican workers into the US mainland and the 1970s return migration.[66] The 1935 study suggests that the construction of an important distinction between the "authenticity" of those on the island and those in the diaspora can be documented as early as the 1930s. In this 1935 example, the key categories of race and class emerge as important concepts deployed to establish and articulate the differences.

The assumption that guides the construction of difference in Cebollero's arguments and is illuminative of the 1930s generation was that the "uniqueness" of Puerto Rican culture and identity was cultivated within the geographic boundaries of the island, for it was the product of generations of isolation. Puerto Rican identity represented a uniqueness more broadly rooted in Latin heritage and civilization, which was defined in opposition to an Anglo-Saxon, North American culture. But, creole elites argued, the Puerto Rican version of a Latin American civilization did not travel well and was easily corrupted, especially when located within the heart of US empire, the mainland. It was from this assumption about the degenerative potential of Puerto Rican cultural and national identities that Cebollero and other creole elites could propose their own versions of derogatory and racist descriptions of Puerto Ricans in the US mainland and Hawaii in the early twentieth century.

More specifically, Cebollero challenged the representativeness of the study sample based on two critical characteristics: race and class. "The extent to which the 'sampling' selected is truly representative of the group is the cornerstone of the whole structure." In addition to the broader questions and assumptions that guided the study, Cebollero's main concern about the sampling's representativeness—which sits at the heart of the distinction between island and diaspora—was more effectively explained through the language of race and class: "Out of the 240 pupils included, 182 were colored or had indications of negro antecedents. This represents 76 per cent of the total."[67] While Cebollero warned that it was unlikely that these figures were correct ("we cannot warrant their authenticity"), they nevertheless undermined the sample's representativeness: "The color distribution of the inhabitants of Puerto Rico, according to the 1930 census, was 74.3 per cent white and 25.7 per cent colored."[68] Cebollero sought authority from the politically constructed and subjective US census figures to conclude that "if the color classification of the 240 pupils included in the investigation is correct, the proportion of white to colored children is approximately the *reverse* of the proportion found in Puerto Rico."[69]

The group of children under study was therefore, by definition, not representative of Puerto Ricans on the island. Instead, based on descriptions of phenotype and color alone, those in the diaspora represented the opposite, the inverse, of what was "typical" of the island population. The diaspora was an illegitimate and inauthentic representative of Puerto Ricans: "This fact is an evidence of the absolute disregard of the principle of 'representativeness,' which should have guided the Chamber of Commerce research workers in selecting the 'sampling' for their study."[70]

Historians Eileen Findlay, Luis Figueroa, and Ileana Rodríguez-Silva have examined how race and class were interconnected in the construction of social hierarchies in Puerto Rico.[71] And the connection between race and class, the racialization of class, has been thoroughly documented and debated in Latin American and Caribbean historiography.[72] Cebollero was better versed in a debate over the markers of class and he dismissed an overt discussion on race. This was a strategy Cebollero deployed to dismiss the value and quality of the study: "A second evidence of the disregard of the researchers . . . for the tenets of correct sampling is to be found in the absence of any occupational analysis of the heads of the families."[73] He dismissed the "inconsequential details" the researchers chose to collect about the parents—whether they were on relief, employed, or at home.

Cebollero, additionally, referenced contemporary arguments within the discipline of psychology to explain the value of occupation and class in a study that intended to measure intelligence. He cited two Columbia University studies to document the "strong link between occupational analysis and social status [May Bere 1924 and Paul Monroe 1925]." He did not challenge the "established fact of psychology that the intelligence levels of various occupations range from very low in such occupations as laborer, miner, teamster, barber, horseshoer, etc., to very high in the professions of engineering, medicine, accountancy, etc." Instead, he reinforced the relationship between class and intellect and questioned whether the Spanish Harlem neighborhood was the best community from which to draw assumptions about the range of classes and intellect in both Puerto Rico and New York: "It is entirely reasonable to suppose that the neighborhood that feeds the school selected may not have supplied a distribution of occupations typical of the Puerto Rican population of New York or Puerto Rico in general."[74]

Within the broader category of class and social status, Cebollero questioned other descriptions of the student group that he believed challenged the sample's representativeness: poverty and retardation. "It is stated in the report that over one-half of the children studied were on relief and that forty-seven per cent were retarded." If these were the group characteristics, after all, how would Cebollero question the low test results? Cebollero cited a 1923 Rudolf Pintner study to confirm his understanding and acceptance that "low intelligence is likely to be very common among the unemployed," that "retardation in school work has been generally associated with low intelligence," and that "all results show the negro decidedly inferior to the white on standard intelligence tests." He was not questioning the link between class, race, and low intelligence. Instead, he was arguing that a sample that was dominated by those characteristics—which he assumed should score low on tests—was not representative of Puerto Ricans on the island: "With such a 'sampling,' the results of psychological tests of mental ability were foredoomed to be inferior. It seems hardly necessary to offer scientific evidence to support our contention."[75]

He was not dismissing the researchers' report that the New York students might have been living in poverty, that many were "negro" or "blacker" than the "typical Puerto Rican," and that as a result they scored low on tests. But those characteristics of the diaspora, Cebollero asserted, were not to be applied to all Puerto Ricans on the island: "To be sure, Puerto Ricans are not seventy-six percent colored, over fifty percent unemployed and forty-seven percent retarded. On the basis of such a 'sampling'—and it can be easily duplicated from among American-born children in almost any state in the Union—a researcher who is not particularly scrupulous about his task, could pronounce any American community inferior, fit for deportation and unworthy of statehood!"[76] In this 1935 example, therefore, Cebollero was crafting an argument about the fundamental "difference" between the diaspora and the island that was based on his interpretation of the categories of race and class. These categories are as important for how they are interconnected in the construction of Puerto Rican social hierarchies as they are for how they have been historically deployed—as a discursive strategy in the construction of difference between island and diaspora.

Cebollero's discussion of race and class differences, however, also informs our second contention about his use of the "sampling" and "representativeness" discussion. He was also providing an example of how the elite, particularly educators and intellectuals, assumed and defended their own self-characterization as a modern and scientific group distinct from the majority of the working class and capable of challenging US (Anglo-Saxon) arguments about racial and intellectual supremacy. Race and class were at the root of Cebollero's construction of the difference between island and diaspora as well as the difference between himself (an elite liberal creole) and the black/working classes.

How was the race and class difference that Cebollero constructed between island and diaspora also a reflection and affirmation of his class position? He spoke as an elite intellectual, the second-in-command of the colonial public school system. Cebollero held a BA from the University of Puerto Rico (1913), had attended Columbia University, and had earned an MA from the University of Chicago (1929). He was serving as an assistant professor of educational administration at the University of Puerto Rico in 1930 when he was appointed to the position of assistant commissioner of the Department of Education of Puerto Rico.[77] With the authority his modern and scientific education granted, Cebollero dismissed Armstrong's research as "unreliable because of its unscientific method," rejected its "unbelievable" conclusions because of its "absolute disregard of the principle of representativeness," and concluded that it was nothing more than a "disturbing" study composed of "inconsequential details." He charged Armstrong with "casting about for evidence" only to find "flimsy support for the sweeping generalizations" in the Porteus and Babcock study, another example of "unwarranted and groundless" research whose sample was also "entirely inadequate": "The amateurish attempts to draw conclusions about racial inferiority on the basis of the studies such as the one conducted under the auspices of the New York State Chamber of Commerce have drawn severe condemnation from *serious* students of race psychology." Cebollero found it "hard to refrain from the suspicion that this is a case of rationalization."[78]

Instead of the rationalization offered by Armstrong and her colleagues, Cebollero supported his arguments by citing conclusions established by "competent psychologists in Puerto Rico" whose studies "attest to the achievements" of Puerto Rican students. Outside of Puerto Rico, he referenced the work of Thomas R. Garth, "one of the most distinguished students of race psychology," and Rudolph Pintner, "the world-famous psychologist of Columbia University," to dismiss the "ignorance" and "unscientific tendency to draw hasty conclusions" in Armstrong's "unreliable" and "wasteful" study. Cebollero reserved rational thought and scientific knowledge for himself (and, by extension, other intellectuals, researchers, and educators in Puerto Rico) while denying the racial eugenicists' and immigration restrictionists' validity.

Cebollero's discussion of the study, the diaspora, and the island was also an expression of the increasingly nationalist and anticolonial 1930s elite. His references to the invalid and unscientific nature of the study demonstrated his own training as well as his right, responsibility, and capacity to challenge Armstrong's study. Cebollero's familiarity with modern science, with education and psychology studies and theories, attested more broadly to the new generation of teachers and administrators that staffed and controlled Puerto Rico's public school system, a more defiantly nationalist group, proponents of their own cultural vision and nationalist project. The 1930s generation of Puerto Rican administrators, in particular, inherited and reproduced the tradition of early twentieth-century educators of promoting their own agenda and vision while aggressively challenging US claims of Puerto Rican inferiority, whether they were made by US administrators within Puerto Rico's school system or by racial eugenicists and immigration restrictionists on the mainland.

"American Citizens of Puerto Rican Birth or Extraction"

In his condemnation of the 1935 study and rejection of the characteristics attributed to the diaspora, Cebollero also contributed to the process of both defining Puerto Rican identity and highlighting the contradictions of citizenship, nation, and empire. When he rejected the derogatory (race, class, and intellect) description of Puerto Ricans, he did so through the language that framed the study—the language of "immigrants" and "national groups." For example, he rejected the assumption that a study of Puerto Ricans in the diaspora could represent the "quality" of those on the island, "for it is as absurd as if a psychological test of the immigrant Italian were to be taken as a measure of the ability of the Roman citizen generally." When he emphasized that Armstrong and her colleagues applied unscientific methods and rejected the support they alleged was present in the Porteus and Babcock Hawaii study, Cebollero referred to Pintner's "definite pronouncement: 'It is only by testing *adequate samplings of national groups within their own countries* that we may approximate some knowledge of racial or national differences in intelligence.'"[79] In the process of rejecting the study's assumptions and conclusions, he argued that national groups cannot be effectively tested outside of their home countries, nor can they be tested in a foreign language. He established and confirmed that Puerto Ricans were a separate "national" group in opposition to the "native" control groups in the United States, that they were native Spanish speakers whose intelligence could not be evaluated through tests with "instructions . . . given in English," and that they maintained a "racial" composition and heritage different from that presented in the diaspora and in the US mainland more broadly.

Cebollero's assertion that the quality of the Puerto Ricans on the island could not be tested in the mainland through the diaspora group in the end reflected his definition of Puerto Ricans as a "national group." It did not deny, however, that Puerto Ricans were also part of the US "nation," members of the US empire, because they were US citizens residing in an unincorporated American colony. In his final denouncement of the study, therefore, he returned to his initial challenge: the study was "useless as a measure of . . . immigration control because Puerto Ricans are American citizens and as such have free access to the country."[80] And he concluded that "it is regrettable that the efforts and expense . . . should have been wasted on a piece of research that is . . . productive of ill-feeling among the American citizens of Puerto Rican birth or extraction residing in the United States and Puerto Rico."[81] He asserted and reminded the researchers that Puerto Ricans, despite his promotion of their distinct national identity throughout his response, were fundamentally US citizens first. In his rejection of the study, Cebollero restated and affirmed Puerto Rico's colonial relationship with the United States and acknowledged Puerto Ricans' location within the modern US empire at the same time that he deployed a more expansive definition of citizenship than Armstrong.

This, ultimately, represents one line of argument proposed by other liberal intellectuals and educators in early twentieth-century Puerto Rico. First, Cebollero asserted the core (and mythic) tenets of Puerto Rico's unique culture and civilization, one rooted in Latin heritage, Spanish language, and geography. And he established that these characteristics defined Puerto Rico as a distinct "national group." Second, he employed a romanticized Puerto Rican vision of the United States as a nation that was potentially a multiracial, multilingual pluralistic society composed of immigrants representing a diversity of national groups, all of whom were protected by the US Constitution. This version of the US nation had been, after all, the vision proposed through Puerto Rico's colonial public schools through the early twentieth-century Americanization policies. This liberal autonomist definition of Puerto Rican national identity and argument for incorporation into the US nation, however, was deeply in contradiction to the vision of nation deployed by the US racial eugenicists and immigration restrictionists who were motivated by their "exclusive nationalism," which sought the protection of the Anglo-Saxon population from nonwhite peoples, immigrants, and colonial subjects.

What does Cebollero's argument imply about citizenship, nation, and empire? His response suggests that in the 1930s the way the prominent concepts of "nation" and "race" were defined, contested, and deployed by different actors depended on their location within the modern US empire of the early twentieth century. Cebollero represents one line of argument within the broader 1930s Puerto Rican debates over nationalism, colonialism, race, and diaspora, just like Armstrong's study represents a particular vision of racial eugenicists and immigration restrictionists who in the 1930s were struggling to protect their agenda in the face of increased immigration from the Caribbean. Cebollero's response also suggests that the conceptualization of the Puerto Rican diaspora was an important site of contestation—a community through which both Puerto Rican intellectuals and US "native nationalists" could define their own group's authenticity. The early twentieth-century diaspora was constructed as an additional contradictory concept—different from both "native" US citizens and "authentic" geographically bounded Puerto Ricans. The diaspora became a location of contradiction and contestation in the process of defining "national identities" within the US empire. Fundamentally, this is one way the diaspora became a key location for the construction of race, class, and national difference.

CONCLUSION

The early twentieth-century Puerto Rican diaspora remains relatively at the margins of historical narratives of both the United States and Puerto Rico. The US literature that examines the history of immigration and racial eugenics rarely turns to the Puerto Rican colonial example for reflection. Meanwhile, histories of 1930s Puerto Rico, when analyzing national and cultural identities or the militant anti-imperial nationalist movement, have rarely reflected on how the diaspora contributed to those processes. The 1930s, however, produced important conversations about national identities in both the United States and Puerto Rico. And both national conversations were forced to engage the expansion of US empire. The 1930s Puerto Rican diaspora was the material consequence of US expansion in the Caribbean—a community born from both exiled anticolonial intellectuals and activists as well as labor leaders, workers, and their families. Sectors of both US and Puerto Rican intellectual circles sharpened their self-identity and national definitions partly through this colonial site of contestation—the diaspora.

Immigration restrictionists and racial eugenicists struggled to maintain support for their policies in the 1930s, particularly as the consequences of US empire in the Caribbean were becoming more evident "at home." Migration and movement have been historically a defining Caribbean characteristic. In the early twentieth century, immigration was a consequence of US economic colonial policies in the region. The black, radical, colonial, and/or foreign immigrants only strengthened the immigration restrictionists' and racial eugenicists' resolve to uphold their position in the US national hierarchy as the scientific voice demanding policies restricting non-Anglo-Saxon immigration in defense of their vision and practice of "exclusive nationalism." The 1930s diaspora became a good case study—through a test on children—to confirm and substantiate their claims that Puerto Rican migration, like all other migration from "the colonial dependencies in the Caribbean," must be stopped. Trevor and Armstrong, additionally, used the children's test results to generate arguments about the inferiority of Puerto Ricans in Hawaii and Puerto Rico. The children represented everything negative (racial degeneracy, poverty, intellectual inferiority) that racial eugenicists and immigration restrictionists argued could only come from the continuous migration of non-Anglo-Saxon populations from the Caribbean.

The Puerto Rican diaspora, however, was also an important site for one sector of the island's intellectual elite who in the 1930s was debating the origins and "uniqueness" of Puerto Rico's national identity within what was a US imperial space. The diaspora challenged the island-based intellectuals who were crafting a definition of cultural nationalism and identity. Cebollero had to denounce the study's intentions, methods, and conclusions, for the US researchers' statements were meant to blanket all Puerto Ricans, not just those in the diaspora. But in the process of denouncing the study, Cebollero also made important contributions to the process of defining a national Puerto Rican identity in the early twentieth century. The diaspora was important as a community conceptualized as one that represented the "inverse" qualities of the island's values and characteristics. Cebollero's rejection of the study required the careful distinction between his own class (the educated, scientific, modern elite) and the working classes of Puerto Rico in the island and the diaspora as well as the wider race and class differences between island and diaspora. In addition, challenging the study in the end demanded that he reinscribe Puerto Rico's colonial relationship to the US Puerto Ricans, whom he defined as "Americans of Puerto Rican birth" and who were simultaneously members of the US nation and empire *and* a distinct "racial" and "national" group. The diaspora highlighted the contradictions of citizenship, nation, and empire in 1930s Puerto Rican conversations and debates.

The 1935 study and Cebollero's response offer historians the opportunity to examine how Caribbean diasporas, created from the policies of US empire in the region, can be brought into the center of debates over "the nation" and the construction of national narratives. The Puerto Rican colonial example suggests how US national identities and US empire were connected. Colonial subjects, even those who become US citizens, can be located within the imagined boundaries of the nation. The example also suggests the geographic limits of island-based history might be broadened to engage and reflect on the legacy of US empire and the role of the diaspora in the construction of national identities.

chapter 5

Parents and Students
Claim Their Rights

The decade of the 1940s marked a new historical moment in the relationship between colonial state building, schools, and citizens. The colonial school system continued to expand. Communities witnessed the building of more schools, hiring of more teachers, and enrollment of more students. However, at the same time, a larger total number of school-age children were not able to attend school. In 1946 the total population of school-age children was 663,376. Fifty-two percent of the children attended schools. The remaining 317,599 did not.[1] The growing school-age population in the 1940s, those inside and outside the classroom, made ever greater demands on the colonial state. A larger total number of students demanded access to the classroom.

This chapter turns its attention to this growing demand for access to schools by students and parents. Demographics alone cannot explain the intensified interest in securing access to schools. The 1940s was a decade of great social, economic, and political change in Puerto Rico. Colonial reformers, embodied in the newly founded Partido Popular Democrático (PPD, Popular Democratic Party), emerged with a social justice agenda that gained support from the majority of the working class. A change from the radical politics and state violence of the 1930s, the PPD came to power through the support of the working class. The PPD carried out a successful political campaign, and its representatives were elected to the colonial legislature. The new representatives of the colonial state had made promises to the working class during their campaigns. Parents and students had been listening to those promises. Access to schools was one of them. The new intensity behind the demands for access to education in the 1940s was also a reflection of the dynamic social change of the populist era.

When they approved and funded public law no. 55 in 1949, Puerto Rican legislators generated a new scholarship opportunity for poor, talented, public schoolchildren. They could not have imagined the overwhelming response the scholarship would generate. By supporting the scholarship, they also, significantly, fostered great hope and aspiration. In theory, public schools had been free and open to all students since 1899. In practice, a limited number of working-class children could pursue the privilege of attending school. Sending a child to school meant withdrawing his or her labor from the home, field, or factory. The new scholarship, however, allowed parents and children to imagine they might receive the bit of support and assistance they required to finally pursue a public education. The opportunity was also celebrated by extended family and the broader community as well as teachers, social workers, and principals. Once the scholarship fund was founded and publicized, students and parents aggressively pursued it. In the process, they declared their rights as citizens and clarified their expectations of the colonial state. The colonial state, meanwhile, as represented through the bureaucracy of the Department of Education in the 1940s, struggled to meet the demands of the citizenry—access to public schools.

By the late 1940s it had become increasingly clear to working-class parents and students that the colonial state, now represented by the PPD, was unable to implement the promised reforms that would guarantee their children access to public schools. Parents and students wrote letters of complaint, in which they made their demands as citizens before the colonial state. Through these letters, historians are able to document parent and student visions for schools and the role of education in their lives. Their voices, which were harder to document in the earlier years of the twentieth century, emerge loudly and confidently. Student voices, first and foremost, undermined the derogatory characterizations teachers and colonial state officials had proposed about poor students and parents in earlier generations.

Since the 1910s, teachers had crafted an image of students as obstacles. Students and their parents required reform and regeneration at the hands of teachers. Otherwise, students and parents would prove to be the primary challenge to the progress of the *patria*. Teachers proposed that it was their responsibility (the profession) to pursue literacy campaigns, promote physical education, and rebuild the home through the school for the benefit of the *patria*. Rarely were students or parents characterized as enthusiastic participants in this process of regeneration. Instead, it appeared that students and poor families had become unwilling targets of colonial reform. However, the student and parent voices that emerged in the 1940s challenge the characterizations earlier proposed by teachers and state officials. In fact, student letters turn traditional arguments upside down. Instead, they suggest that it was the failure of the colonial state to satisfy the demands of the working class that really challenged the citizenship-building project and the ability of the *patria* to progress.

In addition, student letters allow historians to understand how the working class negotiated with the colonial state. In the early twentieth century, teachers overcame great obstacles to promote their vision of citizen and nation within colonial schools. This practice of negotiation produced two results. It allowed teachers to make the best of a difficult situation (colonialism). Teachers were able to promote their agenda for schools within the colonial school system. However, this process of negotiating with and participating in colonial schools meant that teachers also contributed to the process of consolidating colonialism.

The colonial state that emerged in the early twentieth century had evolved through several stages: encounter, 1898–1917; Americanization and reform, 1917–30; and crisis and reconstruction, 1930–40. At each of these historical cycles, the colonial state had not merely imposed its visions upon teachers and schools. Instead, US and Puerto Rican colonial administrators were forced to respond to the demands and interests of intermediate actors. The colonial state was dynamic. It had evolved under the leadership of different generations of colonial administrators (Americans and Puerto Ricans, conservative and liberal) and had equally been shaped by the constant demands of intermediate actors such as teachers, nurses, and social workers.

In the 1940s, as student letters suggest, the colonial state came under increasing pressure from the working class. The practice of negotiating with the colonial state (embodied in the history of teachers) became broader (more inclusive and participatory) during the populist era of the 1940s. The voice of students and parents emerged more frequently and loudly. And just like in each of the prior historical cycles of colonial state building, colonial administrators were forced to address the demands of their constituency. Schoolchildren and parents were direct participants in this process of negotiation. They inserted themselves into the conversation. The demands they made regarding their right to an education suggests that in the 1940s schools remained at the core of the relationship between the colonial state and its citizens.

Luis Muñoz Marín and the Partido Popular Democrático

The political platform and project proposed by Muñoz Marín and the PPD in the late 1930s and 1940s fall within the broader framework of populism in the Caribbean and Latin America.[2] Muñoz Marín, the charismatic leader, was particularly adept at speaking to "the people" through "simple" and direct language intended to engage their immediate concerns. The images of the historic 1938 campaign, for example, highlighted how Muñoz Marín represented himself as one of the people, a *jíbaro*, someone the working class and rural communities could trust and support. He generated alliances with rural households, targeting the support of the male head of the family in particular. The PPD in the 1940s provided a radical alternative to the traditional politics of the early twentieth century. It campaigned on a vision for social justice, through the platform of *pan, tierra, y libertad* (bread, land, and liberty), while intentionally removing the island's political status question from the debate. The PPD platform, in addition, proposed a vision for agrarian reform that was dependent on each citizen's commitment to maintaining the integrity of the vote. The right of the citizen to uphold the value of the franchise, to restrain from "selling his vote," was central to the PPD's campaign. The reciprocal relationship between citizen and colonial state (now embodied through Muñoz Marín's public persona) was promoted and consolidated through the 1938 campaign, the publication and distribution of popular literature (pamphlets and newspaper) in the 1940s, and the founding of a community school extension program (radio and film) intended to reach and serve rural students and adults.[3]

The political project of the 1940s culminated in the founding of the Estado Libre Asociado (ELA, Free Associated State) of Puerto Rico in 1952. The ELA, a modern reinterpretation of the traditional colonial relationship between Puerto Rico and the United States, intended to address several concerns and critiques about the island's lack of political sovereignty that had arisen among different political sectors within the island and the international community. The ELA was meant to represent a newly negotiated "compact" between Puerto Rico and the United States. And the process of approving the ELA constitution, in particular, highlighted the representation of popular will through elected officials in the legislature, the debates during the constituent assembly, and the approval of the compact through the vote. The ELA, however, was generated during a political crisis for both the United States and colonial reformers. Puerto Rico's colonial status garnered attention and critique during the decolonization processes of the late 1940s and early 1950s. The ELA, and particularly the democratic process by which it was constituted and approved, intended to demonstrate to the United Nations and the international community that the island's relationship to the United States could no longer be defined as strictly colonial.

The ELA further institutionalized the island's long tradition of autonomist ideology and reform politics. The Puerto Rican constituency approved its own constitution and elected local and islandwide politicians while remaining politically and economically connected to the United States. While the new ELA status represented the autonomist ideology of the PPD, it faced critique and disapproval from dissenting nationalists and proannexationists. Both political camps argued that the new ELA compact changed little of the fundamentally colonial relationship between the United States and Puerto Rico.[4] However modern and reformed, Puerto Rico was not yet independent. The United States retained sovereignty.

Although the ELA government was a modern version of a colonial state, it was accompanied by a carefully crafted narrative of nation, nationalism, and national identity. The ELA marked the beginning of a collaboration between the PPD leadership and influential intellectuals, artists, and academics, who worked together to craft the language and vision of cultural nationalism. Puerto Rico, despite lacking political sovereignty, was promoted as a culturally distinct and unique island and people who satisfied all requirements of a "nation."[5]

The ELA of the 1950s was a central part of Puerto Rico's new "modernizing" project. And the local public school was the location through which the new vision of nation and citizen was promoted to the new generation of students. As the colonial state invested in public schools, the total number of classrooms grew from 3,273 in 1930 to 4,310 by 1946, and the number of employed schoolteachers increased from 4,451 to 8,881.[6] The expansion of schools was intended to accommodate the growing school-age population and the greater demand for access to schools. The rapid expansion of the public school system, however, could not satisfy the growing demand.

The Department of Education reorganized in the 1940s and generated creative ways to provide schooling to the majority of the population through the founding of the community extension program. The extension program intended to reach a broader segment of rural communities, particularly adults, by providing greater access to educational films and radio programs. In the 1950s public schools also meant to prepare the working-class population for the radical changes the island was undergoing through the state-sponsored industrialization project known as Operation Bootstrap. Operation Serenity complemented Operation Bootstrap as an educational program that addressed the social and cultural changes rural students faced in new urban settings through migration and new household consumption patterns. Schools and classrooms in the 1940s and 1950s continued to be a central site through which the modern colonial state, the ELA, intended to promote its new cultural definition of Puerto Rican citizen. Schools, however, were also a location that students and parents, who identified with the discourse of progress and modernity promoted by Muñoz Marín, claimed as their own. It was through schools, or through appeals to access schools, that parents and students demanded the right to fully participate in the formation of the new, modern Puerto Rico of the 1950s.

While the historical scholarship of 1940s and 1950s Puerto Rico has critically examined the political maneuvering and economic projects born from that generation of colonial reformers, few have proposed an analysis of what the new "nation" meant for the nonelite. "The people" whom Muñoz Marín and the PPD targeted in the 1938 campaign, the working-class supporters of the PPD in the 1940s, were receptive to the new language of social justice, citizenship, and nation. At the same time, however, they generated high expectations of the newly founded colonial state. At the core of their definitions of the relationship between citizen and the colonial state was reciprocity. They demanded the right to access schools. Through the acquisition of public instruction they intended to improve their family's social position. As citizens, theirs was the right to gain literacy and a public education. When they demanded access to public schools in the 1940s and early 1950s, parents and students were also defining their rights as citizens, making their claims on the colonial state, seeking reciprocity. Colonial reformers were not the only historical actors crafting and imagining the modernizing intentions of the 1950s colonial state. This process was also defined and driven by the unflinching demands of parents and students through their sharp critiques against government corruption and inefficiency and by their claims on the state to fulfill its obligations and promises to its citizenry.

The contribution of this chapter, therefore, is twofold. First, it provides a close analysis of the "bottom-up" politics of the 1940s colonial state from the perspective of colonial citizens rather than state officials. It offers a critique of the colonial state through the analysis of the expectations of students and parents for access to public instruction. Second, the critique of the 1940s colonial state builds from the assumption that the PPD and the ELA were extensions of the history of colonial reform of the early twentieth century. A half century of negotiating imperial polices led to the founding of the PPD and the ELA. Neither represented a radical departure from the history of imperial policies.

LAS BECAS (THE SCHOLARSHIPS)

Carlos Maestre Serbiá of the Department of Education was appointed secretary of the new Central Scholarship Committee in 1949.[7] Each municipality founded a local scholarship committee, which selected, investigated, and ranked students and then submitted its recommendations to Maestre Serbiá in San Juan. Local scholarship committees were composed of prominent local educators and parents. The municipal superintendent of schools served as president and the school principal as secretary. The six additional members included the school director, the president of the parents' association, the president of the local chapter of the

Children's Red Cross, a social worker, and a teacher of vocational agriculture. Students who earned a 3.5 GPA or higher, were enrolled in public school, and demonstrated financial need were eligible for the competition. Scholarships were offered in three different categories: funds for clothing and shoes, sustenance, and transportation. The lucky winners received a one-time annual disbursement of $25. Archival documents suggest the legislature never allocated enough funds to award scholarships to all the children who met the criteria and appealed for funds. Only one in three of those nominated by local committees were ultimately selected by the central office.

The new scholarship program also generated greater bureaucracy within the Department of Education. The central scholarship committee established rules and regulations for local municipal committees. In May local committees requested application materials, which they filled out and returned to the department by August. That month, the central committee reviewed local recommendations and chose awardees. Local officials then notified student winners that they would be receiving the scholarship that school year. Within the boxes of mail and paper-work generated by this process are letters written by children, parents, and their allies (teachers, social workers, school principals) to the department or governor, letters containing appeals for funding that often fell outside the parameters of the scholarship committee. The funding of the new law and the scholarship committee bureaucracy inadvertently generated a process that recorded the voices, visions, and goals of children and parents. When they appealed for support, they made claims on the state as members of the "deserving poor," the constituency that the political leader Muñoz Marín had been addressing for years through political campaigns, radio, film, newspapers, and pamphlets. Children presented themselves first as citizens of the country, with rights and obligations. They emerge from the archives as political subjects that forced engagement with the colonial state of the late 1940s and early 1950s.

When the Department of Education advertised the new scholarship in the newspaper, El mundo, on December 1, 1949, it was immediately inundated with requests and appeals from students and parents. Many more children than the department could fund sent letters appealing for help. Noemí Reyes (pseudonym) of Barranquitas, a student, immediately wrote to inquire about any type of help that might be available from the department, whether or not she met scholarship requirements: "In yesterday's newspaper I learned that the Department of Instruction wishes to provide assistance to high school students who have not been able to continue their studies. I would like to kindly request an opportunity to apply."[8] Jorge Castro of Arecibo, a parent, wrote directly to the department seeking support for his daughter. Castro stated bluntly: "I appeal to you because I am a poor man and I must take advantage of the opportunity provided by the government of Puerto Rico. . . . School vacation is quickly approaching, and I do not have the means to provide for her. . . . Please help me in this request so that my daughter does not have to abandon her studies because of what I cannot offer her."[9]

Parents and students wrote the commissioner of education or appealed directly to the governor (don Luis) or his wife (doña Ines). Student and parent responses to the sudden opportunity to receive financial support to attend school were intense and sustained, suggesting that many members of the working class felt an urgency toward the opportunity and privilege of accessing education in the late 1940s and 1950s. For many of the nonelite and non–middle class, public school was a prohibitive expense.

This urgency, the appeal for support, and the demand for the state to intervene and fulfill its obligation to provide all of its citizens equal access to a public education are evident in the few letters that survived in the archives. The letters tell us much about the everyday struggles of the poor and working class. Just as powerfully, in their own words, the letter writers express how this struggle never impeded their intentions and ambitions to attend school. The letters document how students and parents persistently reached out to local and island representatives of the colonial state and the Department of Education and demanded they "do their part" and fulfill their promise to the poor by making schools accessible to all. In addition, students and parents deploy everyday definitions of honor in family, labor, and education as well as expressions of commitment to their community and nation. Students and parents describe the communities in which they lived, the relationships they established with teachers and other school staff, and the sacrifices extended families made to support the one or two children who were particularly gifted or showed promise for success in school.

Beyond the individual and personal requests, the appeals children and parents made as a group documented how the poor and working class maintained specific expectations from the colonial state of the late 1940s and early 1950s. The letters reproduced and were framed within a narrative that engaged the discourse and promises of Muñoz Marín and the PPD. Yet, more significantly, they suggest how the working class and poor were also empowered by that narrative, how they claimed its intentions as their own and used its promises to negotiate for their rights. The persistent demands, and the colonial state's inability to satisfy them, suggest how schools continued to serve as a central location where the state and its citizens negotiated the definitions of rights, obligations, and citizenship. Student demands daily tested the discursive promises for social justice and equality that Muñoz Marín and the PPD proposed for all Puerto Ricans in the late 1930s and 1940s.

LAS CARTAS (THE LETTERS)

What did students and parents write in their letters? What did they request? Individual letters appealed for financial support. While public school attendance was free, an education was not equally accessible to all. Going to school required resources to which the majority of the working class did not always have access—money for transportation, clothing and shoes, and/or school lunches. Students and parents wrote to express their commitment to attend school, to explain their family's financial restrictions, and to justify their expectations that the colonial state should intervene. They asked the state to help them in whatever capacity it could by providing scholarship money for transportation, clothing, shoes, food, and books. In their letters, they claimed equal access to schools as their right. They proposed the argument that if they did not have the material resources to gain and maintain access to schools, it then became the responsibility of the colonial state to intervene on their behalf.

Children and parents who were informed of the scholarship requirements or who had been in conversation with local school officials wrote the commissioner or governor to request specific types of support. One of the first obstacles students who lived in the countryside had to overcome was the cost of transportation. Parents had to pay for their children to be transported from their rural home to a more centralized rural school or to the only available school in the town center. This was a terrible expense, especially for families of agricultural workers who were seasonally employed. If families did not have funds to pay for transportation at the start of the school year, they turned to their community for informal sources of credit and lending. They borrowed money from friends, family, and *pudiente* (wealthy) members of the community. Nevertheless, not all families had access to informal sources of credit.

This was the challenge Diego López and his family faced in Aguada. In a letter to the commissioner, López explained that his father, "a poor cane cutter, does *not* earn enough to send me and my two siblings to school because I live in the country (rural), and transportation costs are high."[10] López, in his second year of high school, had applied twice for the scholarship, yet he had not been chosen. Nevertheless, he wrote to appeal with urgency, for soon he had to decide whether to withdraw from school because of his "terrible economic situation": "Father told me that if I do not receive the scholarship this year, he would not allow me to finish the school year, and I would not be allowed to return to school. I am very interested in school. In the future I would like to be able to help my parents and be a good citizen. Father does all he can so I can stay in school, but I know this is beyond his means."[11] Despite his father's sacrifices and best efforts, despite his commitment to attending school in the interests of and for the benefit of his family and community, López and many other children of agricultural workers lived under precarious conditions, on the verge of withdrawing from school because transportation costs were too high.

Letters requesting money to purchase school clothes and shoes was the second most common request. This was the reason Micael García of Arecibo wrote the

A schoolroom in a rural school, Cidra, Puerto Rico, January 1938. The chalkboard, bookshelf, wooden and iron desks, and new hardwood floors suggest it was a modern and recently constructed school. The feet of two children are visible. Both are barefoot.

commissioner. García's request was specific and direct. In 1949 he received the clothing and shoes scholarship, and "had it not been for the help you provided, I would not have been able to continue my studies." In 1950 he received the transportation scholarship instead. However, that was not enough support for him to stay in school. A third-year high school student in Arecibo, García explained: "I am so poor that . . . despite the fact that the municipality pays for my transportation costs, I can no longer attend because the school clothes I was able to purchase last year with your support are now useless."[12] García's case was typical of other students who did not have the resources to purchase the clothing and shoes required to attend school.

Sometimes students wrote the department because they had yet more immediate needs that fell under the sustenance scholarship option. Students were informed they had won the scholarship in August, which allowed them to make the decision to attend school for one more year, knowing they would be receiving financial support. Unfortunately, the Department of Education bureaucracy was slow to disburse student checks. Six months after being notified she would be receiving the scholarship, Cristal Osorio of Ceiba wrote to the department to inquire about the status of her check: "My father has been without work for three months. For this reason, I inform you that I do not know how I can attend school after the winter break. I am short of clothes and shoes. Plus, during the day at school I often feel dizzy because I have had very little food. Those are the only reasons that would force me to stay home and lose my studies. My only hope is to be able to help my parents in the future."[13] Students like Osorio were forced to make important decisions. Osorio understood that she was living under "poor conditions" and that her father's unemployment meant that necessities like food were limited. Without the immediate support of the Department of Education, she would be forced to withdraw from school. Luisa Belinda Alvarez from Bayamón appealed for a scholarship based on her hard work and financial need while highlighting that access to food was also a concern: "I am a girl who sacrifices in order to study. I have to leave for school without eating breakfast. And sometimes when I come home after school, I have to go to bed without dinner."[14] School social workers alerted department staff that children were not eating enough, were not able to concentrate or stay awake during classes, and could not afford to bring lunch with them to school. The most immediate need—food—was always present in student appeals to the Department of Education.

Children eligible to receive the scholarship requested assistance in these specific categories: transportation, clothing and shoes, and sustenance. However, children also wrote to appeal for a number of other immediate material necessities. Often these requests, unfortunately, arrived outside of application guidelines and funding deadlines. Students, therefore, only received a letter acknowledging their request and asking them to be in contact with local officials to apply the next academic year. This must have been of little consolation to Marisol Santiago of Aguada, who wrote the commissioner to inquire about the status of her scholarship application. She explained that she had already been forced to withdraw from a class because she could not purchase the required book. Without support from the department she would not be able to continue to attend: "About nine months ago I applied for a scholarship through your department. However, I have not yet heard anything about this matter. I am a high school student, and, as my scholarship application confirms, my financial situation is dire. My father passed away, and my mother does not have a job with which to help me purchase clothes, shoes, and books. Just recently, I had to withdraw from one of my classes because they required a book that I have not been able to purchase. I hope you will consider my application and send me the assistance you think I deserve."[15] When Santiago received no response, her mother pursued the case with a second letter, explaining that "my daughter has very good grades, and I understand that the department is awarding scholarships to poor children with a strong GPA." Despite her explanation that she was "a widow with five children to support and . . . only received assistance in the form of $7.50 from the government" and that "this is my eldest daughter at home and I am doing everything humanly possible so that she can study to see if one day we can leave behind this misery we are going through," the only response she received was the suggestion that she contact her local scholarship committee.[16] The documents do not answer whether Santiago graduated from high school, despite her and her mother's best efforts to secure financial support from the colonial state.

Students also wrote the commissioner and governor with general requests for support and assistance. Children who were on the verge of homelessness, living with extended family or community members, appealed for support. Their letters revealed such financial and familial instability that, although they did not receive scholarship money, their cases were turned over for investigation to local social workers and the social welfare department. This was the case of Ricardo Morales of Cidra. Morales was not living with his parents when he wrote Muñoz Marín for help. His father, he said, was a drunk and physically abusive of his mother and brothers. Morales's mother left home to work in the United States and distributed her children under the care of godparents and other family members.[17] However, when Morales wrote the governor, he was no longer living at the original residence his mother arranged with his godmother. Instead, the social worker reported that he had been traveling between towns looking for work. At night he slept on an abandoned ranch, and during the day he assisted the local pharmacist in exchange for clothing and food.[18] According to Morales, because the work was inconsistent, he usually spent most of the day wandering through town and begging for food: "Well, sometimes I do not go to school because I do not have anything to get me there. Sometimes I spend the day in the town without eating. This is why I need you to help me a little bit. Even if it's just to help me buy clothes, shoes, and food. Please do me that favor."[19] Morales wanted to attend school, but he required money to purchase clothing, shoes, and food. He concluded his letter with a postscript in which he declared: "I want to improve myself. Thank you."[20] This type of appeal required the intervention of social workers, for fundamentally, Morales was homeless and without adult supervision. In lieu of his parents, who were unavailable to satisfy his basic needs, Morales tried to get support and protection from the colonial state, specifically governor Muñoz Marín. The commissioner of education could offer little if any help, other than to refer the case to the social welfare department.

Finally, many students and parents wrote requesting simple forms of immediate help so they could continue to attend school. Whether or not they were eligible for this particular scholarship, they wrote because they needed urgent assistance and they were on the verge of withdrawing. This is the simplicity and directness Gabriel Pérez of Isla Verde articulated in his brief letter to the commissioner. Pérez did not appeal for a scholarship but rather for a pair of shoes. He was not asking the governor and the state to address the structural problems that he reported left his parents unemployed. He simply wanted to continue to attend school but could not do so without shoes. At his parents' behest, he would be forced to withdraw unless someone from San Juan could help him. Pérez wrote: "My dear sir: This note is to inform you that I am a poor student that needs your help. My name is Gabriel Pérez and I am in the ninth grade. I have not attended school for the last three days because I do not have shoes. Well, my parents are not working right now. There are no jobs in our community [caserío (shantytown)]. . . . Sir, I wish you could see my situation from my perspective and that you would send me a pair of shoes because I want to study. My parents are asking me to leave school, but I pray to God that one day I can be of use to society."[21]

Student letters represented a variety of direct requests for support from the colonial state. Poor students and parents struggled to find ways to cover basic school expenses. Public school was free but nevertheless prohibitive for the poor and working class who did not have the resources to pay for clothing, shoes, books, and transportation. They turned for support to representatives of the colonial state—the commissioner of education and the governor. They frankly and honestly stated their case and, in turn, expected due attention and a quick and efficient response.

POOR BUT NO ORPHAN: REPRESENTATIONS OF
SELF, FAMILY, AND COMMUNITY

When parents and students wrote the commissioner or the governor requesting support, they were careful to present themselves in humble yet honorable terms. They were honest and frank about their family's limited material and financial resources. When mothers wrote to the commissioner or directly to doña Ines, they explained that they were widows or that their husbands were incapacitated and could not work. Fathers, especially the ones who could not work, wrote and requested support for their children. Students wrote when they felt their parents did not have the financial resources to support them or as a challenge to their parents' request that they withdraw from school.

Students, however, were careful to express honor and respect for their parents. If the father was employed, the child explained that despite his labor and commitment to supporting the child's education, the family's living expenses exceeded the father's wages. A working-class parent who elected to send his or her child to school was making the sacrifice to forgo that child's labor in the home, field, or factory and instead to provide for the additional expenses the child's schooling incurred. Students acknowledged that their parents were doing everything possible to keep them in school but that it was simply no longer feasible. Student stories suggest that despite the number of schools the Department of Education founded throughout the island in the 1940s, the high cost of living, low wages, and poverty of the majority of laborers, particularly rural wage workers, made attending public schools prohibitive for the majority of the poor and a privilege of the middle class and elite.

Letters suggest, for example, great differences in opportunities for the children of the rural laborer and the artisan, especially when the parent wanted to send more than one child to school. Marisela Espinoza of Aguadilla was married to an artisan, a carpenter. Together they were supporting three children through school. Their eldest daughter was in her final year in the social work program at the University of Puerto Rico. Espinoza was inquiring about a change in her daughter's scholarship, a change that denied her a monthly stipend due to low grades. Without the support, her daughter would not be able to finish her degree: "The only one who works in this house is my husband. He is a carpenter and does not have permanent work. When he finds work, he earns $12 to $15 per week. We are a family of eight with three children in school, one in high school, one at university, and one in elementary school. For this reason, unless you do something to help my daughter, she will have wasted her years at school. Please investigate this case further. God will repay you."[22] Although Espinoza struggled to keep her children in school, children of artisans had more opportunity to attend than those of the working class or poor.

Compare Espinoza's appeal to the one Pedro Sánchez of Caguas made to the commissioner. Sánchez explained that he had to choose which two of his four daughters he could send to school the next academic year:

> Distinguished sir, I regret to bother you, however, the urgency of our situation forces me to demand your attention. I am a father and head of household. For more than four years now I have been suffering from a chronic disease that affects both of my legs. For this reason, I am physically unable to work. Out of the four daughters I now have in school, I plan to send two of them next year. And for this I need your help. I want my eldest daughter, who will begin her fourth year of high school, to finish her studies. My other daughter is going into ninth grade and wants to study sewing. It is impossible for me to help them the way I wish I could. This is why I turn to you, shelter my hopes in you. I hope you will give this case the attention it deserves. I will remain eternally grateful.[23]

While class differences shaped children's opportunities, parent letters also attest to how parents never mediated the value they placed on acquiring an education.

If the parent of the child was not employed, the author of the letter was careful to provide a clear explanation. There were no jobs in Pérez's neighborhood, Sánchez was physically incapacitated, and Santiago's mother was a widow. Parents wanted no confusion about their family's intention to work and provide for themselves. When they wrote, they clarified any misunderstandings from previous letters and offered personal references to confirm the claims about their family's condition. This was the intention of Dionisia Cruz of Adjuntas. Cruz wrote to inquire whether her son might qualify to receive some assistance to attend school. She realized, however, that a misunderstanding had developed at some point and that administrators were making reference to her son as a *huérfano de padre*. Cruz wanted to clarify that while her son was poor, he was no orphan. She wrote to the commissioner of education:

> In a copy of a letter sent by Juana Rodríguez Mundo, the director of Economic Assistance at the UPR, to you regarding my son . . . I noticed an error or misinterpretation. She reports that my son's father passed away [*huérfano de padre*]. Luckily, that is not the case. His father is alive. But he is a veteran of the First World War and is 100 percent physically incapacitated. He receives a $60 pension from the federal government, which serves as our only stable source of income. We survive on that and with the little bit I earn through my labors. Because of these conditions, I must

secure a scholarship for my son. He is so interested in going to school, but our resources do not allow for it. I wish to make this clarification now to avoid problems in the future. My son is not an orphan, he is just poor.[24]

Cruz's letter suggests, like many others, that the working poor who appealed to the state to support their right to attend public school did so without compromising their identity, their claims to honor in their family units, their history of having served their country and nation. Cruz's letter proposed that while she might be poor, she had very important things in her life—an intelligent and ambitious son and a husband who was an injured war veteran. Cruz's clarifications were typical of other letters by parents who invited investigations into their family's financial conditions or who provided the names of school principals and town mayors as personal references who could testify in support of their claims.

The way children and parents crafted their letters suggests they only appealed for help from the colonial state when parents were physically incapable of working, earning wages, and sending their children to school. They wrote as a last resort when they could not turn elsewhere for help. This was how Esperanza Martínez from Camuy explained her case to the governor: "I respectfully address you to let you know that I am a student at the José Julián Acosta school in Camuy. And because I am an orphan, I cannot continue my studies, for I am poor. My hopes and dreams are to study. I want to be able to work in the future to help my little brother, who is four and a half years old. My father died about three and a half years ago and my mom about two and a half. Since then I have been living with my uncles. I am only 15 years old and will enter third grade. I hope that you will attend to my case as quickly as possible."[25] Mártinez proposed the argument that she must study if she were ever going to be capable of providing a better life for herself and her younger brother. Letters appealing to the commissioner and governor were framed by the language of honor, the work ethic, and the struggle to attain more than what was accessible to them given the material limitations of their class.

As they appealed for support, they presented their case with humility and honor while demonstrating pride in family and their academic achievements. Parents noted that their daughters were "brilliant," that their child had "earned" the scholarship, and that they were "claiming their daughter's right to a scholarship."[26] Estefania Hernández of Aibonito sent a telegram to the commissioner of education because she believed her daughter had negligently been overlooked for the scholarship. She was direct and to the point: her daughter was "very poor with brilliant grades. I claim my daughter's rights. Especially because she does not have a father and I do not have the means to provide for her education."[27]

When Sofía Rodríguez of Cayey wrote to inquire about when her daughter's scholarship check would be disbursed, she highlighted that her daughter had earned the scholarship "because she was so intelligent."[28] In his appeal, López boldly stated: "I believe I deserve the scholarship because my grades are more than satisfactory."[29] Parents were humbled by the limitations of their class but never wavered in their intention to send their children to school, and they asked for support when they knew they could not provide for their children. Children declared their intention to better themselves, provide for their siblings, and help their parents. Together these letters proposed the argument that, as citizens, parents and students claimed their right to attend schools, to become productive citizens, and to contribute to their community and "maybe even their country."[30] They saw themselves as worthy of requesting and receiving the support of the colonial state, for they were proud of their efforts and achievements.

"Do Your Part": Student Demands on the State

Student demands on the state were greater than individual requests for scholarship and funds. As a group, this generation of schoolchildren was asking the colonial state to "do its part"—to follow through on its promises to support the poor and make it possible for them to exercise their full citizenship rights by attending public school. None accepted that poverty should keep them out of school, and the state had the responsibility to mediate that. When schoolchildren in particular wrote directly to the governor for help, they expected him to understand the type of poverty they lived in, especially in the countryside.

Ernesto Castro of Barranquitas eloquently demonstrated this level of intimacy between himself, whom he designated as a representative of the poor, and the governor: "Dear don Luis: First, let me offer you my most cordial and fraternal greetings. I wish to share with you a problem related to my school career, whose solution will depend on the attention you are able to provide. I refer to the problem that most students, who are inspired by their ambition to succeed and to help their family and community and to create their future, face. He finds himself hindered by the economic situation he was born into, as a member of a poor and humble family."[31] Castro intended to remind Muñoz Marín that his plight was the same as that of many other poor children. They wrote to Muñoz Marín as members of the poor and expected him to respond in the capacity he had cultivated in his speeches as the "father of the poor." Castro had an ambition to attend school, and it was, therefore, in the interests of Muñoz Marín to support him. He called on the governor to do his part by contacting the community of leaders in the colonial state to facilitate for Castro the help he required: "And this being my economic situation, I beg you to generously take interest and provide whatever financial assistance you or your friends or a social welfare institution can provide, so that I can continue to study, which is my goal. I would appreciate your prompt response so that I can be assured that my simple and humble request has found a happy reception. I thank you with anticipation for the great favor that I hope you have the goodness to grant me."[32] Castro's letter testified to how children advocated for themselves by crafting an appeal for assistance that employed Muñoz Marín's discourse of the poor and demanded help from the governor (and his friends).

Students also offered enticements and negotiations they were sure would get the attention of Muñoz Marín. Martínez, the orphan from Camuy, made a proposition to the governor that reflected the familial intimacy children often displayed in their letters to Muñoz Marín. After explaining that she and her brother were orphans who had been taken in by her uncle, she offered the governor a deal. Martínez wrote under the assumption that the governor would be invested in supporting her intention to study: "I hope you will address my problem as quickly as possible. I believe that today he who studies has the right to work. That is why I think you, our governor, should be interested in helping." She confessed that her school grades averaged from Bs to Cs. However, she promised Muñoz Marín that if he took an interest in her case, "by next year, I will earn As and Bs. And at the end of each semester I promise to send you my report card, signed by the principal of my school."[33] Through this personal offer—to improve her grades, report directly to the governor, and accept him as accountable for her success—she assumed the right to establish a personal relationship with Muñoz Marín. She responded to the discursive assertion he had established—that he was the father of the poor—and made claims on that relationship.

Martínez's assumption that, as a poor child and citizen, she had a right to establish a personal relationship with Muñoz Marín was typical rather than exceptional. Esteban Castillo from Coamo not only assumed this personal connection to Muñoz Marín but made requests of the governor as he would have of any family or community member who had the means and interest to support his studies:

Dear governor: The purpose of this letter is to tell you that I am a sixth-grade student who has very good grades in all of my classes. My parents are very poor and do not have the means to send me to school, to buy me the clothes and notebooks that I need. I am interested in continuing my studies. I very much like painting. But I do not have the resources to stay in school. I would like for you to do your part and help me somehow. Maybe that way in the future I will be one of the island's distinguished men. I hope you will help me.[34]

Castillo was direct—he expected the governor to do his part, contribute, cooperate. Students demanded this exchange from Muñoz Marín because they believed, according to their letters, that together they would create tomorrow's citizens. Castillo and Martínez were demanding reciprocity. They maintained expectations of the governor, understood they were together in a "national" struggle for the improvement of the poor and of Puerto Rico. When the children understood their parents could not do more, they demanded Muñoz Marín intervene.

In their writings, children deployed the very concepts that Muñoz Marín had proposed during the election campaign to gain their parents' support—the idea of the productive citizen who contributed to the community and the greater good of the *patria*. Students had also heard Muñoz Marín's campaign message. Their letters intended to remind Muñoz Marín of his promises to and visions for the poor. Students reported to him and described how they had done everything they could but could not get further without his help. Their appeal, their expectation that Muñoz Marín would contribute, would meet them halfway, was a call for the colonial state to be responsive to the needs of the poor. Their letters proposed that, working together as a community of citizens, they could fulfill their own ambitions and Muñoz Marín's vision for Puerto Rico. This was a collective vision.

Children coming home from school on a road near Manatí, Puerto Rico, December 1941.

Agustina Fuentes of Cayey wrote a brief letter that clearly articulated this relationship between students, Muñoz Marín, and the *patria*. She began by using
language that established familiarity and deference: "Dear sir and governor, I
pray this letter finds you in perfect health and in the company of your dear family." She humbly apologized for her "forwardness" and stated her situation: "Well,
I have dared to contact you myself directly, although I am a student, because
I need to share with you my problem. I am a young lady, 17 years old, in ninth
grade. I want to continue studying through my fourth year of high school, for I
want to be a registered nurse. My parents do not have the economic means to
help me." Fuentes wanted to attend high school, her parents could not support
her, but she had faith that Muñoz Marín would: "I want to be successful with your
help. I will accept any help you can provide. And I will be deeply grateful because
I am really in a quite difficult situation. I want to succeed and one day declare,
'I, Agustina Fuentes, was able to succeed thanks to the help of our governor, who
was the bread of the poor.'" Fuentes had faith that her success and her dreams
could be attained thanks to the generosity and support of Muñoz Marín. She concluded the letter by restating their assumed intimate and familial relationship:
"I remain your humble servant and friend. You are like a father to us."[35]

Students were not passively absorbing political discourses; rather, they were
dreamers, workers, citizens, and intellectuals. In their letters, fathers and mothers
do not fail, as teachers had proposed in the 1910s and 1920s. Instead, parents are
prevented from providing all they desire, despite their formidable efforts. It then
became the responsibility of the state to contribute to familial, community, and
national progress. Students defined a new kind of progress for the *patria*. They
established a familial partnership with Muñoz Marín and the colonial state. Parents were already productive citizens. Schools were not creating them. Instead,
schools allowed students to reach their full potential. The arguments students and
parents proposed undermined some of the characterizations articulated by educators in the 1910s and 1920s, suggesting that children came from fragile homes
with allegedly degenerate fathers and mothers.

The Colonial State's Response

How did the state respond to the multiple and persistent requests of the many students and parents who needed urgent financial support to attend public schools?
State responses, despite the good intentions of the scholarship and its administrators, were at best underwhelming, ineffective, distant, and disappointing. Most
of the requests, despite the urgency portrayed in the letters, received the standard
response. Secretary Maestre Serbiá wrote the customary and solemn reply. The

department could not provide anything other than advice. Students were directed to contact the local scholarship committee and request that their names be placed on the list of applicants for the next academic year. We can only imagine that students found this response to a personal appeal insufficient and disappointing. This was the response Pérez, who wrote the letter requesting the commissioner to send him a pair of shoes, received two months after making his request.

Students, parents, and staff became increasingly aware of the inefficiency and ineffectiveness of the state as the academic year progressed. Students received notification in August that they had been awarded the scholarship. For many, this news allowed them to make the decision to attend school one more year instead of withdrawing and joining the labor force. Because scholarship checks did not arrive immediately, however, students and parents were forced to turn to their informal community sources of lending and credit. They borrowed money to pay for transportation, or they bought clothing and supplies on credit. Families covered school expenses as best they could and anxiously waited for the scholarship check to arrive.

However, some years it took the staff at the Department of Education six to eight months to process the applications and disburse students' checks. When students had not yet received their checks by December or even March of the spring semester, they found themselves in a difficult situation. By then creditors had come to collect on their debts. Without the resources to pay back the money borrowed, students anxiously wrote to the commissioner, demanding that their checks be disbursed immediately. Letters written by López and García were typical of the majority of scholarship recipients who inquired about their checks. They wrote when they were on the verge of withdrawing from school. They begged for confirmation that the Department of Education was going to follow through on its promises.

The case of Alberto Negrón from Bayamón demonstrates the hardships the late disbursement of checks caused students and their families as well as the resourcefulness of students who were not shy in their demands for their rightful share from the Department of Education. In October of the school year, Negrón wrote his first inquiry to the commissioner of education: "Dear sir: I write to inform you that although I am a scholarship student, we are two months into the school year and I have not yet received my scholarship. I have to purchase my tickets [transportation] every day and I do not have the money. For this reason, I have had to miss several days of school. These absences are affecting my grade and will ruin my academic record. . . . I think it best that you send my scholarship money, if you can, at the beginning of the school year. When you delay months in sending us our money . . . we have to find a way to cover the expenses of transportation, clothes, and other things. But we do not have those resources and are forced to miss school and eventually to abandon it altogether."[36] Negrón's appeal to the commissioner was clear: when checks were late, students had to borrow money to acquire the supplies and expenses required to attend school. But some students did not have access to local and informal credit and were forced to withdraw. The late disbursement of checks was a hardship for students, and, Negrón suggested, the department should reconsider the way it processed scholarships in order to better address students' needs.

On October 10 Secretary Maestre Serbiá responded to Negrón's letter, explaining that it took the department time to process the checks of so many students throughout the island. Maestre Serbiá concluded his letter with the suggestion that Negrón "kindly wait a bit longer."[37] Two months later, however, the scholarship check had still not arrived. Negrón's father visited the school social worker, Graciela Rivera Ávila, to inquire about the status of the check. The social worker, who had little information for Negrón's father, wrote secretary Maestre Serbiá to investigate the case: "The father . . . informed us that his son has not received the money assigned to him in the scholarship. I know well and can attest to the precarious economic situation that his family is going through as well as the sacrifices they make so that Alberto can continue in school. This is why I thought it best I write, to get to the root of this delay."[38]

Secretary Maestre Serbiá replied that he expected checks to be disbursed by December 15.[39] Two weeks later, on December 26, when the check had not yet arrived, Negrón wrote a second letter to Secretary Maestre Serbiá. Negrón apologized for "bothering" Maestre Serbiá a second time, but Negrón had not yet received his check, and at this point in the academic year, he simply wanted confirmation of whether or not he was to receive it. If not, he needed to immediately withdraw from school: "I need to know if the scholarship has not been approved so I can abandon school. If it is approved, I wish to know why you have not sent me my money. They have been coming to collect the money I borrowed to pay for my tickets [transportation]. Plus, I need to purchase clothes and shoes in order to attend class. Without the scholarship money, I must immediately withdraw from school, because my economic condition is somewhat dire. I hope you will forgive me for bothering you. I expect a quick response."[40]

This was the predicament in which many scholarship students found themselves. Six months into the school year, when they had not yet received their scholarship check, they were faced with creditors who came to collect debts, they lacked the funds to purchase their school supplies (including food), and they did not have the privilege of time to attend one more semester in case checks arrived. It was at this point, faced with the inefficiency and unresponsiveness of the

Department of Education, that working-class students were forced to withdraw from school. Despite Negrón's two letters, his father's inquiry, and the social worker's intervention, the Bayamón school district scholarship checks were not disbursed until March of that academic year. The inefficiency and bureaucracy of the Department of Education in the late 1940s and early 1950s must have left students and parents, like Negrón and maybe Fuentes, disillusioned with the promises of the colonial state.

Not all students were as deferential and respectful in their letters of inquiry to Maestre Serbiá. Some were simply indignant at the inefficiency of the Department of Education and defiant over the consequences of the late disbursement of checks. Rosario Gallardo of Gurabo proved to be as resourceful as Negrón and his father in her determination to inquire about the status of her scholarship check. Gallardo was granted a scholarship in the fall of 1950, but her file traveled a different bureaucratic route. Her original scholarship, funded by the University of Puerto Rico, was transferred to the new scholarship program in the Department of Education. This caused some delays in the disbursement of her check that fall semester. Meanwhile, the rest of the scholarship students in Gurabo, except Gallardo, had received their checks. Gallardo began by inquiring at the Student Services Office at the University of Puerto Rico, which forwarded her letters to the Department of Education. In her December 22, 1950, letter to the Student Services Office, Gallardo expressed anxiety and concern about not being able to repay the money she had borrowed for school expenses. She needed her scholarship check immediately: "Right now I spend $1 per week on transportation and other school expenses. You have access to my application materials, which confirm that my family does not earn enough to pay for these expenses. . . . I hope you will do everything in your power to help me receive that money, because I owe all of it for the [bus] tickets. I borrowed this money because of the promise that I was receiving the scholarship. How can you do this to me now? I hope you will do everything within your reach to help my case."[41]

Two weeks later, her request not attended to, Gallardo wrote a second letter directly to the Department of Education. More upset than ever, she was worried that her file had been overlooked. It was January, and Gallardo felt burdened by debt collectors, by her father's unemployment, by the economic hardship she and her family had to endure. On January 5, 1951, she shared these concerns with the commissioner of education and demanded an explanation for what she understood to be the department's negligence.

Dear Sir, I write to inquire as to why my scholarship was not disbursed in December 1950, as expected. I have the right to inquire about my case, since the rest of the students received their scholarship checks. I am as poor, maybe even more poor than, some of the students who have already received their money. I barely get by [*estudiando a pulmón*]. My dad was a day laborer during the cane season. The rest of the year we hardly survive. He is no longer a cane cutter because he fell ill and can no longer work. We were defending ourselves with the insurance money he received. But, now that he cannot work, what will become of us? At least I had the scholarship money coming, which could help me pay for transportation and other school expenses. What can I do now that you have taken away that money without any explanation? I expect that if you had a reason for taking it away from me, you should have notified me a long time ago. Now, I owe that money and have no hope of paying it back. If you don't believe what I am describing to you, you are welcome to come visit our home.[42]

Gallardo, dismayed by the department's inefficiency, offered the critique that bureaucratic negligence had generated great hardship and stress for her and her family. She demanded her rightful share: "I am as poor, maybe even more poor than, some of the students who have already received their money." Gallardo had come to believe that the Department of Education's promise to fund scholarships was simply a farce, an abuse of trust, a broken contract.

Finally, five days later, on January 10, Secretary Maestre Serbiá responded to Gallardo's inquiries. Her file had been reviewed, all paperwork was now in order, and her check was in the mail. It was exceptional that her complaints and demands had generated a response from the department. However, Maestre Serbiá offered Gallardo a suggestion at the conclusion of his letter: "You have the right to inquire why your check was not disbursed with the rest of the students in your school. It is, nevertheless, important that you remain calm and make your request with a modicum of respect."[43] Maestre Serbiá, like other administrators, demanded that students demonstrate respect and decorum in their exchanges with department staff. The comment also suggested, however, that he did not empathize with the anxiety and stress students and their families experienced as they waited for the department to disburse scholarship checks, a period that forced them to contemplate the possibility that they might soon have to withdraw from school altogether.

The bureaucracy of the department, the delays in the disbursement of checks, forced students to be as resourceful as possible. Negrón's father sought the support of the school social worker. Gallardo wrote to staff at both the University of Puerto Rico and the Department of Education until her case was resolved. Student questions and demands also forced school staff, like principals, social workers, and teachers, to serve as allies in students' negotiations with the department.

Letters written by social workers, for example, attest to the persistent demands students made on the colonial state to keep its promises and follow through on the disbursement of student checks. Aurora Maldonado, the vocational counselor in the town of Barceloneta, wrote Maestre Serbiá in February of the school year. She was concerned that, six months into the school year, the children in her school district had not yet received their scholarship checks: "I would appreciate an explanation as to why the students who were awarded a scholarship in this school have not yet received anything. They visit my office every day and ask me about it. I cannot provide them with a satisfactory response."[44]

Local scholarship committee members advocated for their students in other ways. María Arroyo, the superintendent of schools in Barranquitas, for example, wrote the Department of Education to challenge the small number of scholarships granted to her school district. She and the committee, aware that the legislature had allocated $40,000 to be distributed in scholarships that year, had estimated that the town of Barranquitas had the right to more than three scholarships. Arroyo and the scholarship committee questioned the fairness of the distribution of scholarships and asked that the department reconsider the number made available for Barranquitas: "The Barranquitas Scholarship Committee has asked me to bring to your attention our request that the final decision by the Central Scholarship Committee about the number of scholarships made available to our town be reconsidered, considering the total amount of funds designated island wide. . . . We have heard from unofficial sources that other towns with similar school enrollment numbers as ours were awarded two middle school and two elementary school scholarships."[45]

The Department of Education was unable to respond to all the requests it received for support. Some letters attested to how local school administrators found other ways to satisfy the needs of their constituencies. This was how Pedro Sánchez's appeal was resolved. Sánchez, the *padre de familia* who wrote the commissioner for help because he had to send two of his four daughters to school, did not receive support from the Department of Education. However, Charles Miner, the superintendent of schools in Caguas, was able to secure funds to help Sánchez purchase books so that his daughters could attend school. In his letter updating the commissioner about the case, Miner did not describe how he acquired the money or who donated the support. Nevertheless, Miner's letter suggests that in some cases school administrators worked outside the limits of the Department of Education to address the demands of their students.[46]

Finally, when students did not get results through local channels, they mobilized as a group and appealed to the commissioner of education. This was the case of the six scholarship students in Guayama in the fall of 1949. Four months into the school year, the students had not yet received their scholarship checks. Therefore, on December 7 they sent a letter of inquiry, signed on behalf of the "Scholarship Students of Guayama," to the commissioner.[47] They received a response promising the checks would be in the mail as of December 15. The students' letter did not survive in the archives. Unfortunately, we do not know how they presented their case. However, the archives document that, sadly, the checks did not arrive in December as promised, because in March 1950, Thayda Rivera, a visiting teacher in Guayama, wrote the commissioner one more time: "The Guayama students who were awarded scholarships by the Department of Instruction but who have not yet received their money stop by my office every day to ask when their money will arrive, since a few of the students have already received checks. They are anxious to know when they will receive theirs. In general, they are very poor and have spent the entire school year waiting for that assistance, acquiring debts to pay for their school expenses, under the belief that they will receive their scholarship checks."[48] The visiting teacher's letter attested to the children's persistent daily inquiries about the status of their checks as well as to the financially precarious condition most had to endure. The Guayama example documents the resourcefulness of students and their allies as they struggled to hold the state accountable for its promises to make public instruction available to all. It also attests to the solidarity children developed in the face of the department's inefficiency and bureaucracy. Their persistent inquiries about the status of their checks forced first the superintendent of the school district and second a visiting teacher to intervene on their behalf.

Student pleas and demonstrations of solidarity, however, also suggest that, despite its best intentions, the colonial state of the late 1940s and early 1950s was not capable of delivering on its promises to the poor and working class. Letters in the archives not only document students' desperation and urgency as they inquired about the status of scholarship checks. They also record the choices many scholarship students made when checks arrived late. Often, local scholarship committees returned checks to the Department of Education and explained that male students, like Mateo Cristóbal of Fajardo, had dropped out of school to join the US Army.[49] The example of Julián Esteves of Vieques attested to the mobility of working-class families. The Vieques committee reported that, by the time the check arrived, his family had moved to the neighboring island of Santa Cruz in search of work.[50] Young girls like Carolina Hernández of Bayamón were forced to leave their homes and live with extended family, where they exchanged domestic labor for food and housing. This was the explanation Cecilia Rivera, the school social worker, provided when she returned Hernández's check: "We regret to return the $25 check. . . . When we attempted to locate her and inquired about her family, we learned that the child did not return to school at the beginning of this year. She was adopted by an uncle, who in exchange for providing her sustenance, requires her domestic services." Hernández's mother proved unable to care for her, for the mother "is insane, wandering the streets." Rivera powerfully and simply acknowledged the decision Hernández had to make: "The child was lucky to find a home that opened its doors to her, and she must secure that, even if in exchange she sacrifices the opportunity to receive an education."[51] Finally, local committees wrote many letters to the central scholarship office reporting that the scholarship recipient had withdrawn from school by the time the check arrived.

The limited state response to the constant and persistent student appeals suggests that a longer-term and broader consequence was a redefinition of the relationship between citizens (students, parents, educators) and the colonial state (the Department of Education). Student letters initially highlighted an awareness of a personal and familial relationship with the colonial state's main representative, Muñoz Marín. However, as a result of the unresponsiveness and inefficiency of the department, student letters reflected a sense of disillusionment and disappointment. Students and parents, as they struggled to find support for their right to attend public school, also recognized the limits of the colonial state. It was incapable of delivering the services and support that it had promised through its popular campaign since the late 1930s.

Conclusion

The brief letters written by students and their parents tell us much about the relationship between working families, public schools, and the colonial state in the late 1940s and early 1950s.

First, the rights of the poor defined by Muñoz Marín and the PPD in 1940 were at the core of students' letters. Significantly, however, student expectations and demands suggest that they too were redefining the concept of citizen and deploying what they understood to be their right—access to public schools. Students and their families located access to public schools at the top of their agendas. They valued education as a requirement for better employment and for the ability to contribute to their families, communities, and country in the future.

Second, the working class and poor saw it as the responsibility of the colonial state to support their right to attend school. The wages earned by many working-class families were insufficient to cover household expenses. The additional costs of attending school, in the form of transportation, clothing, shoes, and supplies, made it financially prohibitive for many. However, students and parents argued that this did not deny them the right to attend school. Overcoming that gap in income became the responsibility of the colonial state. Its representatives had to intervene to make sure that the state's promise of the right of all to attend school was fulfilled.

Third, the persistent demands of the working class to access schools might have forced the colonial state to reevaluate its commitment to public instruction, to imagine ways to expand services and access, to try to become more efficient and responsive to student needs, although it is difficult to measure and evaluate these changes. Working-class students, as well as their parents and allies, every day held the representatives of the colonial state accountable for their promises.

Nevertheless, the colonial state of the 1940s and 1950s demonstrated great commitment to the expansion of public schools. The social justice agenda of Muñoz Marín and the PPD promised the poor the right to access schools. Despite its best intentions, nonetheless, the colonial state was incapable of fulfilling its promises. It could not satisfy popular demand for public schools, for access to teachers, for scholarships, for shoes. It could not, ultimately, help generate enough jobs and wages to allow working families to provide the funds required to cover school expenses. Nevertheless, the state was able to help select one thousand scholarship recipients each year. While the Department of Education helped the lucky few finish their degrees when they otherwise might not have been able to, its inefficiency suggested an inability to respond to the demands of the majority of requests it received. Students and parents, unable to secure financial support or to wait for the department bureaucracy to disburse scholarship checks, likely made the difficult and painful decision to withdraw from school.

Finally, student letters suggest that schools represented a critical location through which the citizenry and the colonial state came together. Citizens made demands for access to education. They consistently held the state accountable for its promises to the poor. It was a site through which the citizens and the state daily negotiated their rights and responsibilities. This was a heritage of early twentieth-century politics when teachers and others incessantly negotiated their visions with the requirements of the colonial state.

Education, Nation, and Empire

EDUCATION AND STATE IN LATIN AMERICA AND THE CARIBBEAN

Twentieth-century Latin American nation-building projects looked to schools and teachers.[1] The practice of defining national identities, forging citizens, and establishing the relationship between citizen and state required the collaboration of teachers and schools. It was in the classroom that teachers—civil servants incorporated into federal governments—daily practiced nation building. Schools were central, in particular, to new revolutionary states that sought to consolidate and institutionalize national ideologies. For example, secular schools and federal teachers were at the core of nation-building goals in 1930s and 1940s Mexico. It was through the classroom that revolutionary Mexico would "form a new state."[2] The new Cuban revolutionary state of the 1960s and the Sandinista Nicaraguan state in the early 1980s prioritized literacy and public schools.[3] Newly founded revolutionary governments partially fulfilled their promises of social justice to their supporters and citizens by prioritizing adult literacy, rural education, and basic instruction.

Historians of modern Mexico proposed the framework for understanding the relationship between schools and the modern state.[4] Mexico in the 1930s and 1940s personified the negotiation between state and citizen, between federal intentions and local demands. The new Cardenista administration of the 1930s and 1940s sought the consolidation of the nation through the expansion of secular schools. The process of founding new schools throughout the vast regions of Mexico was intended to cultivate a sense of belonging to the nation among its citizens. They imagined that territorial consolidation could be accomplished through schools. The diverse regions of Mexico could be incorporated under one flag. Defining national boundaries and ideologies in the postrevolutionary period also implied promoting a new "racial" definition of citizen, a definition informed by the intellectual constructions of *mestizaje*. Elite intellectuals, based in the central Distrito Federal, imagined Mexico's regions were occupied by "racial others" of various indigenous heritages. For intellectuals in the service of the new state and nation, the question became how to transform the "internal" racial others into modern, progressive, and constructive citizens of the unified nation. Elite educators found promise in the new generation of teachers that was deployed across the nation. Teachers were charged with bringing modern visions of citizen and nation, as defined by elite intellectuals in Mexico City, to rural areas. In this way, they contributed to the process of creating modern citizens who were invested in supporting the new nation-state. The intention of the new revolutionary state was to consolidate the nation, integrate regions under one flag, promote a racial vision of the modern citizen, and do so through the expanding authority of the central state.

At the same time, however, Mexican history documents how central state visions were deeply challenged by local communities. While some embraced the promises that modern forms of education might have potentially brought to their communities, others deeply resented how elite ideologies that originated in the Federal District served to undermine local understandings of religion, family, and honor. Local communities and actors were shaped by specific histories. Deeply held religious or patriarchal beliefs could not be supplanted by the ideas promoted by "outsiders" or from the "top down." Local reactions to federal policy were informed by a range of factors, including the entrenchment of religion in communities, how indigenous and ethnic identities were embedded in local contexts, and the level of suspicion toward federal policy or toward the intentions of those from outside the region. Teacher practices, their professionalism and openness (or lack thereof) to local demands and concerns, also shaped the process. While some communities rejected national visions and projects, others saw the opportunity to promote their local agendas through the school and found ways to appropriate and redefine the role of secular education in communities. In this way, teachers and local actors were actively engaged in the hegemonic processes that informed nation building.

Access to public schools was also at the core of the Cuban state's vision of social justice. The Cuban Revolution of 1959 and the process of consolidating and institutionalizing the new revolutionary state in the 1960s faced a set of international challenges different from those posed to the Cárdenas administration a generation earlier. Nevertheless, when the new Cuban state committed to battle the nation's illiteracy rate, especially adult illiteracy, it engaged in nation-building practices similar to those of Mexico. Combating illiteracy was fundamental to the state's vision to "uplift" the new Cuban citizen—to forge the "new man." In the early stages of Cuba's successful popular literacy campaign, young teachers and others volunteered to serve the new nation by traveling from Havana to rural provinces, taking residence with a rural family, and teaching literacy to both young children and adults. As middle-class teachers increasingly abandoned the island in the 1960s, however, other literate professionals were required to contribute to the national project by teaching literacy. Young teachers taught both literacy and state ideology from the speeches and writings of Ernesto Guevara's *Venceremos* (We will win).[5]

Cuba's literacy campaign shared two practices with Mexico's school project. In both countries, schools were in the service of the nation. Teaching literacy meant promoting state ideology. This was a requirement in the process of forging citizens. A socialist education became a foundation of adult literacy and children's elementary education. In addition, however, as the new revolutionary state engaged in the rapid expansion of secular schools, it "discovered" its rural areas. Teachers, the new state agents, were young men and women, often of middle-class or intermediate backgrounds, raised in towns and cities. Often it was these urban teachers, deployed to rural areas, who were awakened to the material challenges of rural life. It was through their eyes that the urban middle classes and elites learned of housing and work conditions in rural areas. In this way, the expansion of schools and literacy campaigns also served to educate more privileged urban citizens to the material realities of rural life and to the challenges that many of the new nation's citizens faced.

The nation's commitment to rural areas was also at the heart of Nicaragua's National Literacy Crusade. The crusade earned the 1980 UNESCO Prize in Literacy. Twenty-five percent of the country's population was mobilized, and teachers became "militants of a political cause."[6] The Nicaraguan example prominently documented how literacy and schools were at the heart of a structural transformation of government. Schools were the venues through which the new Sandinista state engaged in the processes of policy making and institution building and the formation of a revolutionary society. Fundamentally, the Nicaraguan case study foregrounded a Freirian (Paulo Freire, *Pedagogy of the Oppressed*) vision of popular education. Teaching literacy was one part of a "bilateral" process between student and teacher. Adults were partners, not simple receptors of knowledge. Sandinista educators acknowledged that adult students often had much to teach as well. Teachers were revolutionary agents committed to a rural campaign meant to abolish adult illiteracy with the promise to create a new nation. At the same time, teachers were expected to be open to the histories of local communities and to adapt to local conditions.

These Latin American examples attest to the centrality of secular public schools in the nation-building process. In each case, a revolutionary state harnessed its central authority and prioritized teaching literacy, building schools, and providing the majority of its citizens access to a public education. On the one hand, schools, education, and literacy served the interests of the state to create citizens who supported its ideologies and policies. On the other, rural communities demanded literacy and access to schools as their right. It was one way a revolutionary state could partially fulfill its promise of social justice. Nevertheless, education was never a top-down practice. Local actors and teachers negotiated state visions with the particularities of local communities. In this way, the negotiated process of schooling in a new revolutionary state was a practice in nation building and a contribution to a hegemonic process.

EDUCATION AND STATE IN PUERTO RICO

Puerto Rico's early twentieth-century history of education, teachers, and schools shares much with these Latin American examples. The new American colonial state in Puerto Rico post-1898 founded a secular public school system that was intended to generate support for new state policies. Schools and teachers were at the center of the colonial state's project to consolidate its authority outside of San Juan, throughout the island's disparate regions. While policy-making decisions were centralized in the administrative center of San Juan, they intended to reach out to other smaller urban centers, including Ponce, Mayagüez, Fajardo, and Guayama. Through these regional urban centers, the Department of Education tackled the additional challenge of reaching rural communities. Regional urban cities and towns established their own administrative centers and reinforced their authority over the more dispersed rural towns and their schools. Teachers were also important contributors to the authority of the new American colonial state. Thousands of new teachers were incorporated into the colonial bureaucracy as civil servants. They were supervised and patrolled by principals and inspectors, who in turn were under the authority of central administrators in San Juan. Through this centralized and hierarchical bureaucracy, Puerto Rico's Department of Education became an administrative arm of the American colonial state. Its agents responded to the interests of the state—to centralize and consolidate state authority throughout the island's regions and across the urban/rural divide.

Puerto Rico's history, however, sharply diverged from other Latin American examples in one important aspect. The founding of secular schools in Mexico, Cuba, and Nicaragua attested to the successes of revolutionary governments. It was a practice in the institutionalization of the goals and promises of revolutionary states. Meanwhile, Puerto Rico became an example of how a modern empire founded and consolidated a colonial state in the Caribbean. Clearly, the American colonial state was not a Latin American revolutionary state, for fundamentally, as a colony the island would serve the interests of the metropole, while in the revolutionary state new schools and state policy were created to serve the interests of its citizenry.

The American colonial state was revolutionary, nevertheless, in other ways. The new colonial state was revolutionary in that it intended to supplant traditional economic and political structures. The economy was more directly and efficiently incorporated into US private corporate interests. The political system was reorganized so that US political appointees held supreme authority (i.e., the Executive Branch established with the Foraker Act), although there was partial representation through the elected officials in the lower house. It was a revolutionary moment in the history of the island. After four hundred years of Spanish colonialism, and after the dynamic cycles of nineteenth-century Puerto Rican political history, the new US imperial authority established its own regime.

Like in Mexico, Cuba, and Nicaragua, schools were at the center of the new state political project. Secular public schools were established with the intention to provide "lessons in civilization" to all. Agents of the American state imagined that US values, culture, and traditions would supplant local ones. The example of new lessons in civilization is where Puerto Rico also diverged from other Latin American examples. Mexico intended to create its new modern citizens through the incorporation of multiple indigenous ethnicities into its national polity. Cuba and Nicaragua both promoted state ideologies of the "new man" and social justice. These countries looked to schools as the location through which national identities could be supported and nurtured, where citizens could be incorporated into a national vision of justice for all. The new American colonial state in Puerto Rico wanted to generate new "colonial" identities meant to support the larger intentions of US empire. The goal was for local students to embrace their new location as "tropical Yankees" in the larger US imperial hierarchy.[7]

While the new American colonial state represented a rupture from the practices of a negligent and declining Spanish authority and while schools were one location through which the new colonial state attempted to generate support and establish its authority among colonial subjects, these are, nevertheless, narratives and comparisons that remain too simple, narrow, and monolithic. The history of schools, teachers, and students presented here suggests that the relationship between empire, colonial state, and education was more complex, contradictory, and negotiated.

EDUCATION AND EMPIRE

Latin American case studies suggest that local actors in dynamic communities forcefully promoted their values and visions through schools. Local actors re-shaped top-down ideologies imposed from capital cities when they did not complement local ideas and interests. In addition, however, Puerto Rico's history suggests that local actors mediated the ideological visions and intentions of US empire and the colonial state. Puerto Ricans shared a long history. The island and its people were not a blank slate onto which US imperial intentions could be uncritically inscribed. Turn-of-the-century Puerto Rican educators had goals and visions for public schools, and it was these teachers' visions through which imperial intentions were filtered. Teaching was a demanding occupation, and educators participated in dramatic changes in curriculum and pedagogy. Late nineteenth-century teachers carried forward the tradition of defending their practice and commitment to students before a colonial state. The new generation of teachers that took over the classroom in the 1910s and 1920s directed public schools in the 1930s and 1940s when they replaced US administrators. The children of the socially descending coffee elite of the late nineteenth century came into the same professional space as the children of urban artisans and other intermediate occupations.

The multiple generations of teachers that led public schools came into the classroom with already existing creole identities, identities informed by local race, gender, and class hierarchies. These were, nevertheless, identities that were also transformed by the experience of teaching. Teachers, as individuals and as a group, faced the challenge of redefining gender norms, of finding a balance between traditional and "modern" definitions. Some embraced what they understood to be progressive pedagogy (i.e., modern physical education) when they imagined it could lead to the regeneration of the race. They felt empowered to bring progress to rural residents, to cleanse the urban poor, and to sanitize the environment. They cultivated competing visions of "the nation" or, rather, a national type of identity for Puerto Ricans. They imagined ways to continue to promote local agendas while maintaining a broader relationship with the US empire. Those employed within the colonial school system articulated support for increased autonomy for the island, or a colonial form of nationalism. They also engaged in the process of defining the parameters of national identities. Therefore, diaspora communities became locations through which to further clarify the differences between "authentic" members of the "community" and those "corrupted" in the "belly of the beast." Parents and students were not absent from these processes. In the 1940s their demands for access to public schools were also a declaration of their rights as citizens. In these different contexts, already existing local conversations engaged with the visions of imperial actors. Generations of teachers were at the heart of this story of negotiation.

The many stories of how local actors negotiated US colonial school policies, of how they mediated imperial intentions, suggest two conclusions about empire, state, and education. First, in many ways, the reactions of Puerto Ricans to the intentions of the American colonial state draw similarities with other Latin American case studies and their nation-building processes. The early twentieth-century Puerto Rican example, the way local teachers proposed visions and challenged the new state, was a familiar practice. While Puerto Rican teachers were engaged in similar types of nation-building practices, they did so within the dominant framework of empire. In other words, the Puerto Rican case study challenges traditional definitions of colonialism and nationalism. It challenges the assumption of a linear evolution from colony to nation. It provides the alternative example of an enduring form of colonial nationalism. Today's cultural nationalism and the status of the Estado Libre Asociado (ELA, Free Associated State) are products of historical negotiations between local actors and the empire.

Second, the process of negotiating with the American colonial state in the first half of the twentieth century also suggests that the US empire was malleable enough to adapt to local demands and conditions. It was not monolithic in its practice and governance. It was expanding, adapting, and transforming according to multiple local examples on the mainland, in the Caribbean, and in the Pacific. In Puerto Rico, for example, it was dynamic enough to produce different definitions of citizenship.[8] Puerto Ricans moved through newly created and defined political categories—colonial subject, Puerto Rican citizen, and US citizen (with restrictions). In practice, schoolteachers reproduced a type of colonial citizenship. Fundamentally, the history of teachers, parents, and students suggested that teachers deeply informed imperial intentions and colonial policies through their daily practice. They did so during the early moment of encounter with the new American colonial state at the turn of the century, throughout the periods of colonial reform in the 1910s and 1920s, and again in the late 1940s and early 1950s as a new generation of colonial reformers founded and institutionalized the ELA.

Notes

ACKNOWLEDGMENTS

1. Trías Monge, *Puerto Rico.*
2. Burnett and Marshall, *Foreign in a Domestic Sense.*

INTRODUCTION: *HACER PATRIA*

1. E. San Millán, "Letter/clippings," Series Oficina del Gobernador (SOG), General File #3024, box 778, Archivo General de Puerto Rico (AGPR).
2. Other banners read: "Donde una escuela se abre, una cárcel se cierra" (Where you open a school, you close a jail); "Si suprimimos la enseñanza, queda suprimido el hombre" (When we suppress instruction, we suppress man); "Necesitamos mejores edificios escolares" (We need better school buildings); "Los niños necesitan escuelas" (Children need schools); "Autoridades, ¡vigilad por la educación de los niños!" (Authorities, guard the children's education); "Recordad que salísteis de la escuela; dadnos esa misma oportunidad" (Remember, you are the product of schools; Grant us the same opportunity); "Nosotros estamos contentos porque tenemos escuelas" (We are happy because we have schools) (E. San Millán, "Letter/clippings").
3. E. San Millán, "Letter/clippings."
4. "Distinguidos compatriotas: A nuevos tiempos, nuevas ideas. Por el espíritu de las ideas están mantenidas las instituciones y ellas, las ideas, obedeciendo a las invariables leyes del progreso, evolucionan eternamente. Comienza hoy una era de un gran valor moral, al igual que espiritual, para el progreso de nuestra Sociedad. Distinta hoy, a los del ayer: El Tiempo, las Circunstancias y los Medios. Tenemos trascendentales cuestiones que resolver; tales como El Social, El Económico, El Cultural, El Político, etc. La Clase Magisterial Puertorriqueña, FACTOR innegable en la evolución progresiva del

Pueblo de Puerto Rico, jamás permanecerá indiferente ante esos problemas" (Manuel Ortiz de Renta, "Letter/clippings," SOG, General File #3024, box 778, AGPR, emphasis in original).

5. Stepan, *The Hour of Eugenics"*; Appelbaum, Macpherson, and Rosemblatt, *Race and Nation.*

6. Scarano, *Puerto Rico*; Ayala and Bernabe, *Puerto Rico*; Bernabe, *Respuestas al colonialismo*; Clark, *Puerto Rico*; Burnett and Marshall, *Foreign in a Domestic Sense*; Estades Font, *La presencia militar*; García Muñiz, *La estrategia*; Trías Monge, *Puerto Rico.*

7. Navarro-Rivera, *Universidad de Puerto Rico*; Navarro-Rivera, "The Imperial Enterprise"; Navarro, *Creating Tropical Yankees*; Negrón de Montilla, *La americanización.*

8. Adams, *Education for Extinction*; Archuleta, Child, and Lomawaima, *Away from Home*; Child, *Boarding School Seasons*; Lindsey, *Indians at Hampton Institute*; Lomawaima, *They Called It Prairie Light*; Moody-Turner, *Black Folklore*; Negrón de Montilla, *La americanización.* On early twentieth-century immigration and race, see Daniels, *Guarding the Golden Door*; King, *Making Americans*; Ngai, *Impossible Subjects*; Smith, *Civic Ideals.*

9. Negrón de Montilla, *La americanización.*

10. Vaughan, *Cultural Politics*; Vaughan, *The State*; Bronfman, *Measures of Equality*; Dávila, *Diploma of Whiteness*; Dawson, *Indian and Nation*; Lewis, "The Nation"; Milanesio, "Gender and Generation"; Palmer and Rojas Chaves, "Educating Señorita"; Stepan, *"The Hour of Eugenics."*

11. The premier example of the expansion of a public school system in the service of the nation and its citizens is postrevolutionary Mexico. See Vaughan, *Cultural Politics.*

12. Briggs, *Reproducing Empire*; Findlay, *Imposing Decency*; Thompson, *Imperial Archipelago*; Thompson, *Nuestra isla*; Rodríguez-Silva, *Silencing Race.*

13. Gómez Tejera and Cruz López, *La escuela puertorriqueña*; International Institute of Teachers College, Columbia University, *Survey*; López Yustos, *Historia documental*; Maldonado Jiménez, *Historia y educación*; Navarro-Rivera, *Universidad de Puerto Rico*; Navarro, *Creating Tropical Yankees*; Negrón de Montilla, *La americanización*; Osuna, *A History of Education*; Tirado, *Cien años de educación.*

14. On the idea of the middle class in Latin America, see Owensby, *Intimate Ironies*; Parker, *The Idea of the Middle Class.*

15. Dávila, *Diploma of Whiteness*; Lewis, "The Nation"; Milanesio, "Gender and Generation"; Palmer and Rojas Chaves, "Educating Señorita"; Vaughan, *Cultural Politics.*

16. Azize Vargas, *La mujer en la lucha*; Findlay, *Imposing Decency*; Roy-Féquière, *Women, Creole Identity*; Matos Rodríguez, *Women and Urban Change.*

17. De la Fuente, *A Nation for All*; Ferrer, *Insurgent Cuba*; Joseph and Nugent, *Everyday Forms*; Mallon, *Peasant and Nation*; Sanders, *Contentious Republicans.*

18. See authors brought together in McCoy and Scarano, *Colonial Crucible.*

19. Go, *The American Colonial State*; Joseph and Legrand, *Close Encounters*; Kramer, *The Blood of Government*; LaFeber, *The New Empire*; McCoy and Scarano, *Colonial Crucible*; Pérez, *Cuba in the American Imagination*; Renda, *Taking Haiti*; Silva, *Aloha Betrayed*; Thompson, *Imperial Archipelago.*

20. Chinea, *Race and Labor*; Cubano Iguina, "Visions of Empire"; Figueroa, *Sugar, Slavery, and Freedom*; Findlay, *Imposing Decency*; García, "I Am the Other"; Guerra, *Popular Expression*; Martínez-Vergne, *Shaping the Discourse*; Rodríguez-Silva, *Silencing Race*; Scarano, "The Jíbaro Masquerade"; Schmidt-Nowara, *Empire and Antislavery*.

21. Pedreira, *Insularismo*; Flores, *Divided Borders*; González, *El país de cuatro pisos*; Roy-Féquière, *Women, Creole Identity*.

22. Díaz Quiñones, *La memoria rota*; Duany, *The Puerto Rican Nation*; Flores, *The Diaspora Strikes Back*; Janer, *Puerto Rican Nation-Building Literature*.

23. Findlay, *Imposing Decency*; Figueroa, *Sugar, Slavery, and Freedom*.

24. With the exception of Walsh, "'Advancing the Kingdom.'" Her work provides a careful analysis of Americanization as a negotiated ideology. See also Torres-González, *Idioma, bilingüismo y nacionalidad*.

25. See heroic interpretations presented in Gómez Tejera and Cruz López, *La escuela puertorriqueña*. See also the work of Rubén Maldonado Jiménez, who does not romanticize national identity constructions. He presents the professional history of resistance before the new US colonial officials. See Maldonado Jiménez, *¿Hasta cuándo?*; and "La persecución política."

26. Navarro, *Creating Tropical Yankees*.

27. We must note, however, that she also analyzed a variety of other government sources such as "circular letters" and legislative records. See Department of Education, *Annual Report*.

28. Pérez, *Cuba in the American Imagination*; Renda, *Taking Haiti*.

29. Azize Vargas, *La mujer en la lucha*; Baerga, *Género y trabajo*; Findlay, *Imposing Decency*.

30. Specifically, I mean Florencia Mallon's definition of hegemony as both a process and an endpoint. She conceptualizes it as dynamic, changing, and not simply imposed from above. See Mallon, *Peasant and Nation*.

31. Vaughan, *Cultural Politics*.

32. Bederman, *Manliness and Civilization*; Cooper and Stoler, *Tensions of Empire*; Guha, *A Subaltern Studies Reader*; McClintock, *Imperial Leather*; Scott, *Weapons of the Weak*; Stoler, *Carnal Knowledge*; Stoler, McGranahan, and Perdue, *Imperial Formations*; Trouillot, *Silencing the Past*.

33. Dávila, *Sponsored Identities*; Duany, *The Puerto Rican Nation*.

34. Dávila, *Sponsored Identities*; Duany, *The Puerto Rican Nation*.

35. Academia Puertorriqueña de la Lengua Española, *La enseñanza del español*; Barreto, *Language, Elites, and the State*; Barreto, *Politics of Language*; Cebollero, *A School Language Policy*; Torres-González, *Idioma, bilingüismo y nacionalidad*.

36. Pérez, *The Near Northwest Side Story*.

37. Miller, *Historia de Puerto Rico*.

38. Maldonado Jiménez, *Historia y educación*.

39. Maldonado Jiménez, *La persecución política del magisterio*.

40. Osuna, *A History of Education*.

CHAPTER 1. THE POLITICS OF EMPIRE, EDUCATION, AND RACE

1. Scarano, *Puerto Rico.*

2. Scarano, *Puerto Rico*; Ayala and Bernabe, *Puerto Rico*; Schmidt-Nowara, *Empire and Antislavery*; Cubano Iguina, "Visions of Empire"; Cubano Iguina, *Rituals of Violence*; Picó, *1898—la guerra.*

3. Scarano, "Liberal Pacts"; McCoy and Scarano, *Colonial Crucible*; Thompson, *Imperial Archipelago*; García, "I Am the Other"; Duany, *The Puerto Rican Nation.*

4. Thompson, *Imperial Archipelago*; Burnett and Marshall, *Foreign in a Domestic Sense*; Trías Monge, *Puerto Rico.*

5. Ayala, *American Sugar Kingdom.*

6. Guerra, *Popular Expression.*

7. Findlay, *Imposing Decency*; Guerra, *Popular Expression*; Negrón de Montilla, *La americanización.*

8. Navarro, *Creating Tropical Yankees.*

9. Gómez Tejera and Cruz López, *La escuela puertorriqueña*, 152.

10. Dubois, *A Colony of Citizens.*

11. Lasso, *Myths of Harmony*; Thurner, *From Two Republics*; Guardino, *The Time of Liberty.*

12. Scarano, *Puerto Rico.*

13. Chinea, *Race and Labor.*

14. Kinsbruner, *Not of Pure Blood*, table 2.1, 28, table 2.2, 29.

15. Picó, *Libertad y servidumbre.*

16. Bergad, "Toward Puerto Rico's Grito de Lares."

17. Cubano Iguina, *El hilo en el laberinto.*

18. Picó, *Libertad y servidumbre*; Findlay, *Imposing Decency*; Rodríguez-Silva, *Silencing Race*; Figueroa, *Sugar, Slavery, and Freedom.*

19. Graham, *House and Street.*

20. Findlay, *Imposing Decency.*

21. Rodríguez-Silva, "*Libertos* and *Libertas.*"

22. Chinea, *Race and Labor*; Figueroa, *Sugar, Slavery, and Freedom.*

23. Alonso, *El gíbaro.*

24. Zeno Gandía, *Obras completas*; Janer, *Puerto Rican Nation-Building Literature*; Rodríguez-Silva, *Silencing Race.*

25. Stepan, "*The Hour of Eugenics.*"

26. Osuna, *A History of Education.*

27. Scarano, *Puerto Rico.*

28. Coll y Toste, *Historia de la instrucción pública*; Brau, *Historia de Puerto Rico.*

29. Brau, "Rafael Cordero."

30. Picó, *Educación y sociedad*, 9.

31. McCoy and Scarano, *Colonial Crucible*; Kramer, *The Blood of Government*; Thompson, *Imperial Archipelago*; Pérez, *Cuba in the American Imagination*; Silva, *Aloha Betrayed.*

32. Thompson, *Imperial Archipelago.*

33. Moss, *Schooling Citizens*.

34. Smith, *Civic Ideals*. I take the term *imperial archipelago* from Thompson, *Imperial Archipelago*.

35. Morgan, "Supplemental Report."

36. Adams, *Education for Extinction*.

37. Lomawaima, *They Called It Prairie Light*; Child, *Boarding School Seasons*.

38. Moody-Turner, *Black Folklore*; Navarro, *Creating Tropical Yankees*.

39. Navarro, *Creating Tropical Yankees*, 116.

40. Thompson, *Imperial Archipelago*.

41. For a complementary description, see Thompson, *Imperial Archipelago*.

42. Duany, *The Puerto Rican Nation*.

43. Duany, *The Puerto Rican Nation*; Thompson, *Imperial Archipelago*.

44. Go, *The American Colonial State*.

45. Navarro, *Creating Tropical Yankees*.

46. Cooper and Stoler, *Tensions of Empire*; McCoy, Scarano, and Johnson, "On the Tropic of Cancer."

47. McClintock, *Imperial Leather*.

48. Go, *The American Colonial State*.

49. Osuna, *A History of Education*, 120.

50. Osuna, *A History of Education*, 121.

51. Miller, *Historia de Puerto Rico*, 373.

52. García, "I Am the Other."

53. López Yustos, *Historia documental*, 101; Coll y Toste, *Historia de la instrucción pública*, 197.

54. Renda, *Taking Haiti*, 90–91.

55. Renda, *Taking Haiti*, 115–16.

56. Miller, *Historia de Puerto Rico*, 373.

57. Miller, *Historia de Puerto Rico*, 371.

58. The five initial members included Victor S. Clark, George G. Groff, Henry Huyke, José Saldaña, and Roberto H. Todd. See Suárez-Santa, "Los primeros 10 años."

59. Scarano, *Puerto Rico*, 654–58.

60. Suárez-Santa, "Los primeros 10 años"; Santiago Molina, "Comparación de las leyes."

61. Negrón de Montilla, *La americanización*.

62. Navarro, *Creating Tropical Yankees*, 116.

63. Liu, "Education"; Bergee, "Ringing the Changes."

64. http://www.washingtonhistory.com/Histories/Washington_HH.pdf, 9.

65. Navarro, *Creating Tropical Yankees*, 44.

66. Negrón de Montilla, *La americanización*, 23–24.

67. Navarro, *Creating Tropical Yankees*, 44.

68. explorepahistory.com/hmarker.php?markerId=1150.

69. explorepahistory.com/hmarker.php?markerId=1150.

70. López Yustos, *Historia documental*; Negrón de Montilla, *La americanización*.

71. Lake Mohonk Conference of Friends of the Indian and Other Dependent Peoples, *Proceedings*, 163.

72. Lake Mohonk Conference of Friends of the Indian and Other Dependent Peoples, *Proceedings*, n.p.

73. Lake Mohonk Conference of Friends of the Indian and Other Dependent Peoples, *Proceedings*.

74. Negrón de Montilla, *La americanización*, 54. In the 1903 legislation, twenty-five students would be funded for four years to study in the United States, and twenty students would be sent to study industry and return to Puerto Rico. Section 68 of the 1903 law specified the twenty-five, but section 71 clarified that they could be boys or girls. See *Las leyes y resoluciones*.

75. *Las leyes y resoluciones*.

76. Navarro-Rivera, "The Imperial Enterprise," 183.

CHAPTER 2. *EL MAGISTERIO* (THE TEACHERS)

1. Rodríguez-Silva, *Silencing Race*; Findlay, *Imposing Decency*; Figueroa, *Sugar, Slavery, and Freedom*.

2. Salvador Brau quoted in Delano and Delano, *En busca*, 40.

3. Puente Acosta, *Biografía*.

4. Figueroa quoted in Delano and Delano, *En busca*, 30.

5. "El miserable estado de abyección y de desprecio que arrastraba la infeliz raza" (quoted in Márquez Calderón, "Labor educativa," 10).

6. "Marcado con el sello de la degradación (piel negra . . .)" (Sotero Figueroa quoted in Ferrer Canales, "Significación del Rafael Cordero," n.p.).

7. Puente Acosta, *Biografía*, 2.

8. Findlay, *Imposing Decency*; Figueroa, *Sugar, Slavery, and Freedom*; Rodríguez-Silva, *Silencing Race*.

9. Daubón, "El maestro Rafael"; Sellés Solá and Osuna, *Lecturas históricas*; Gómez Tejera and Cruz López, *La escuela puertorriqueña*; López Yustos, *Historia documental*; Puerto Rico, Department of Education, *Rafael Cordero*.

10. This argument is made explicit in all twentieth-century narratives about maestro Rafael. For the 1940s interpretation, see Gómez Tejera and Cruz López, *La escuela puertorriqueña*. For the 1960s, see Puerto Rico, Department of Education, *Rafael Cordero*. For the 1990s, see López Yustos, *Historia documental*; "Labor educativa."

11. "Sobreponiéndose a sus limitaciones sociales y económicas, logro iniciar la educación de gran parte de los forjadores de la sociedad de Puerto Rico en el siglo 19" (Márquez Calderón, "Labor educativa," 1).

12. Márquez Calderón, "Labor educativa," 1.

13. Hoganson, *Fighting for American Manhood*; Bederman, *Manliness and Civilization*.

14. Salvador Brau quoted in Delano and Delano, *En busca*, 40.

15. Márquez Calderón, "Labor educativa," 3.

16. Delano and Delano, *En busca*, 30.

17. Brau, "Rafael Cordero," 271.

18. The narrative history in Delano and Delano, *En busca,* provides a positive interpretation of Celestina's own history and in relation to her brother.

19. Maldonado Jiménez, "La persecución política"; Maldonado Jiménez, "Los maestros(as)."

20. "Libro de actas, 1910–1915, Libro #1," March 23, 1910, Meeting Minutes, Private Archives of the Asociación de Maestros de Puerto Rico, San Juan (hereafter AMPR Private Archives), 1.

21. "Asociación de Maestros de Puerto Rico: Francisco Vincenty," *PRSR* 1 (April 1917): 40.

22. "Appendix VII: Report of the Commissioner of Education, 1921," in Department of Education, *Annual Report* (1921), 376.

23. Andrews, *Blacks and Whites*; De la Fuente, *A Nation for All*; Ferrer, *Insurgent Cuba*; Appelbaum, Macpherson, and Rosemblatt, *Race and Nation.*

24. Dietz, *Economic History*; Scarano, *Puerto Rico.*

25. The 1920 US census data I use in the following discussion are based on the households containing an individual enumerated as a teacher from the group of individuals sampled in the Puerto Rico Census Project. For an explanation of the methodology of the sampling of census data, see Velyvis, Thompson-Colón, and Winsborough, "Public Use Samples."

26. The 1920 Puerto Rico census project sampled 379 teachers. Out of those households that included teachers, 185 were headed by an individual who reported a gainful occupation. Ninety-eight of the heads of households reported an occupation of *ninguna/o.* Teachers were heads of households in fifty-two of the units and were *huespeds* or *alojados* in forty-four. The following discussion is based on households in which an individual was reported as a relative or a spouse of a gainfully employed head of household.

27. A minority of teachers resided with heads of households at the margins of the intermediate groups. For example, on one end of the spectrum, only 6 percent of teachers were married to or children of members of the professional elite, including doctors, surgeons, and lawyers. On the other end, only 4.3 percent of teachers were residing with heads of households enumerated as agricultural or industrial unskilled wageworkers. This suggests that in 1920 descendants of the island's traditional professional elite or the working class represented only a small percent of the teaching force. The middle-class status of the teaching force is also reinforced by the number of teachers who were related or married to a head of household whose occupation was enumerated as a "nongainful occupation" but who employed one or more servants. In the teaching sample, the nongainful occupation status primarily represented female heads of households reported as widowed or elderly. It did not signify unemployment as much as an elite or middle-class status of a head of household with property or wealth who chose not to work. Twenty-four percent of the teachers related or married to a nongainfully employed head of household also lived with household servants in the capacity of cooks, nannies, and seamstresses. This occupational distribution of households with teachers is restricted to 1920 census data.

28. Stepan, *"The Hour of Eugenics"*; Appelbaum, Macpherson, and Rosemblatt, *Race and Nation*.

29. Stepan, *"The Hour of Eugenics,"* 9–17.

30. Vaughan, *Cultural Politics*; Bronfman, *Measures of Equality*; Dávila, *Diploma of Whiteness*; Dawson, *Indian and Nation*; Lewis, "The Nation"; Milanesio, "Gender and Generation"; Palmer and Rojas Chaves, "Educating Señorita"; Stepan, *"The Hour of Eugenics."*

31. Santiago Negroni used the phrase "hogar, escuela, patria" in a speech he presented at the AMPR annual conference in December 1916 ("Asociación de Maestros de Puerto Rico: Extracto del memorial y mensaje del presidente de la Asociación de Maestros, Sr. Negroni, a la sexta asamblea anual, celebrada en los días 27, 28, y 29 de diciembre," *PRSR* 1, no. 2 [February 1917]: 30–32).

32. Rodríguez-Silva, *Silencing Race*; Bernabe, *Respuestas al colonialismo*.

33. Picó, "Origins."

34. United States Bureau of the Census, *Thirteenth Census*, table 38, 594–607.

35. The historiography on race as social constructions in the Caribbean and Latin America is well established. As an introduction to the debates and the literature, see Appelbaum, Macpherson, and Rosemblatt, "Introduction."

36. Findlay, *Imposing Decency*; Rodríguez-Silva, *Silencing Race*.

37. Del Moral, "Race in Puerto Rico."

38. Gerardo Sellés Solá, "A los honorables presidentes del Senado y Cámara de Representantes y las honorables Comisiones de Instrucción de la Legislatura Insular," *PRSR* 5, no. 8 (April 1921): 42; Sellés Solá, "El español en Puerto Rico."

39. Sellés Solá, "El español en Puerto Rico"; Círculo de Supervisión y Administración Escolar de Puerto Rico, *Don Gerardo Sellés Solá, in memoriam* (1956). Sellés Solá was a professor in (1931–46) and dean of (1933–35) the College of Education at the UPR.

40. Gerardo Sellés Solá, "Carta circular no. 6," *PRSR* 5, no. 9 (May 1921): 34–37.

41. Stepan, *"The Hour of Eugenics."*

42. Sellés Solá, "Carta circular no. 6," 35, 37.

43. Gerardo Sellés Solá, "La Asociación de Maestros hace importantes recomendaciones y peticiones en beneficio del país," *PRSR* 7, no. 9 (May 1923): 40–48.

44. Sellés Solá, "La Asociación de Maestros," 43–44.

45. Sellés Solá, "La Asociación de Maestros," 43.

46. Sellés Solá, "A los honorables presidentes," 42.

47. Sellés Solá, "A los honorables presidentes," 42.

48. Sellés Solá, "Carta circular no. 6," 35.

49. Sellés Solá, "Carta circular no. 6," 34.

50. Sellés Solá, "Carta circular no. 6," 35.

51. Sellés Solá, "Carta circular no. 6," 35.

52. González Ginorio, *Lectura infantil*; González Ginorio, *Manual de maestro*.

53. That movement, nevertheless, emerged in a more organized form in the 1930s.

54. José González Ginorio, "Educación doméstica: Para padres y maestros. Parte 2," *PRSR* 1, no. 10 (December 1917): 33.

55. José González Ginorio, "Educación doméstica: Para padres y maestros," *PRSR* 1, no. 8 (October 1917): 10.

56. González Ginorio, "Educación doméstica," 12.

57. José González Ginorio, "Mensaje del Presidente, Sr. José González Ginorio, leído ante la Asociación de Maestros de Puerto Rico, reunida en su décima asamblea ordinaria," *PRSR* 5, no. 6 (February 1921): 17.

58. José González Ginorio, "Manifiesto del nuevo presidente de la Asociación de Maestros de Puerto Rico," *PRSR* 4, no. 6 (February 1920): 55.

59. Lorenza Brunet del Valle, "La escuela rural," *PRSR* 5, no. 1 (September 1920): 23.

60. Brunet del Valle, "La escuela rural," 25.

61. González Ginorio, "Manifiesto," 54.

62. See the discussion in chapter 1. See also Thompson, *Imperial Archipelago*; Navarro, *Creating Tropical Yankees*; Duany, *The Puerto Rican Nation*.

63. "Libro de actas, Asambleas anuales, 1916 al 1925, Libro #4," Meeting Minutes, AMPR Private Archives, emphasis added.

64. Negrón de Montilla, *La americanización*; Navarro, *Creating Tropical Yankees*.

65. Bernabe, *Respuestas al colonialismo*.

66. Sellés Solá, "Carta circular no. 6."

67. Scarano, *Puerto Rico*; Ayala, *American Sugar Kingdom*; Bernabe, *Respuestas al colonialismo*.

CHAPTER 3. CITIZENSHIP, GENDER, AND SCHOOLS

Portions of this chapter will be published as "Colonial Citizens of a Modern Empire: Illiteracy, Masculinity, and War" in *The New West Indian Guide* 87 (2013).

1. Stoler, McGranahan, and Perdue, *Imperial Formations*, 8, 9, 10.

2. Paralitici, *No quiero mi cuerpo pa' tambor*.

3. Ayala and Bernabe, *Puerto Rico*, 73.

4. Scarano, *Puerto Rico*, 721.

5. Azize Vargas, *La mujer en la lucha*.

6. Findlay, *Imposing Decency*; Barceló Miller, *La lucha*.

7. Barceló Miller, *La lucha*.

8. Matos Rodríguez and Delgado, *Puerto Rican Women's History*; Barceló Miller, *La lucha*; Findlay, *Imposing Decency*; Azize Vargas, *La mujer en Puerto Rico*; Azize Vargas, *La mujer en la lucha*; Acosta Belén, *The Puerto Rican Woman*.

9. García, "I Am the Other"; Barceló Miller, *La lucha*.

10. Rodríguez-Silva, *Silencing Race*.

11. Barceló Miller, *La lucha*.

12. Bobonis and Toro, "Modern Colonization."

13. Carey Hickle, "Illiteracy among the Recruits," *PRSR* 3, no. 3 (November 1918): 4–8; W. G. Coxhead, "Educational Work in Camp Las Casas," *PRSR* 3, no. 1 (September 1918): 50–51.

14. Hickle, "Illiteracy among the Recruits."

15. Hickle, "Illiteracy among the Recruits"; José Padín, "¡Ese sesenta y cinco y medio por ciento!," *PRSR* 1, no. 2 (February 1917): 6; Luis García Casanovas, "¿Cómo puede llevarse a cabo una campaña efectiva contra el analfabetismo de nuestra población rural?," *PRSR* 3, no. 9 (May 1919): 9–10.

16. Hickle, "Illiteracy among the Recruits," 7.

17. H., "Federal Aid and Education in Porto Rico," *PRSR* 4, no. 3 (November 1919): 3–7.

18. Miguel M. Toro, "Mi cuarto a espadas," *El mundo*, April 12, 1919, 8.

19. This was a common argument. See as an example García Casanovas, "¿Cómo puede llevarse?"

20. This critique became part of a mainstream pedagogic argument when it was supported by the 1925 Columbia University study of the island's schools. See International Institute of Teachers College, Columbia University, *Survey*.

21. Sellés Solá, "El español en Puerto Rico"; International Institute of Teachers College, Columbia University, *Survey*.

22. José C. Díaz, "Por nuestros analfabetas," *PRSR* 3, no. 7 (March 1919): 53.

23. Díaz, "Por nuestros analfabetas," 54.

24. Carlos Rivera Ufret, "Contra el analfabetismo," *PRSR* 4, no. 3 (November 1919): 10.

25. Paul G. Miller, "Address of the Commissioner of Education, Honorable Paul G. Miller," *PRSR* 2, no. 2 (February 1918): 26–32.

26. Miller, "Address of the Commissioner."

27. Torregrosa Rivera, "Suggested Program"; Arán, *Course of Study*.

28. The long-term consequence was the reorganization and emphasis on physical education in public schools for both boys and girls. See Paul G. Miller, "Circular Letter No. 32," December 1, 1920, SOG, General File #3024, box 778, AGPR; Pedro Gil, "Educación física," *PRSR* 4, no. 10 (June 1920): 12–18; Arán, *Course of Study*; Torregrosa Rivera, "Suggested Program"; Torregrosa Rivera, "Study of Certain Phases"; E. Santiago Márquez, "En bien de la instrucción," *El mundo*, November 8, 1919, 2; Lucila Santoni, "Higiene práctica," *PRSR* 4, no. 8 (April 1920): 25–29.

29. R. B. Pérez Mercado, "Conferencias rurales," *PRSR* 4, no. 5 (January 1920): 45–46; Genaro Concepción, "Lo que significa la guerra para el jíbaro puertorriqueño," *PRSR* 3, no. 3 (November 1918): 45–48.

30. Concepción, "Lo que significa," 46.

31. Concepción, "Lo que significa," 46.

32. Concepción, "Lo que significa," 46.

33. Francisco Vincenty, "Mensaje e informe del presidente-administrador, Sr. Francisco Vincenty, a la octava asamblea de la Asociación," *PRSR* 3, no. 8 (April 1919); Francisco Vincenty, "Informe presentado a los Comités de Instrucción de la asamblea legislativa," *PRSR* 3, no. 9 (May 1919): 61–65.

34. García Casanovas, "¿Cómo puede llevarse?" 12. Paul G. Miller, "Message of the Commissioner of Education, Dr. P. G. Miller, to the Porto Rico Teacher's Association,"

PRSR 3, no. 8 (April 1919). Teachers often turned to legislators to demand compulsory attendance laws and the persecution of parents who failed to send children to school. Since the early twentieth century, teachers had demanded stronger compulsory attendance laws. See Victor M. Suárez, "A Simple Method of Increasing Rural Enrollment," *PRSR* 3, no. 6 (February 1919): 8–17; San Juan, Junta Escolar, *Informe*, 18–20. This request, however, was matched by colonial administrators' interests in school attendance. The question of legislating mandatory attendance and enforcing it was presented as the best way to protect children from being abused as illegal forms of labor in both factories and fields. See Paul G. Miller, January 31, 1917, SOG, File "Enero 31/1917," Document #1500, box 686, AGPR; "Child Labor and School Attendance," *PRSR* 4, no. 3 (November 1919): 8–9; "Ley regulando el trabajo de mujeres y niños, y protegiéndolos contra ocupaciones peligrosas," *PRSR* 4, no. 3 (November 1919): 62–65.

35. Dietz, *Economic History*.

36. Julio B. Ortiz, "Sobre el analfabetismo," *El mundo*, October 29, 1919, 8; Coloma P. de Casablanca, "Cooperación del hogar y la escuela," *PRSR* 14, no. 1 (September 1929): 29, 48; Suárez, "A Simple Method."

37. Padín's 1917 critique foreshadowed the anticolonial, pronativist economic reform policies he advocated for when he became Puerto Rico's commissioner of education in 1930. See "First Class Citizenship," *PRSR* 1, no. 4 (April 1917): 1–2.

38. "83 escuelas nocturnas se establecerán en la Isla," *El mundo*, September 17, 1919, 2; Rivera Ufret, "Contra el analfabetismo," 10.

39. Bernabe, *Respuestas al colonialismo*; Barceló Miller, *La lucha*.

40. "La Universidad Popular en Puerto Rico. Importante proyecto de ley," *El mundo*, April 21, 1919, 4.

41. "Por la cultura de Puerto Rico," *El mundo*, March 15, 1919, 3.

42. M. Saavedra, "El único camino para combatir el analfabetismo," *El mundo*, October 24, 1919, 7.

43. Rivera Ufret, "Contra el analfabetismo."

44. Saavedra, "El único camino."

45. Pedro P. Arán, "Report on Physical Education," *PRSR* 10, no. 1 (September 1925): 34–35.

46. Sellés Solá, "Carta circular no. 6," *PRSR* 5, no. 9 (May 1921): 34–37.

47. Carlos V. Urrutia, "Cultura física," *PRSR* 6, no. 4 (December 1921): 16.

48. Gil, "Educación física," 12.

49. Gil, "Educación física," 18, emphasis in original.

50. Gerardo Sellés Solá, "A los honorables presidentes del Senado y Cámara de Representantes y las honorables Comisiones de Instrucción de la Legislatura Insular," *PRSR* 5, no. 8 (April 1921): 35–43; Sellés Solá, "Carta circular no. 6," 34; Antonio G. Martínez, "El problema de los niños," *El mundo*, December 3, 1919, 9; Félix Matos Bernier, "Los brotes de la vida," *El mundo*, January 13, 1921, 6; Rafael Martínez Marrero, "Cuestiones pedagógicas. Después de las 4 p.m.," *El mundo*, August 13, 1919, 10.

51. Francisco Faberllé, "Physical Culture up to the Present Time," *PRSR* 10, no. 4 (December 1925): 29–30.

52. Gil, "Educación física," 14–15.

53. Sellés Solá, "Carta circular no. 6," 34; Alfredo Silva, "Lo que juegan los niños de Puerto Rico," *PRSR* 10, no. 4 (December 1925): 34–35.

54. Bary, *Child Welfare*.

55. Bary, *Child Welfare*, 67.

56. Ismael Ramos, "Notes on Physical Culture," *PRSR* 10, no. 5 (January 1926): 39.

57. "Información escolar," *PRSR* 9, no. 1 (September 1925): 36. Antonio Sarriera, "Acuerdos aprobados por la Asociación de Maestros de Puerto Rico en la última asamblea anual celebrada durante los días 27, 28, 29 y 30 del mes de diciembre del año mil novecientos veinte," *PRSR* 5, no. 7 (March 1921): 39.

58. Gil, "Educación física," 13.

59. Physical education instruction and training was founded and finding its way in the 1920s. It would develop more fully into a profession that meant to address the needs of the majority of the population in the late 1930s.

60. The other two *jinetes* were Cosme Beitía Sálamo and Gacho Torres.

61. Beitía Sálamo attended Ponce High School, where he excelled in track and field and baseball. One of the "four leaders" of baseball in the 1920s, he founded the professional baseball team known as Puerto Rico Sports. Beitía Sálamo earned a bachelor's degree from the University of Puerto Rico, a master's degree in physical education from Columbia University, and a law degree from the University of Puerto Rico. He was the first professor of physical education at the University of Puerto Rico. In 1929 he founded the Liga Atlética Intercolegial. He was also a first lieutenant in the Regimiento 65 de Infantería and a member of the National Guard of Puerto Rico. Fortier Méndez also attended Ponce High School, where he was both a student and the coach of the school's baseball team. Fortier Méndez served in World War I as a second lieutenant in the US Army. He retired from the military as an infantry captain. Fortier Méndez was one of the first professors of physical education in the 1920s, assigned to the Guayama High School. See Tomasini, "Honor a los maestros," 18–22, 92–94.

62. Gerardo Sellés Solá, "Certamen anual de la Asociación," *PRSR* 6, no. 3 (November 1921): 44–46.

63. Sellés Solá, "Carta circular no. 6," 35.

64. Urrutia, "Cultura física," 17.

65. In the 1950s the new ELA Department of Education established a scholarship program that awarded children a small amount of money to pay for items working-class parents might not be able to afford, specifically, clothing and transportation. See chapter 5.

66. Urrutia, "Cultura física," 17.

67. Julio Fiol Negrón, "Girls Also Have Their Share in Physical Education," *PRSR* 13, no. 9 (May 1929): 44.

68. Generosa Fernández, "Niñas escuchas," *PRSR* 11, no. 3 (November 1926): 43.

69. Elizabeth Lutes, "Natural Dancing," *PRSR* 11, no. 9 (May 1927): 39–41.

70. Urrutia, "Cultura física," 17.

71. AMPR Board of Directors Meeting, Meeting Minutes, AMPR Private Archives.

72. José González Ginorio, "Manifiesto del nuevo presidente de la Asociación de Maestros de Puerto Rico," *PRSR* 4, no. 6 (February 1920): 53–56.

73. Sellés Solá, "A los honorables presidentes," 35–43.

74. Carey Hickle, "The Need of Better Trained Teachers, Part 1," *PRSR* 1, no. 8 (October 1917): 19–28; Carey Hickle, "The Need of Better Trained Teachers, Part 2," *PRSR* 1, no. 9 (November 1917): 23–35.

75. Miller, January 31, 1917, 3.

76. Paul G. Miller, "The Commissioner's Message to the Teachers' Association of Porto Rico," *PRSR* 1, no. 1 (January 1917): 10–15; "Courses for Rural Teachers at the College of Agriculture and Mechanic Arts," *PRSR* 1, no. 3 (March 1917): 8.

77. Francisco Vincenty, "Mensaje e informe del presidente-administrador, Sr. Francisco Vincenty, a la novena asamblea de la Asociación," *PRSR* 4, no. 6 (February 1920): 37–47.

78. "News Notes: The Summer Schools," *PRSR* 1, no. 5 (May 1917): 49.

79. González Ginorio, "A los lectores," n.p.

80. Del Rosario, *Mis cinco años*, 85.

81. M. Benítez Flores, "Deficiencias de nuestro sistema educativo: Cómo corregirlas," *PRSR* 2, no. 2 (February 1918): 64–79.

82. Barceló Miller, *La lucha*.

83. Lorenza Brunet del Valle, "Ideales de la escuela moderna," *PRSR* 3, no. 9 (May 1919): 16.

84. Lorenza Brunet del Valle, "Ética profesional en el magisterio," *PRSR* 2, no. 3 (March 1918): 26.

85. Lorenza Brunet del Valle, "La escuela rural," *PRSR* 5, no. 1 (September 1920): 25.

86. Brunet del Valle, "La escuela rural," 25–26.

87. Brunet del Valle, "Ideales," 18.

88. The text of the letter read: "Onorable Gobernador, Mi objeto es para decirle como an nombrado a Carlo Urrutia inperto [inspector] de aqui un hombre tan in moral que hiso una profesora en sinta y sela llebo abibir a Bayamon como querida con su Senora y luego sedibosio de Su Senora para casarse con la querida y tanbien de sonrro una nina de un sapatero su Sora tenia una prima en la misma casa y tanbien la hiso en sinta se lla Mariana tiene una hija yo siento ese nombramiento por mis hijas que estan en las escuelas cuendo era ayudante aqui se enseserraba en un salon con una maestra en la escuela de la Rosa el Senor Geique [Huyke] no sabe lo que aecho con nombrar a Arrutia es un hombre muy inmoral para imperto de escuela" (document no. 923/1, August 14, 1922, SOG, Appointment File #923, box 685, AGPR).

CHAPTER 4. TESTING FOR CITIZENSHIP IN THE DIASPORA

1. Sánchez Korrol, *From Colonia to Community*.

2. Armstrong, Achilles, and Sacks, *Report*.

3. Armstrong, Achilles, and Sacks, *Report*, 1–2.

4. See comparative examples of Mexican and Filipino communities in the United States that suffered deportation and decolonization schemes in the early twentieth century: Ngai, *Impossible Subjects*; Daniels, *Guarding the Golden Door*.

5. Ngai, *Impossible Subjects*.

6. Duany, *The Puerto Rican Nation*; Thompson, *Nuestra isla y su gente*; Flores, *Divided Borders*.

7. In the historical literature of Puerto Ricans on the island and in the diaspora, *diasporicans* have been constructed as outsiders to the imagined Puerto Rican nation since the great 1950s migration. The authenticity debates gained ground in the 1970s. Here I argue, however, that the process of constructing the *diasporicans* as outside of the nation began earlier, during the historical moment when the parameters of Puerto Rican national identity were being proposed in the 1930s. See Díaz Quiñones, *La memoria rota*; Flores, *Divided Borders*; Flores, *The Diaspora Strikes Back*; Pérez, *The Near Northwest Side Story*.

8. Ngai, *Impossible Subjects*; Daniels, *Guarding the Golden Door*.

9. Armstrong, Achilles, and Sacks, *Report*, 2.

10. Armstrong, Achilles, and Sacks, *Report*, 1.

11. United States House of Representatives, *Hearing*.

12. Trías Monge, *Puerto Rico*, 91.

13. Laughlin, *Report*; Laughlin and Trevor, *Immigration and Conquest*.

14. Armstrong, *660 Runaway Boys*.

15. Ngai, *Impossible Subjects*, 13.

16. Daniels, *Guarding the Golden Door*, 55.

17. Trevor, *Analysis*.

18. Ngai, *Impossible Subjects*, 22.

19. Ngai, *Impossible Subjects*, 24; King, *Making Americans*.

20. King, *Making Americans*, 173; Stepan, "The Hour of Eugenics."

21. Stepan, "The Hour of Eugenics."

22. Ngai, *Impossible Subjects*, 47.

23. Armstrong, Achilles, and Sacks, *Report*, 1.

24. James, *Holding Aloft*, 12.

25. Armstrong, Achilles, and Sacks, *Report*, 3; International Institute of Teachers College, Columbia University, *Survey*.

26. Hoffnung-Garskof, "The Migrations"; James, *Holding Aloft*.

27. Ayala, *American Sugar Kingdom*.

28. Scarano, *Puerto Rico*; Ayala and Bernabe, *Puerto Rico*.

29. Armstrong, Achilles, and Sacks, *Report*, 3.

30. Armstrong, Achilles, and Sacks, *Report*, 3; Clark, *Porto Rico*.

31. Armstrong, Achilles, and Sacks, *Report*, 3; International Institute of Teachers College, Columbia University, *Survey*.

32. Armstrong, Achilles, and Sacks, *Report*, 3; American Child Health Association, "Porto Rico."

33. Armstrong, Achilles, and Sacks, *Report*, 3.

34. Armstrong, Achilles, and Sacks, *Report*, 3.

35. Armstrong, Achilles, and Sacks, *Report*, 4.

36. Briggs, *Reproducing Empire*, 75.

37. Armstrong, Achilles, and Sacks, *Report*, 4.

38. Sánchez Korrol, *From Colonia to Community*; Vega and Iglesias, *Memoirs of Bernardo Vega*.

39. Armstrong, Achilles, and Sacks, *Report*, 5.

40. Armstrong, Achilles, and Sacks, *Report*, 7.

41. Armstrong, Achilles, and Sacks, *Report*, 5.

42. Armstrong, Achilles, and Sacks, *Report*, 5.

43. Stepan, *"The Hour of Eugenics."*

44. Armstrong, Achilles, and Sacks, *Report*, 5.

45. Thompson, *Nuestra isla y su gente*; Duany, *The Puerto Rican Nation*.

46. Armstrong, Achilles, and Sacks, *Report*, 5.

47. Lomawaima, *They Called It Prairie Light*; Child, *Boarding School Seasons*.

48. Armstrong, Achilles, and Sacks, *Report*, 7.

49. Armstrong, Achilles, and Sacks, *Report*, 8.

50. Porteus and Babcock, *Temperament and Race*.

51. A description of the Puerto Rican community of Hawaii first appears in the "Racial Efficiency Index": "Racially, the Porto Rican is a hybrid of widely different blood strains, a mixture of Spanish, negro, and aboriginal Indian so that in his racial affinities he may be said to out-Mexican the Mexican. He shares the worst qualities of the Portuguese and of the Filipino, so that of all the migrants to Hawaii he is probably the worst timber for citizenship" (Porteus and Babcock, *Temperament and Race*, 107–8).

52. Porteus and Babcock, *Temperament and Race*, v.

53. Armstrong, Achilles, and Sacks, *Report*, 8.

54. Armstrong, Achilles, and Sacks, *Report*, 8.

55. Porteus and Babcock, *Temperament and Race*, 107–8.

56. Armstrong, Achilles, and Sacks, *Report*, 8.

57. Porteus and Babcock, *Temperament and Race*, 116.

58. Armstrong, Achilles, and Sacks, *Report*, 8.

59. Armstrong, Achilles, and Sacks, *Report*, 9.

60. Armstrong, Achilles, and Sacks, *Report*, 8.

61. Porteus and Babcock, *Temperament and Race*, 7.

62. Pedro A. Cebollero, "Reactions of Puerto Rican Children in New York City to Psychological Tests," *PRSR* 20, no. 7 (March 1936): 3–6, 25.

63. Cebollero, "Reactions," 3.

64. Cebollero, "Reactions," 4.

65. A long-standing argument in Puerto Rican historiography and more broadly in the critical empire scholarship is the construction of Puerto Rican identity in opposition to the "other"—Americans. See Duany, *The Puerto Rican Nation*; Díaz Quiñones, *La memoria rota*; Flores, *Divided Borders*.

66. Flores, *Divided Borders*; Duany, *The Puerto Rican Nation*; Pérez, *The Near Northwest Side Story*; Díaz Quiñones, *La memoria rota*.

67. Cebollero, "Reactions," 3.

68. Cebollero, "Reactions," 3–4.

69. Cebollero, "Reactions," 4, emphasis added.

70. Cebollero, "Reactions," 4.

71. Findlay, *Imposing Decency*; Figueroa, *Sugar, Slavery, and Freedom*; Rodríguez-Silva, *Silencing Race*.

72. Andrews, *Blacks and Whites*; De la Fuente, *A Nation for All*; Ferrer, *Insurgent Cuba*; Appelbaum, Macpherson, and Rosemblatt, *Race and Nation*.

73. Cebollero, "Reactions," 4.

74. Cebollero, "Reactions," 4.

75. Cebollero, "Reactions," 4.

76. Cebollero, "Reactions," 4.

77. "The New Assistant Commissioner," *PRSR* 13, no. 3 (November 1930): 7.

78. Cebollero, "Reactions," 5, emphasis added.

79. Cebollero, "Reactions," 5, emphasis in original.

80. Cebollero, "Reactions," 3.

81. Cebollero, "Reactions," 25.

CHAPTER 5. PARENTS AND STUDENTS CLAIM THEIR RIGHTS

1. Osuna, *A History of Education*, appendix 8, table 2, 626, table 6, 628. Government-owned schoolrooms: 3,273 (1930), 4,048 (1940), and 4,310 (1946); teachers: 4,451 (1930), 6,294 (1940), and 8,881 (1946); and public school enrollment: 221,189 (1930), 286,098 (1940), and 349,959 (1946).

2. On populism in the Caribbean, see Turits, *Foundations of Despotism*.

3. Gómez Tejera and Cruz López, *La escuela puertorriqueña*; López Yustos, *Historia documental*.

4. Scarano, *Puerto Rico*; Ayala and Bernabe, *Puerto Rico*.

5. Dávila, *Sponsored Identities*; Duany, *The Puerto Rican Nation*.

6. Osuna, *A History of Education*, 628.

7. In the 1940s the name of the Department of Education was changed to Department of Instruction. It was later changed back to Department of Education. For consistency throughout the book, I have retained the early twentieth-century name, Department of Education. However, I kept the original use of Department of Instruction in quotes of primary documents.

8. Noemí Reyes is a pseudonym. To maintain anonymity, all names of parents and children in this chapter are pseudonyms. N. W. R., Barranquitas, to Francisco Collazo, San Juan, December 2, 1949, transcript in Fondo Departamento de Instrucción, Tarea 57-A-27, Correspondencia Becas, 1950–55, AGPR. All letter transcripts cited hereafter in the endnotes are from this collection.

9. J. C. C., Arecibo, to Departamento de Instrucción, San Juan, March 9, 1950.

10. D. L., Aguado, to Comisionado de Instrucción, San Juan, December 21, 1950, emphasis in original (López underlined the word "no" twice).

11. D. L. to Comisionado de Instrucción.

12. M. G., Arecibo, to Comisionado de Instrucción, San Juan, November 27, 1950.

13. C. O., Ceiba, to Comisionado de Instrucción, San Juan, December 18, 1950.

14. L. B. A. M., Bayamón, to Comité de Becas, Departamento de Instrucción, San Juan, August 21, 1950.

15. M. S., Aguada, to Comisionado de Instrucción, San Juan, February 2, 1951.

16. I. C. v. S., Aguada, to Comisionado de Instrucción, San Juan, January 25, 1951.

17. R. M., Cidra, to Luis Muñoz Marín, San Juan, n.d. [August 1950].

18. C. M., Cidra, to P. D. F., Cidra, November 30, 1950.

19. "Bueno a veces no voy a la escuela porque no tengo y ay veces paso los días sin comer por el pueblo. Asi mismo es que llo nesecito una alludita de Usted aun que me de para comprarme ropa y zapatos y comida. Agame ese favor." (R. M. to Muñoz Marín).

20. R. M. to Muñoz Marín.

21. G. P., Isla Verde, to Mariano Villaronga, San Juan, n.d. [received February 5, 1951].

22. M. E. R., Aguadilla, to Carlos Maestre Serbiá, San Juan, August 3, 1950.

23. P. S., Caguas, to Mariano Villaronga, Comité de Instrucción, San Juan, July 10, 1950.

24. D. R. de C., Adjuntas, to Carlos Maestre Serbiá, San Juan, August 3, 1950.

25. E. M. C., Camuy, to Luis Muñoz Marín, San Juan, June 13, 1950.

26. R. B., Hormigueros, to Comisionado de Instrucción, San Juan, January 26, 1950.

27. E. H. v. E., Aibonito, to Comisionado de Instrucción, San Juan, March 15, 1950.

28. S. R., Cayey, to Oficina de Instrucción, San Juan, December 15, 1950.

29. D. L. to Comisionado de Instrucción.

30. M. G. to Comisionado de Instrucción.

31. E. C., Barranquitas, to Luis Muñoz Marín, San Juan, June 26, 1950.

32. W. C. to Muñoz Marín.

33. E. M. C., Camuy, to Luis Muñoz Marín, San Juan, June 13, 1950.

34. E. C., Coamo, to Luis Muñoz Marín, San Juan, November 20, 1950.

35. A. F. G., Cayey, to Luis Muñoz Marín, San Juan, January 13, 1951.

36. A. N. C., Bayamón, to Oficina del Superintendente de Escuelas, October 4, 1950.

37. Carlos Maestre Serbiá, San Juan, to A. N. C., Bayamón, October 10, 1950.

38. G. R. Á., Bayamón, to Carlos Maestre Serbiá, Comité de Becas, San Juan, December 8, 1950.

39. Carlos Maestro Serbiá, San Juan, to G. R. Á., Bayamón, December 13, 1950.

40. A. N. C., Bayamón, to Jefe de Oficina de Becas, Departamento de Instrucción, San Juan, December 26, 1950.

41. R. G. R., Gurabo, to Universidad de Puerto Rico, Servicios al Estudiante, December 22, 1950.

42. R. G., Gurabo, to Departamento de Instrucción, San Juan, January 5, 1951.

43. Carlos Maestre Serbiá, San Juan, to R. G., Gurabo, January 10, 1951.

44. A. M., Barceloneta, to Comisionado de Instrucción, San Juan, February 21, 1950.

45. M. A., Barranquitas, to Comisionado de Instrucción, San Juan, November 29, 1949.

46. C. M., Caguas, to Mariano Villaronga, San Juan, August 17, 1950.

47. Mariano Villaronga, Commissioner of Education, San Juan, to "Jóvenes becarios de la Escuela Superior," Guayama, December 15, 1950.

48. T. R., Guayama, to Carlos Maestre Serbiá, San Juan, March 15, 1950.

49. J. R. L., Fajardo, to Carlos Maestre Serbiá, San Juan, December 11, 1950.

50. J. R. S., Vieques, to Comisionado de Instrucción, San Juan, October 10, 1950.

51. P. T. N., Bayamón, to Bernardo Huyke, Bayamón, February 5, 1950.

CONCLUSION: EDUCATION, NATION, AND EMPIRE

1. Dávila, *Diploma of Whiteness*; Lewis, "The Nation"; Miller, *Between Struggle and Hope*; Palmer and Rojas Chaves, "Educating Señorita"; Rockwell, *Hacer escuela, hacer estado*; Vaughan, *Cultural Politics*; Vaughan and Lewis, *The Eagle and the Virgin*.

2. Rockwell, *Hacer escuela, hacer estado*, 345.

3. Miller, *Between Struggle and Hope*; *Nicaragua triunfa en la alfabetización*; MacDonald, *Making a New People*; De la Fuente, *A Nation for All*.

4. Rockwell, *Hacer escuela, hacer estado*; Lewis, *The Ambivalent Revolution*; Vaughan and Lewis, *The Eagle and the Virgin*; Vaughan, *Cultural Politics*; Dawson, *Indian and Nation*.

5. MacDonald, *Making a New People*; Horowitz and Suchlicki, *Cuban Communism*.

6. Cardenal, "Objetivos," 36; Harris and Vilas, *Nicaragua*; Miller, *Between Struggle and Hope*.

7. McCoy and Scarano, *Colonial Crucible*; Negrón de Montilla, *La americanización*; Navarro, *Creating Tropical Yankees*.

8. Adams, *Education for Extinction*; Child, *Boarding School Seasons*; Lindsey, *Indians at Hampton Institute*; Lomawaima, *They Called It Prairie Light*; Moss, *Schooling Citizens*; Smith, *Civic Ideals*.

Bibliography

Archival Sources

The primary sources cited are held at the following institutions:
Archivo Central de la Universidad de Puerto Rico, Río Piedras
Archivo General de Puerto Rico (AGPR), San Juan
Archives of the Asociación de Maestros de Puerto Rico (AMPR), San Juan
Colección Puertorriqueña, Biblioteca Lázaro, Universidad de Puerto Rico

Newspapers and Periodicals

Ecos de la escuela superior
Ecos escolares
El hogar
El magisterio moderno
El mundo
El sol: Revista oficial de la Asociación de Maestros
El tiempo
La correspondencia
La democracia
La revista escolar de Puerto Rico/Porto Rico School Review (PRSR)
New York Times
Porto Rico Progress
Problemas sociales y económicos de Puerto Rico
Puerto Rico ilustrado
Puerto Rico infantil

Revista de agricultura de Puerto Rico
Voces juveniles

PUBLISHED PRIMARY SOURCES

Arán, Pedro. *Course of Study in Physical Education for the Public Schools of Porto Rico. Second Grade.* San Juan: Bureau of Supplies, Printing, and Transportation, 1926.

Armstrong, Clairette P. *660 Runaway Boys: Why Boys Desert Their Homes.* Boston: R. G. Badger, 1932.

Armstrong, Clairette P., Edith M. Achilles, and M. J. Sacks. *A Report of the Special Committee on Immigration and Naturalization of the Chamber of Commerce of the State of New York Submitting a Study on Reactions of Puerto Rican Children in New York City to Psychological Tests.* New York: Special Committee on Immigration and Naturalization, Chamber of Commerce of the State of New York, 1935.

Bere, May. *A Comparative Study of the Mental Capacity of Children of Foreign Parentage.* New York, Teachers College: Columbia University, 1924.

Daubón, J. A. "El maestro Rafael." *Revista Puertorriqueña* 5 (1891): 97–99.

Del Rosario, Isaac. *Mis cinco años de maestro rural.* Mayagüez: Imp. de La Voz Escolar, 1920.

Department of Education. *Annual Report of the Commissioner of Education.* Washington, DC: Government Printing Office, 1901–39.

Garth, Thomas Russell. *Race Psychology: A Study of Racial Mental Differences.* New York: Whittlesey House, McGraw-Hill Book Company, 1931.

González Ginorio, José. "A los lectores de este libro." In *Mis cinco años de maestro rural.* By Isaac del Rosario. Mayagüez: Imp. de La Voz Escolar, 1920.

———. *Lectura infantil. Libro primero. (Luis y Ana).* New York: D. C. Heath, 1916.

———. *Manual de maestro: Método racional para enseñar a leer y escribir el castellano.* New York: D. C. Heath, 1918.

Huyke, Juan B. "José Padín." In *Esfuerzo propio: Entrevistas con portorriqueños que se han formado por su propio esfuerzo.* San Juan: Negociado de Materiales, Imprenta y Transporte, 1922.

International Institute of Teachers College, Columbia University. *A Survey of the Public Educational System of Porto Rico.* New York: Bureau of Publications, 1926.

Lake Mohonk Conference of Friends of the Indian and Other Dependent Peoples. *Proceedings of the . . . Annual Meeting of the Lake Mohonk Conference of Friends of the Indian and Other Dependent Peoples.* [New York]: Lake Mohonk Conference, 1904.

Las leyes y resoluciones de la primera sesión de la segunda asamblea legislativa de Puerto Rico. San Juan: Tip. "El País," 1903.

Laughlin, Harry H. *A Report of the Special Committee on Immigration and Alien Insane Submitting a Study on Immigration-Control.* New York: Chamber of Commerce of the State of New York, 1934.

Laughlin, Harry H., and John B. Trevor. *Immigration and Conquest: A Study of the United States as the Receiver of Old World Emigrants Who Become the Parents of Future-Born*

Americans. New York: Special Committee on Immigration and Naturalization, Chamber of Commerce of the State of New York, 1939.

Masini, Juan, Santiago Negroni Jr., J. M. Vivaldi, and Andres Mattei, eds. *Historia ilustrada de Yauco*. Yauco: Yauco Printing Company, 1925.

Miller, Paul G. *Historia de Puerto Rico*. New York: Rand McNally, 1922.

Monroe, Paul. *A Survey of the Educational System of the Philippine Islands by the Board of Educational Surveys: Created Under Acts 3162 and 3196 of the Philippine Legislature*. Manila: Bureau of Printing, 1925.

Pintner, Rudolf. *Intelligence Testing*. Holt, 1923.

Porteus, S. D., and M. E. Babcock. *Temperament and Race*. Boston: Badger, 1926.

Puente Acosta, Lorenzo. *Biografía del maestro Rafael Cordero*. Puerto Rico: Imprenta de Acosta, 1868.

Rosario, José C. *La escuela rural*. San Juan: Imp. Venezuela, 1936.

Rowe, L. S. *The United States and Puerto Rico*. New York: Longmans, Green, 1904.

Rural Life in Puerto Rico. San Juan: Department of Education, 1934.

San Juan, Junta Escolar. *Informe de la Junta Escolar de San Juan, 1903–1904*. San Juan: Tipografía "El País," 1904.

Trevor, John B. *An Analysis of the American Immigration Act of 1924*. New York: Carnegie Endowment for International Peace, 1924.

United States Bureau of the Census. *Fifteenth Census of the United States: 1930*. Washington, DC: Government Printing Office, 1931.

———. *Fourteenth Census of the United States, 1920*. Washington, DC: Government Printing Office, 1922.

———. *Thirteenth Census of the United States Taken in the Year 1910*. Vol. 3. Washington, DC: Government Printing Office, 1917.

United States House of Representatives. *Hearing before the Committee on the Territories, House of Representatives, Seventy-Fourth Congress, First Session on H.R. 1394. A Bill to Enable the People of Puerto Rico to Form a Constitution and State Government and Be Admitted into the Union on an Equal Footing with the States*. Washington, DC: Government Printing Office, 1935.

Zeno, Francisco M. *Cuestiones sociales: El obrero agrícola de Puerto Rico*. San Juan: La Correspondencia de Puerto Rico, 1922.

Unpublished Manuscripts, Dissertations, and Theses

American Child Health Association. "Porto Rico: An Inquiry into the Health, Nutritional and Social Conditions in Porto Rico as They May Affect Children." Unpublished manuscript, 1930.

Del Moral, Solsiree. "Race in Puerto Rico, 1898–1930: A Preliminary Analysis of the Island's Population, Occupation, and Agriculture Censuses." Master's thesis, Columbia University, 1997.

Hoff, John Van Rensslaer. "Abridgement of Report of the Board of Charities of Porto Rico for the Period Ending June 30, 1900, Embracing the Work of Porto Rico Relief." Unpublished manuscript, 1900.

"Labor educativa: Maestro Rafael Cordero de Molina." Unpublished manuscript, Facultad de Educación, Universidad de Puerto Rico, Recinto de Río Piedras, 1992.

Maldonado Jiménez, Rubén. "Los maestros(as): Actitudes y polémicas ante la invasión norteamericana a Puerto Rico (1898–1901)." PhD diss., Universidad de Puerto Rico, 1996.

Márquez Calderón, Juanita. "Labor educativa: Maestro Rafael Cordero de Molina." Unpublished manuscript, Facultad de Educación, Universidad de Puerto Rico, Recinto de Río Piedras, 1992.

Osuna, John Joseph. "Education in Porto Rico." PhD diss., Columbia University, 1923.

Picó, Fernando. "Educación y sociedad en el Puerto Rico del siglo 19: Consideraciones en torno a la escolarización primaria y sus limitaciones." Unpublished manuscript, Centro de Estudios de la Realidad Puertorriqueña, San Juan, February 1983.

Quiñones de Gómez, Virginia. "El instituto civil de segunda enseñanza en Puerto Rico en el siglo 19." Master's thesis, Universidad de Puerto Rico, Río Piedras, 1965.

Santiago Molina, Aida Iris. "Comparación de las leyes que rigen el sistema educativo desde el 1903 hasta el presente." Unpublished manuscript, Universidad de Puerto Rico, Facultad de Ciencias Sociales, Escuela Graduada de Administración Pública, Río Piedras, Puerto Rico, 1996.

Sellés Solá, Gerardo. "El español en Puerto Rico en los últimos treinta años." Master's thesis, Universidad de Puerto Rico, 1931.

Sosa, Héctor Hiraldo. "La Segunda Unidad Rural y sus implicaciones educativas dentro del Departamento de Instrucción Pública pasado y presente." PhD diss., Universidad de Puerto Rico, 1983.

Suárez-Santa, Sandra I. "Los primeros 10 años de legislación educativa bajo el régimen norteamericano y su impacto en la educación moderna." Master's thesis, Facultad de Educación, Recinto de Río Piedras, Departamento de Estudios Graduados, Universidad de Puerto Rico, 1981.

Tomasini, Juan B. "Honor a los maestros de educación física y propulsores del deporte puertorriqueño." Unpublished manuscript, 1992.

Torregrosa Rivera, Felicio Miguel. "A Study of Certain Phases of Physical Education for Boys in the Public High Schools of Puerto Rico." Thesis, Syracuse University, 1938.

———. "Suggested Program of Physical Education and Recreation for the Rural Schools of Puerto Rico." Unpublished manuscript, n.d.

Veve de Margarida, Manuela. "Gerardo Sellés Solá: Contribución a la educación en Puerto Rico." PhD diss., Universidad de Puerto Rico, 1967.

Walsh, Ellen. "'Advancing the Kingdom': Missionaries and Americanization in Puerto Rico, 1898–1930s." PhD diss., University of Pittsburgh, 2008.

Published Sources

Academia Puertorriqueña de la Lengua Española. *La enseñanza del español y del inglés en Puerto Rico: Una polémica de cien años.* San Juan: La Academia, 1998.

Acosta Belén, Edna, ed. *The Puerto Rican Woman.* New York: Praeger, 1986.

Adams, David Wallace. *Education for Extinction: American Indians and the Boarding School Experience, 1875–1928.* Lawrence: University Press of Kansas, 1995.

Alegría Ortega, Idsa E., and Palmira N. Ríos González, eds. *Contrapunto de género y raza en Puerto Rico.* Río Piedras: Centro de Investigaciones Sociales, 2005.

Alonso, Manuel A. *El gíbaro: Cuadro de costumbres de la isla de Puerto Rico.* Biblioteca Popular. San Juan: Instituto de Cultura Puertorriqueña, 1988.

Anderson, Benedict. *Imagined Communities: Reflections on the Origin and Spread of Nationalism.* London: Verso, 1983.

Anderson, Warwick. *The Cultivation of Whiteness: Science, Health, and Racial Destiny in Australia.* New York: Basic Books, 2003.

Andrews, George Reid. *Blacks and Whites in São Paulo, Brazil, 1888–1988.* Madison: University of Wisconsin Press, 1991.

Appelbaum, Nancy P., Anne S. Macpherson, and Karin Alejandra Rosemblatt. "Introduction: Racial Nations." In *Race and Nation in Modern Latin America,* edited by Nancy P. Appelbaum, Anne S. Macpherson, and Karin Alejandra Rosemblatt, 1–31. Chapel Hill: University of North Carolina Press, 2003.

Archuleta, Margaret L., Brenda J. Child, and K. Tsianina Lomawaima, eds. *Away from Home: American Indian Boarding School Experiences, 1879–2000.* Santa Fe: Museum of New Mexico Press, 2000.

Ayala, César J. *American Sugar Kingdom: The Plantation Economy of the Spanish Caribbean, 1898–1934.* Chapel Hill: University of North Carolina Press, 1999.

Ayala, César J., and Rafael Bernabe. *Puerto Rico in the American Century: A History since 1898.* Chapel Hill: University of North Carolina Press, 2007.

Azize Vargas, Yamila. *La mujer en la lucha.* Río Piedras: Editorial Cultural, 1985.

————, ed. *La mujer en Puerto Rico.* Río Piedras: Ediciones Huracán, 1987.

Baerga, María del Carmen, ed. *Género y trabajo: La industria de la aguja en Puerto Rico y el Caribe Hispánico.* 2nd ed. San Juan: Editorial de la Universidad de Puerto Rico, 1995.

Barceló Miller, María de Fátima. *La lucha por el sufragio femenino en Puerto Rico, 1896–1935.* Río Piedras: Ediciones Huracán, 1997.

Barreto, Amílcar A. *Language, Elites, and the State: Nationalism in Puerto Rico and Quebec.* Westford: Praeger, 1998.

————. *The Politics of Language in Puerto Rico.* Gainesville: University Press of Florida, 2001.

Bary, Helen V., US Children's Bureau. *Child Welfare in the Insular Possessions of the United States. Part 1. Porto Rico.* Washington, DC: Government Printing Office, 1923.

Bederman, Gail. *Manliness and Civilization: A Cultural History of Gender and Race in the United States, 1880–1917.* Chicago: University of Chicago Press, 1995.

Bergad, Laird W. "Toward Puerto Rico's Grito de Lares: Coffee, Social Stratification, and Class Conflicts, 1828–1868." *Hispanic American Historical Review* 60 (November 1980): 617–42.

Bergee, Martin J. "Ringing the Changes: General John Eaton and the 1886 Public School Music Survey." *Journal of Research in Music Education* 35, no. 2 (Summer 1987): 103–16.

Bernabe, Rafael. *Respuestas al colonialismo en la política puertorriqueña, 1899–1929*. Río Piedras: Ediciones Huracán, 1996.

Bobonis, Gustavo J., and Harold J. Toro. "Modern Colonization and Its Consequences: The Effects of U.S. Educational Policy on Puerto Rico's Educational Stratification, 1899–1910." *Caribbean Studies* 35, no. 2 (July–December 2007): 30–76.

Borges, Dain. "'Puffy, Ugly, Slothful and Inert': Degeneration in Brazilian Social Thought, 1880–1940." *Journal of Latin American Studies* 25, no. 2 (May 1993): 235–56.

Brau, Salvador. *Historia de Puerto Rico*. Río Piedras: Editorial Edil, 1973.

———. "Rafael Cordero." In *Disquisiciones sociológicas y otros ensayos*. Río Piedras: Universidad de Puerto Rico, 1956.

Briggs, Laura. *Reproducing Empire: Race, Sex, Science, and U.S. Imperialism in Puerto Rico*. Berkeley: University of California Press, 2002.

Bronfman, Alejandra. *Measures of Equality: Social Science, Citizenship, and Race in Cuba, 1902–1940*. Chapel Hill: University of North Carolina Press, 2004.

Burnett, Christina Duffy, and Burke Marshall, eds. *Foreign in a Domestic Sense: Puerto Rico, American Expansion, and the Constitution*. Durham, NC: Duke University Press, 2001.

Cardenal, Fernando. "Objetivos de la Cruzada Nacional de Alfabetización." In *Nicaragua triunfa en la alfabetización: Documentos y testimonies de la cruzada nacional de alfabetización*, 27–36. San José: Departamento Ecuménico de Investigaciones, 1981.

Cebollero, Pedro A. *La política lingüístico-escolar de Puerto Rico*. San Juan: Baldrich, 1945.

———. *A School Language Policy for Puerto Rico*. San Juan: Imprenta Baldrich, 1945.

Child, Brenda J. *Boarding School Seasons: American Indian Families, 1900–1940*. Lincoln: University of Nebraska Press, 1998.

Chinea, Jorge Luis. *Race and Labor in the Hispanic Caribbean: The West Indian Immigrant Worker Experience in Puerto Rico, 1800–1850*. Gainesville: University Press of Florida, 2005.

Círculo de Supervisión y Administración Escolar de Puerto Rico. *Don Gerardo Sellés Solá, in memoriam*. San Juan, 1956.

Clark, Truman R. *Puerto Rico and the United States, 1917–1933*. Pittsburgh: University of Pittsburgh Press, 1975.

Clark, Victor S., ed. *Porto Rico and Its Problems*. Washington, DC: Brookings Institution, 1930.

Coll y Toste, Cayetano. *Historia de la instrucción pública en Puerto Rico hasta el año de 1898*. San Juan: Boletín Mercantil, 1910.

Cooper, Frederick, and Ann Laura Stoler, eds. *Tensions of Empire: Colonial Cultures in a Bourgeois World*. Berkeley: University of California Press, 1997.

Cruz Monclova, Lidio, and Antonio J. Colorado. *Noticia acerca del pensamiento político de Puerto Rico, 1808–1952*. Mexico City: Editorial Orión, 1955.

Cubano Iguina, Astrid. *El hilo en el laberinto: Claves de la lucha política en Puerto Rico, siglo XIX*. Río Piedras: Ediciones Huracán, 1990.

———. *Rituals of Violence in Nineteenth-Century Puerto Rico: Individual Conflict, Gender, and the Law*. Gainesville: University Press of Florida, 2006.

———. "Visions of Empire and Historical Imagination in Puerto Rico under Spanish Rule, 1870–1898." In *Interpreting Spanish Colonialism: Empires, Nations, and Legends*, edited by Christopher Schmidt-Nowara and John M. Nieto-Phillips, 87–108. Pittsburgh: University of Pittsburgh Press, 1999.

Cuesta Mendoza, Antonio. *Historia de la educación en el Puerto Rico colonial*. Mexico City: M. L. Sánchez, 1946.

Daniels, Roger. *Guarding the Golden Door: American Immigration Policy and Immigrants since 1882*. New York: Hill and Wang, 2004.

Dávila, Arlene M. *Sponsored Identities: Cultural Politics in Puerto Rico*. Philadelphia: Temple University Press, 1997.

Dávila, Jerry. *Diploma of Whiteness: Race and Social Policy in Brazil, 1917–1945*. Durham, NC: Duke University Press, 2003.

Dawson, Alexander S. *Indian and Nation in Revolutionary Mexico*. Tucson: University of Arizona Press, 2004.

De la Fuente, Alejandro. *A Nation for All: Race, Inequality, and Politics in Twentieth-Century Cuba*. Chapel Hill: University of North Carolina Press, 2001.

Delano, Jack, and Irene Delano. *En busca del maestro Rafael Cordero*. Río Piedras: Editorial de la Universidad de Puerto Rico, 1994.

Díaz Quiñones, Arcadio. *La memoria rota*. Río Piedras: Ediciones Huracán, 1993.

Díaz Soler, Luis M. *Puerto Rico: Sus luchas por alcanzar estabilidad económica, definición política y afirmación cultural, 1898–1996*. Isabela: Isabela Printing, 1998.

Dietz, James L. *Economic History of Puerto Rico: Institutional Change and Capitalist Development*. Princeton, NJ: Princeton University Press, 1986.

Duany, Jorge. *The Puerto Rican Nation on the Move: Identities on the Island and in the United States*. Chapel Hill: University of North Carolina Press, 2002.

Dubois, Laurent. *A Colony of Citizens: Revolution and Slave Emancipation in the French Caribbean, 1787–1804*. Chapel Hill: University of North Carolina Press, 2004.

Estades Font, María Eugenia. *La presencia militar de Estados Unidos en Puerto Rico, 1898–1918: Intereses estratégicos y dominación colonial*. Río Piedras: Ediciones Huracán, 1988.

Fernández Méndez, Eugenio. *Salvador Brau y su tiempo: Drama y paradoja de una sociedad*. San Juan: Universidad de Puerto Rico, 1956.

Ferrer, Ada. *Insurgent Cuba: Race, Nation, and Revolution, 1868–1898*. Chapel Hill: University of North Carolina Press, 1999.

Ferrer Canales, José. "Significación del Rafael Cordero, maestro puertorriqueño." In *Rafael Cordero: Presencia y vigencia*. San Juan: Instituto de Cultura Puertorriqueña, 2000.

Figueroa, Luis A. *Sugar, Slavery, and Freedom in Nineteenth-Century Puerto Rico*. Chapel Hill: University of North Carolina Press, 2005.

Findlay, Eileen. *Imposing Decency: The Politics of Sexuality and Race in Puerto Rico, 1870–1920*. Durham, NC: Duke University Press, 1999.

Flores, Juan. *The Diaspora Strikes Back: Caribeño Tales of Learning and Turning*. New York: Routledge, 2009.

———. *Divided Borders: Essays on Puerto Rican Identity*. Houston: Arte Público Press, 1993.

Freire, Paulo. *Pedagogy of the Oppressed*. New York: Continuum, 1970.

García, Gervasio L. "I Am the Other: Puerto Rico in the Eyes of North Americans, 1898." *Journal of American History* 87 (June 2000): 39–64.

García Muñiz, Humberto. *La estrategia de los Estados Unidos y la militarización del Caribe*. Río Piedras: Instituto de Estudios del Caribe, Universidad de Puerto Rico, 1988.

Go, Julian. *The American Colonial State in the Philippines: Global Perspectives*. Durham, NC: Duke University Press, 2003.

Gómez Tejera, Carmen, and David Cruz López. *La escuela puertorriqueña*. Sharon: Troutman Press, 1970.

González, José Luis. *El país de cuatro pisos y otros ensayos*. Río Piedras: Ediciones Huracán, 1989.

Graham, Richard, ed. *The Idea of Race in Latin America, 1870–1940*. Austin: University of Texas Press, 1990.

Graham, Sandra Lauderdale. *House and Street: The Domestic World of Servants and Masters in Nineteenth-Century Rio de Janeiro*. Cambridge: Cambridge University Press, 1988.

Guardino, Peter. *The Time of Liberty: Popular Political Culture in Oaxaca, 1750–1850*. Durham, NC: Duke University Press, 2005.

Guerra, Lillian. *Popular Expression and National Identity in Puerto Rico: The Struggle for Self, Community, and Nation*. Gainesville: University Press of Florida, 1998.

Guha, Ranajit, ed. *A Subaltern Studies Reader, 1986–1995*. Minneapolis: University of Minnesota Press, 1997.

Harris, Richard L., and Carlos M. Vilas, eds. *Nicaragua: A Revolution under Siege*. London: Zed Books, 1985.

Helg, Aline. *Our Rightful Share: The Afro-Cuban Struggle for Equality, 1886–1912*. Chapel Hill: University of North Carolina Press, 1995.

Hoffnung-Garskof, Jesse. "The Migrations of Arturo Schomburg: On Being Antillano, Negro, and Puerto Rican in New York 1891–1938." *Journal of American Ethnic History* 21 (Fall 2001): 3–49.

Hoganson, Kristin L. *Fighting for American Manhood: How Gender Politics Provoked the Spanish-American and Philippine-American Wars*. New Haven, CT: Yale University Press, 1998.

Horowitz, Irving Louis, and Jaime Suchlicki, eds. *Cuban Communism*. 10th ed. New Brunswick, NJ: Transaction Publishers, 1998.

James, Winston. *Holding Aloft the Banner of Ethiopia: Caribbean Radicalism in Early Twentieth-Century America*. New York: Verso, 1998.

Janer, Zilkia. *Puerto Rican Nation-Building Literature: Impossible Romance*. Gainesville: University Press of Florida, 2005.

Joseph, Gilbert M., ed. *Reclaiming the Political in Latin American History: Essays from the North*. Durham, NC: Duke University Press, 2001.

Joseph, Gilbert M., and Catherine C. Legrand, eds. *Close Encounters of Empire: Writing the Cultural History of U.S.–Latin American Relations*. Durham, NC: Duke University Press, 1998.

Joseph, Gilbert M., and Daniel Nugent, eds. *Everyday Forms of State Formation: Revolution and the Negotiation of Rule in Modern Mexico*. Durham, NC: Duke University Press, 1994.

King, Desmond. *Making Americans: Immigration, Race, and the Origins of the Diverse Democracy*. Cambridge, MA: Harvard University Press, 2000.

Kinsbruner, Jay. *Not of Pure Blood: The Free People of Color and Racial Prejudice in Nineteenth-Century Puerto Rico*. Durham, NC: Duke University Press, 1996.

Kramer, Paul A. *The Blood of Government: Race, Empire, the United States, and the Philippines*. Chapel Hill: University of North Carolina Press, 2006.

LaFeber, Walter. *The New Empire: An Interpretation of American Expansion, 1860–1898*. Ithaca, NY: Cornell University Press, 1963.

Lasso, Marixa. *Myths of Harmony: Race and Republicanism during the Age of Revolution, Colombia, 1795–1831*. Pittsburgh: University of Pittsburgh Press, 2007.

Lewis, Stephen E. *The Ambivalent Revolution: Forging State and Nation in Chiapas, 1910–1945*. Albuquerque: University of New Mexico Press, 2005.

———. "The Nation, Education, and the 'Indian Problem' in Mexico." In *The Eagle and the Virgin: Nation and Cultural Revolution in Mexico, 1920–1940*, edited by Mary Kay Vaughan and Stephen E. Lewis, 176–95. Durham, NC: Duke University Press, 2006.

Lindsey, Donald F. *Indians at Hampton Institute, 1877–1923*. Urbana: University of Illinois Press, 1995.

Liu, Goodwin. "Education, Equality, and National Citizenship." *Yale Law Review* 116, no. 2 (November 2006): 330–411.

Lomawaima, K. Tsianina. *They Called It Prairie Light: The Story of Chilocco Indian School*. Lincoln: University of Nebraska Press, 1994.

López Yustos, Alfonso. *Historia documental de la educación en Puerto Rico, 1503–1970*. San Juan: Sandemann, 1985.

MacDonald, Theodore. *Making a New People: Education in Revolutionary Cuba*. Vancouver, BC: New Star Books, 1985.

Maldonado Jiménez, Rubén. *¿Hasta cuándo? La lucha de los maestros por justicia salarial, antes y después de la invasión de Estados Unidos a Puerto Rico, 1880–1900*. San Juan: Ediciones Nueva Provincia, 1998.

———, ed. *Historia y educación: Acercamiento a la historia social de la educación en Puerto Rico*. San Juan: Editorial de la Universidad de Puerto Rico, 2001.

———. "La persecución política a los maestros: 1868–1901." In *Historia y educación: Acercamientos a la historia social de la educación en Puerto Rico*, edited by Rubén Maldonado Jiménez, 163–206. San Juan: Editorial de la Universidad de Puerto Rico, 2001.

———. *La persecución política del magisterio en Puerto Rico*. Toa Alta: Editorial Nueva Provincia, 2006.

Mallon, Florencia. *Peasant and Nation: The Making of Postcolonial Mexico and Peru*. Berkeley: University of California Press, 1995.

Martínez-Vergne, Teresita. *Shaping the Discourse on Space: Charity and Its Wards in Nineteenth-Century San Juan, Puerto Rico*. Austin: University of Texas Press, 1999.

Matos Rodríguez, Félix V. *Women and Urban Change in San Juan, Puerto Rico, 1820–1868.* Gainesville: University Press of Florida, 1999.

Matos Rodríguez, Félix V., and Linda C. Delgado, eds. *Puerto Rican Women's History: New Perspectives.* Armonk: M. E. Sharpe, 1998.

McClintock, Anne. *Imperial Leather: Race, Gender, and Sexuality in the Colonial Contest.* New York: Routledge, 1995.

McCoy, Alfred W., and Francisco A. Scarano, eds. *Colonial Crucible: Empire in the Making of the Modern American State.* Madison: University of Wisconsin Press, 2009.

McCoy, Alfred W., Francisco A. Scarano, and Courtney Johnson. "On the Tropic of Cancer: Transitions and Transformations in the U.S. Imperial State." In *Colonial Crucible: Empire in the Making of the Modern American State,* edited by Alfred W. McCoy and Francisco A. Scarano, 3–33. Madison: University of Wisconsin Press, 2009.

Milanesio, Natalia. "Gender and Generation: The University Reform Movement in Argentina, 1918." *Journal of Social History* 39, no. 2 (2005): 505–29, 601.

Miller, Valerie. *Between Struggle and Hope: The Nicaraguan Literacy Crusade.* Boulder, CO: Westview Press, 1985.

Moody-Turner, Shirley. *Black Folklore and the Politics of Racial Representation.* Jackson: University Press of Mississippi, 2013.

Morales Carrión, Arturo. *Puerto Rico: A Political and Cultural History.* New York: W. W. Norton, 1983.

Morgan, T. J. "Supplemental Report on Indian Education." In *House Executive Document* no. 1, 51st Cong., 1st sess., serial 2725 (1889). In *American Indians,* edited by Nancy Shoemaker, 93–97. Malden: Blackwell Publishers, 2001.

Moss, Hilary J. *Schooling Citizens: The Struggle for African American Education in Antebellum America.* Chicago: University of Chicago Press, 2009.

Navarro, José Manuel. *Creating Tropical Yankees: Social Science Textbooks and U.S. Ideological Control in Puerto Rico, 1898–1908.* New York: Routledge, 2002.

Navarro-Rivera, Pablo. "The Imperial Enterprise and Educational Policies in Colonial Puerto Rico." In *Colonial Crucible: Empire in the Making of the Modern American State,* edited by Alfred W. McCoy and Francisco A. Scarano, 163–74. Madison: University of Wisconsin Press, 2009.

———. *Universidad de Puerto Rico: De control político a crisis permanente, 1903–1952.* Río Piedras: Ediciones Huracán, 2000.

Negrón de Montilla, Aida. *La americanización en Puerto Rico y el sistema de instrucción pública, 1900–1930.* San Juan: Editorial de la Universidad de Puerto Rico, 1998.

Ngai, Mae M. *Impossible Subjects: Illegal Aliens and the Making of Modern America.* Princeton, NJ: Princeton University Press, 2004.

Nicaragua triunfa en la alfabetización: Documentos y testimonios de la cruzada nacional de alfabetización. San José: Departamento Ecuménico de Investigaciones, 1981.

Osuna, Juan José. *A History of Education in Puerto Rico.* 2nd ed. Río Piedras: Editorial Universitaria, 1949.

Owensby, Brian P. *Intimate Ironies: Modernity and the Making of Middle-Class Lives in Brazil.* Stanford, CA: Stanford University Press, 1999.

Palmer, Steven, and Gladys Rojas Chaves. "Educating Señorita: Teacher Training, Social Mobility, and the Birth of Costa Rican Feminism, 1885–1925." *Hispanic American Historical Review* 78, no. 1 (1998): 45–82.

Paralitici, Ché. *No quiero mi cuerpo pa' tambor: El servicio militar obligatorio en Puerto Rico.* San Juan: Ediciones Puerto, 1998.

Parker, D. S. *The Idea of the Middle Class: White-Collar Workers and Peruvian Society, 1900–1950.* University Park: Pennsylvania State University Press, 1988.

Pedreira, Antonio S. *Insularismo: Ensayos de interpretación puertorriqueña.* 2nd ed. San Juan: Biblioteca de Autores Puertorriqueños, 1942.

Pérez, Gina M. *The Near Northwest Side Story: Migration, Displacement, and Puerto Rican Families.* Berkeley: University of California Press, 2004.

Pérez, Louis A., Jr. *Cuba in the American Imagination: Metaphor and the Imperial Ethos.* Chapel Hill: University of North Carolina Press, 2008.

———. "We Are the World: Internationalizing the National, Nationalizing the International." *Journal of American History* 89 (2002): 558–66.

Picó, Fernando. *1898—La guerra después de la guerra.* Río Piedras: Ediciones Huracán, 1987.

———. *Educación y sociedad en el Puerto Rico del siglo 19: Consideraciones en torno a la escolarización primaria y sus limitaciones.* San Juan: Centro de Estudios de la Realidad Puertorriqueña, 1983.

———. *Historia general de Puerto Rico.* Río Piedras: Ediciones Huracán, 1986.

———. *Libertad y servidumbre en el Puerto Rico del siglo XIX.* Río Piedras: Ediciones Huracán, 1982.

Picó, Isabel. "Origins of the Puerto Rican University Student Movement under U.S. Domination (1903–1930)." In *Puerto Rico and Puerto Ricans: Studies in History and Society,* edited by Adalberto López and James Petras, 175–94. New York: John Wiley & Sons, 1974.

Puerto Rico, Department of Education. *Rafael Cordero: "El maestro."* Hato Rey: El Departamento, 1964.

Putnam, Lara. *The Company They Kept: Migrants and the Politics of Gender in Caribbean Costa Rica, 1870–1960.* Chapel Hill: University of North Carolina Press, 2002.

Quintero Rivera, Ángel G. *Patricios y plebeyos: Burgueses, hacendados, artesanos y obreros. Las relaciones de clase en el Puerto Rico de cambio de siglo.* Río Piedras: Ediciones Huracán, 1988.

Quintero Rivera, Ángel, and Gervasio García. *Desafío y solidaridad: Breve historia del movimiento obrero puertorriqueño.* Río Piedras: Ediciones Huracán, 1986.

Rafael Cordero: Presencia y vigencia. San Juan: Instituto de Cultura Puertorriqueña, 2000.

Renda, Mary A. *Taking Haiti: Military Occupation and the Culture of U.S. Imperialism, 1915–1940.* Chapel Hill: University of North Carolina Press, 2001.

Rockwell, Elsie. *Hacer escuela, hacer estado: La educación posrevolucionaria vista desde Tlaxcala.* Zamora, Michoacán: Centro Público de Investigación, 2007.

Rodríguez-Silva, Ileana. "*Libertos* and *Libertas* in the Construction of the Free Worker in Postemancipation Puerto Rico." In *Gender and Slave Emancipation in the Atlantic World,* edited by Pamela Scully and Diana Paton, 199–222. Durham, NC: Duke University Press, 2005.

————. *Silencing Race: Disentangling Blackness, Colonialism, and National Identity.* New York: Palgrave Macmillan, 2012.

Roy-Féquière, Magali. *Women, Creole Identity, and Intellectual Life in Early Twentieth-Century Puerto Rico.* Philadelphia: Temple University Press, 2004.

Sánchez Korrol, Virginia E. *From Colonia to Community: The History of Puerto Ricans in New York City.* Berkeley: University of California Press, 1994.

Sanders, James E. *Contentious Republicans: Popular Politics, Race, and Class in Nineteenth-Century Colombia.* Durham, NC: Duke University Press, 2004.

Scarano, Francisco A. "The Jíbaro Masquerade and the Subaltern Politics of Creole Identity Formation in Puerto Rico, 1745–1823." *American Historical Review* 101, no. 5 (December 1996): 1398–1431.

————. "Liberal Pacts and Hierarchies of Rule: Approaching the Imperial Transition in Cuba and Puerto Rico." *Hispanic American Historical Review* 78, no. 4 (November 1998): 583–601.

————. *Puerto Rico: Cinco siglos de historia.* San Juan: McGraw-Hill Interamericana, 2008.

Schmidt-Nowara, Christopher. *Empire and Antislavery: Spain, Cuba, and Puerto Rico, 1833–1874.* Pittsburgh: University of Pittsburgh Press, 1999.

Scott, James C. *Weapons of the Weak: Everyday Forms of Peasant Resistance.* New Haven, CT: Yale University Press, 1986.

Scott, Joan Wallach. *Gender and the Politics of History.* New York: Columbia University Press, 1999.

Sellés Solá, Gerardo, and Juan José Osuna. *Lecturas históricas de la educación en Puerto Rico.* N.p., 1943.

Silva, Noenoe K. *Aloha Betrayed: Native Hawaiian Resistance to American Colonialism.* Durham, NC: Duke University Press, 2004.

Smith, Rogers M. *Civic Ideals: Conflicting Visions of Citizenship in U.S. History.* New Haven, CT: Yale University Press, 1997.

Stepan, Nancy Leys. *"The Hour of Eugenics": Race, Gender, and Nation in Latin America.* Ithaca, NY: Cornell University Press, 1991.

Stoler, Ann Laura. *Carnal Knowledge and Imperial Power: Race and the Intimate in Colonial Rule.* Berkeley: University of California Press, 2002.

————, ed. *Haunted by Empire: Geographies of Intimacy in North American History.* Durham, NC: Duke University Press, 2006.

————. *Race and the Education of Desire: Foucault's History of Sexuality and the Colonial Order of Things.* Durham, NC: Duke University Press, 1995.

Stoler, Ann Laura, Carole McGranahan, and Peter C. Perdue, eds. *Imperial Formations.* Santa Fe: School for Advanced Research Press, 2007.

Thompson, Lanny. *Imperial Archipelago: Representation and Rule in the Insular Territories under U.S. Dominion after 1898.* Honolulu: University of Hawaii Press, 2010.

————. *Nuestra isla y su gente: La construcción del otro puertorriqueño en "Our island and their people."* San Juan: Centro de Investigaciones Sociales y Departamento de Historia de la Universidad de Puerto Rico, 1995.

Thurner, Mark. *From Two Republics to One Divided: Contradictions of Postcolonial Nation-Making in Andean Peru*. Durham, NC: Duke University Press, 1997.

Tirado, Ramón Claudio. *Cien años de educación y de administración educativa en Puerto Rico: 1900–2000*. Hato Rey: Publicaciones Puertorriqueñas, 2003.

Torres-González, Roamé. *Idioma, bilingüismo y nacionalidad: La presencia del inglés en Puerto Rico*. San Juan: Editorial de la Universidad de Puerto Rico, 2002.

Trías Monge, José. *Puerto Rico: The Trials of the Oldest Colony in the World*. New Haven, CT: Yale University Press, 1997.

Trouillot, Michel-Rolph. *Silencing the Past: Power and the Production of History*. Boston: Beacon Press, 1995.

Turits, Richard. *Foundations of Despotism: Peasants, the Trujillo Regime, and Modernity in Dominican History*. Stanford, CA: Stanford University Press, 2003.

Vaughan, Mary Kay. *Cultural Politics in Revolution: Teachers, Peasants, and Schools in Mexico, 1930–1940*. Tucson: University of Arizona Press, 1997.

———. *The State, Education, and Social Class in Mexico, 1880–1928*. DeKalb: Northern Illinois University Press, 1982.

Vaughan, Mary Kay, and Stephen E. Lewis, eds. *The Eagle and the Virgin: Nation and Cultural Revolution in Mexico, 1920–1940*. Durham, NC: Duke University Press, 2006.

Vázquez Calzada, José. *La población de Puerto Rico y su trayectoria histórica*. San Juan: Universidad de Puerto Rico, 1988.

Vega, Bernardo, and César Andreu Iglesias. *Memoirs of Bernardo Vega: A Contribution to the History of the Puerto Rican Community in New York*. New York: Monthly Review Press, 1984.

Velyvis, Kristen, Theresa Thompson-Colón, and Halliman Winsborough. "Public Use Samples of 1910 and 1920 Puerto Rico Censuses." *Caribbean Studies* 35, no. 2 (July–December 2007): 2–29.

Wade, Peter. *Blackness and Race Mixture: The Dynamics of Identity in Colombia*. Baltimore, MD: Johns Hopkins University Press, 1993.

Wagenheim, Kal, and Olga Jiménez de Wagenheim, eds. *The Puerto Ricans: A Documentary History*. Princeton, NJ: Markus Wiener Publishers, 1994.

Zeno Gandía, Manuel. *La charca*. Hato Rey: Publicaciones Puertorriqueñas, 1996.

———. *Obras completas*. Río Piedras: Ediciones del Instituto de Literatura Puertorriqueña, Universidad de Puerto Rico, 1955.

Index